McGRAW-HILL EDUCATION CLASSICS

EDWARD H. REISNER, *General Editor*

FRENCH LIBERALISM AND EDUCATION
IN THE EIGHTEENTH CENTURY

McGRAW-HILL EDUCATION CLASSICS

EDWARD H. REISNER, *General Editor*

Early Protestant Educators
Edited by FREDERICK EBY

Comenius
Edited by M. W. KEATINGE

Locke
Edited by W. E. SEALOCK

French Liberalism and Education in the Eighteenth Century
Edited by F. DE LA FONTAINERIE

Thomas Jefferson and Education in a Republic
Edited by C. F. ARROWOOD

Pestalozzi
Edited by L. F. ANDERSON

Reports on European Education
Edited by EDGAR W. KNIGHT

Horace Mann
Edited by A. O. NORTON

Henry Barnard on Education
Edited by JOHN S. BRUBACHER

Pioneers of Women's Education
Edited by WILLYSTINE GOODSELL

Francis W. Parker
Edited by EDWARD H. REISNER

Educational Views of Benjamin Franklin
Edited by THOMAS WOODY

Ignatius Loyola and the Ratio Studiorum
Edited by EDWARD A. FITZPATRICK

All in press or in preparation, January, 1932

FRENCH LIBERALISM AND EDUCATION IN THE EIGHTEENTH CENTURY

The Writings of
La Chalotais, Turgot, Diderot, and Condorcet
on National Education

Translated and Edited by
F. DE LA FONTAINERIE

Assistant Professor of Romance Languages
University of Pennsylvania

McGRAW-HILL BOOK COMPANY, INC.

NEW YORK AND LONDON

1932

To
C. B. U.

PREFACE

THE aim of this collection of the educational writings of four prominent liberalists of the eighteenth century is to present their works in their own words, in so far as it is possible to do this in another language. The translator has ever had in mind the Italian adage *Traduttore, traditore* and has endeavored never to traduce the meaning. It has not always been easy to do this and, at the same time, write passably good English. Whenever the one had to be sacrificed to the other, it has always been the form to the sense. It has likewise often been difficult to find just the right word to render the author's meaning and even, at times, to understand in precisely what sense he was using a word. Eighteenth century writers had many personal idiosyncrasies. The translator, in order to obtain a clear idea, has read as much as possible of the other works of the author in question, as well as of those of writers with whom he showed familiarity and who, thus, might have influenced his style or vocabulary. If, in spite of his good will—and it is probable—the translator has failed in any detail, he very humbly begs pardon of those who will not perceive it and enlightenment of those who will.

The essays have been reproduced in their entirety. No omissions have been made except where they consisted of mere lists of books or authors, and in such cases the excision has been indicated in the proper place.

PREFACE

To some, the explanatory notes may seem unnecessarily copious. If the compiler has appeared to underrate the general culture of his readers, he hopes that this may be considered only as an indication of excess of zeal.

The writer desires to acknowledge his indebtedness to Reverend J. B. Bassich, S. J.; to Dr. William Pepper, Dean of the School of Medicine, University of Pennsylvania; to Mr. Roger F. Williams, Attorney at Law, Philadelphia; and to Professor C. Addison Willis, formerly of Girard College, for suggestions in regard to the translation of philosophical, medical, legal, and scientific terms, as well as to Dr. Joseph A. Meredith of Temple University, Philadelphia, who kindly read the manuscript. To these, and to all others who have shown an interest in the work, he wishes to express his sincere thanks.

F. de la F.

PHILADELPHIA,
January, 1932.

CONTENTS

INTRODUCTION

EDUCATION IN FRANCE IN THE EIGHTEENTH CENTURY

BEFORE considering the several projects for educational reform which are presented in this volume, it will perhaps be well to make a brief study of the general subject of education in France in the eighteenth century, in order that we may be able to judge more accurately the justice of the criticisms that are made as well as the opportuneness and feasibility of the reforms advocated.

Albert Duruy, in his work on public instruction and the Revolution states:

> No one has ever contested that there were flourishing colleges and famous universities in France before the Revolution. This would have been an undertaking too daring indeed. One has been content, on the singularly interested testimony of Parliamentarians and Encyclopedists, to condemn as retrograde the instruction given in these colleges.[1]

Rambaud tells us that in France there existed in the eighteenth century, as to-day, three degrees of instruction: primary, which was given in the *petites écoles;* secondary, given in the colleges; and higher, in the universities.[2]

[1] A. DURUY, *L'instruction publique et la Révolution,* p. 3, Hachette, Paris, 1882.

[2] A. RAMBAUD, *Histoire de la civilisation française,* Vol. II, p. 260, Armand Colin, Paris, 1921.

INTRODUCTION

Furthermore, there were the great scientific institutions: the *Collège Royal* or *Collège de France* and the *Jardin du Roi* or *Jardin des Plantes;* and the special schools: the *École des Mines,* the *École des Ponts et Chaussées*—both for engineers; the *École des Jeunes de Langues*—for the study of the languages necessary to diplomacy and commerce; and the two veterinary schools, one at Alfort and one at Lyons, etc.[3]

La Chalotais in his *Essay on National Education,* Turgot in his *Memorial to the King,* and Diderot in his *Plan of a University for the Russian Government*—which is as much a criticism of conditions in France as a plan for Russia—do not, as may be noted, complain of lack of schools, but of the quality or objective of the instruction and the subject matter. With Condorcet, the case is different; as he presented his *Report on the General Organization of Public Instruction* when the Revolution had either suppressed or was about to suppress all institutions of learning and practically put an end to public instruction, there was certainly a lack of them. Before this, all things considered, there does not seem to have been any dearth of educational opportunity.

In the reign of Louis XV, there remained practically only one matter of importance that was not under the direct control of the State. This was education, which continued to be a private affair, or something which concerned the

---

[3] A. RAMBAUD, *op. cit.,* Vol. II, p. 273. There were also the following special schools: schools of artillery, 7; of drawing, mathematics, hydrography, 12; for army cadets, 14; for naval cadets, 3; for the blind, 1; for the deaf and dumb, 1; of singing, 2; of midwifery, 12; and sundry, 12. A. DURUY, *op. cit.,* pp. 48, 49.

Church, or else, in so far as the government was interested in general education, had been tacitly entrusted to the Church.[4]

This did not suit at all those who wished to exalt the State above everything else; for they saw in the Church and in the religious orders formidable opponents to the complete supremacy of the State over the minds of its subjects. From their point of view, there was much justification for their attitude. The Catholic Church has never ceased to be fundamentally an international institution.[5] It could never be relied upon to lend itself, and rarely coerced for a time even into lending itself, to the furtherance of any narrow nationalistic scheme of education; and, as Protestantism was out of the question in France and Jansenism had failed, there was only the international Church with which to reckon. "One may believe," says one writer on the subject,[6] "that Protestantism, if it had triumphed in France, if it had not been hunted out during the religious wars before being exterminated by the revocation of the Edict of Nantes, would have given us what we have hardly obtained to-day after three hundred years of struggle and effort, a strong (national?) organization of primary instruction." Usually the attack was against the

[4] E. H. Reisner, *Nationalism and Education since 1789*, p. 9, The Macmillan Company, New York, 1927.

[5] In this connection, it is interesting to note that the limits of the ecclesiastical divisions did not even coincide with the political boundaries of the kingdom; in some cases French bishops were suffragans of foreign archbishops, and vice versa. See A. Rambaud, *op. cit.*, Vol. II, p. 36.

[6] G. Compayré, *Histoire critique des doctrines de l'éducation en France depuis le seizième siècle*, Vol. I, p. 157, Hachette, Paris, 1898.

Jesuits. In the first place, they had exerted great influence over secondary and higher education; in the second, on account of the form of their organization, they were the most international in spirit of all the teaching orders.

Thus it is in particular with the influence of the clergy upon education that La Chalotais deals in his *Essay on National Education*. Though he is also concerned with many details of curriculum and school administration as well as general educational policy, his main theme is the removal of education from the control of the clergy and the substitution therefor of the control of the State. He is quite as critical as Diderot, for instance, of the neglect of the study of the practical sciences and the emphasis placed upon the study of the Latin language and classical literature. Like Turgot, he suggests the creation of a Royal Committee, at least to study a plan of education and to determine the subjects of study for all the colleges. This committee would be composed principally of statesmen and men of letters, and "the adherents of any special faction should not be included in it." The dominant idea is always that the entire control of education belongs exclusively to the State. For a further and more detailed discussion of the subject, the reader is referred to the introductory remarks on the essay.

The exponents of the new philosophy were naturally utterly opposed to the education given by the Church. The Church taught that man was naturally depraved, and dependent upon divine grace and his own cooperation with it for his salvation. The new philosophy, at least as expressed by Rousseau, held that "man is a being naturally good, loving justice and order." The Church fully admitted the inequality of men as mortals, though it stoutly maintained their equality in the sight of God as souls. According to Condorcet, "the natural order creates in society no other inequalities than those of wealth and education." If these alone were the differences of viewpoint of the two schools of thought, it would be enough to explain why they were completely antagonistic. Therefore, it is unnecessary to enter into further differences of opinion or doctrine to explain why any system of education that would be acceptable to the one could never be so to the other, and why each one saw in the other enemies of humanity.

The idea of a national education controlled by the State and supported by the community had not yet been born. The royal government contented itself with encouraging public instruction, and willingly left the rest to private initiative. The State did not teach. Why should it have done so? It saw teachers and schools provided and maintained everywhere by the free treasury of the successive liberality of faith and charity. These teachers gave it no concern in regard to the guiding of minds, nor these schools in regard to the prosperity of studies. In fact, the State, that is to say the King, had no interest in teaching. He had one interest only: which was that there should be many schools and that these schools should be perfectly orthodox. Let us add that, in demanding that they be thus, he was making use of a right that all governments have asserted. Louis XIV wished that the children be taught a religion which itself taught submission to the prince. The Convention will attempt later in the same way to substitute for the Commandments of God the Declaration of the Rights of Man, and for the catechism, republican ethics.

Thus says De Salvandy, Minister of Public Instruction, in 1847.[7]

However, we must not overlook the fact that the royal government had, at a certain moment, interested itself more directly in popular education, and what we may call obligatory instruction had been decreed. Two ordinances of Louis XIV, in 1694 and 1698, respectively, and one of Louis XV, in 1724, required regular attendance at school. In reality, it was a matter of religion or politics—very certainly in the first two cases at least. These edicts followed close upon the revocation of the Edict of Nantes, and concerned above all the religious instruction of children, particularly those of parents of the "so-called reformed religion." The teachers were placed under the direct authority of the parish priests. These ordinances do not appear to have been carried out.[8]

In general, the King's government left all matters pertaining to education in the hands of local bishops and the religious orders. From the viewpoint of the time, there was nothing irregular in this proceeding. The clergy were considered the proper ones to teach, and education, except in special cases, was no more an affair of the government than the sale of fuel would be in our own time; indeed less so, as we fully realize that fuel is a prime necessity for all, which education was certainly not considered at that time.

The practical defect of this system was that it resulted in a great inequality of educational opportunity. Some

[7] Quoted from the *Moniteur* of April 12, 1847, by A. Duruy, *op. cit.*, p. 6.

[8] A. Rambaud, *op. cit.*, Vol. II, p. 260.

dioceses were well provided; others very scantily. It was probably, partly at least, to remedy this situation that Turgot proposed the creation of a Royal Council of National Education, under the direction of which would be placed the academies, the universities, the colleges, and the primary schools. In this *Memorial,* Turgot advocates moral and social instruction which would make the people "clearly understand their obligations to society and to the King's authority which protects it, the duties which these obligations impose upon them and the interest which they have in fulfilling these duties, both for the public welfare and for their own." Though he would undoubtedly seem to wish to subject all education—other than religious—to the direct control of the State, unlike La Chalotais, Turgot does not indicate any intention of excluding either the regular or secular clergy from teaching. This, however, may well be because he was fully aware that Louis XVI would hardly have looked with favor upon such a proposal.

In 1843, Abel-François Villemain, who was at that time Minister of Public Instruction, submitted to the King a report on the existing state of secondary instruction in France. A part of this report deals with the comparative state of secondary education in 1789 and in 1842.[9] We have here a complete analysis of the statistics regarding secondary schools before the Revolution. This is an official document, prepared by the highest educational authority

[9] *Exposé des motifs et projet de loi sur l'Instruction Secondaire présenté à la Chambre des Pairs, le 2 février 1844, par M. Villemain, Ministre de l'Instruction Publique, précédé du Rapport au Roi en date du 3 mars 1843, sur l'état de cette instruction en France, et de divers discours relatifs au même sujet,* p. 52, Paul Dupont, Paris, 1844.

in the kingdom and submitted to the head of the nation himself, as well as to the country at large. Therefore, the figures given therein may be accepted as being the most reliable available; and, in all probability they are highly accurate. The following extracts are from this report.

The first difference is in the number even of the colleges. This number, in the last century, from the year 1763 on,[10] was 562 establishments for a population of 25 million souls. To-day, in France, of which the population has increased by more than a third, the number of Royal and Communal Colleges does not exceed 368. But we must observe that under the old monarchy, in consequence of the great number of establishments depending upon the universities or corporations dedicated to teaching, there existed very few private institutions. The exact figures cannot be given to-day; but we know that these establishments were rare and without importance, and that the 72,747 students who frequented the former colleges constituted almost the total number of the children who were then receiving a liberal education. . . .

In fact, formerly, everything in the traditions and in the customs contributed to liberal education; everything was prepared for it and favored it: the number of scholarships and aids of all kinds, the free tuition in a great number of establishments, the extremely moderate costs of all the others. Thus, in the 562 colleges which existed toward the middle of the last century, there were 525 scholarships reserved for candidates for the priesthood, 2724 non-specified scholarships, and a great number of special private foundations which afforded, by means of remission of fees or of pecuniary rewards accorded as prizes, the benefits of an education totally or partially gratuitous to 7199 children. Furthermore, the instruction was

---

[10] That is, after the suppression of the Jesuit colleges.

imparted without any remuneration whatever in many colleges, especially in all the colleges in Paris since 1719. The number of day students who profited by the free tuition in the former colleges in Paris and in the various provinces is estimated at 30,000. To sum up, the total number of students who received their education or instruction either entirely or partially gratuitously exceeded 40,000. This state of affairs was not a gift of the government, but the result of the generosity of several centuries, and was, so to say, the expression itself of that civilization which, since the middle ages, had carried so far the glory of France in letters and sciences. It was thanks to such foundations that education had spread, had become secularized. . . .[11]

Without doubt, the abundant means of obtaining a liberal education free, which so many accidental causes had produced under the *ancien régime,* could not to-day be systematically reestablished by the State. The creation even of the 6000 scholarships decreed by the Emperor remained well below the large number of foundations which had been accumulated before 1789. . . .

Between 500 and 600 colleges in which a liberal education [12] was given to some 73,000 is indeed a very respectable number both of colleges and of students, for the time and in a population of 25 million; and when we note that over one half of the total number of students (40,000) were holders of scholarships of some sort or were at least exempt

[11] Lavisse states that the Revolution took from the Colleges 30 million of revenue. E. Lavisse, *Histoire de France depuis les origines jusqu'à la Révolution,* Vol. IX, Part I, p. 166, Hachette, Paris, 1910.

[12] Rambaud states that in these colleges were taught French, Latin, Greek and the elements of the sciences. See A. Rambaud, *op. cit.,* Vol. II, p. 264.

from the payment of tuition, we certainly cannot complain of either lack of interest in education or of lack of encouragement of poor students. Furthermore, since these 40,000 students must have been prepared somehow and somewhere to enter these institutions of secondary instruction, there must have existed adequate means of acquiring elementary instruction free or nearly so. Therefore the statement made in the *Cambridge Modern History:* "The multitude of splendid foundations made a liberal education cheap and often gratuitous" [13] would seem to be fully justified.

In Buisson's *Dictionnaire de pédagogie,* the total number of colleges existing at the beginning of the Revolution is given as 564; and it is further stated: "To this number we must add, even after the closing or the assignment to the universities of the numerous colleges which had been held by the Jesuits, a large number of ecclesiastical colleges belonging to the Oratorians, the Benedictines, the Minims, the Lazarists, the Congregation of St. Joseph and other religious communities." [14]

There were in 1789 twenty-one universities. (By universities, we must understand only what we should call in the United States, graduate schools.) Of these, fourteen had all four faculties (Arts, Law, Medicine and Theology). The University of Strasbourg had two Faculties of Theology: the one Catholic, and the other Protestant. In some cases among the remaining number, there was no Faculty

---

[13] *Cambridge Modern History,* Vol. VIII, p. 260.
[14] F. Buisson, *Dictionnaire de pédagogie et d'instruction primaire,* Part I, Tome I, p. 1051, Hachette, Paris, 1886–1887. (The article is by A. Rambaud.)

of Arts, in others, none of Medicine or of Theology; but
the Faculty of Law was always to be found.[15]

In these universities almost the same degrees were con-
ferred as to-day: the Baccalaureate (in the Faculty of Arts,
the Masters of Arts replaced the Bachelors), the Licence—
which gave the right to teach, and the Doctorate—which
was obtained only after publicly defending a thesis.[16] The
value of these degrees would depend a great deal upon the
university at which they had been obtained—just as to-day.
In some cases the examinations seem to have been somewhat of a farce; though perhaps we should not give too
much credit to the semi-facetious anecdotes that are related
on the subject. We know, however, that there was serious
ground for complaint and that strenuous efforts were made
to force the delinquent universities to put their house in
order; for, in 1754, the University of Bourges was threatened with suppression, as had been the case with the University of Cahors some few years previously.[17]

Much has been written about the narrow and inadequate
education afforded by these colleges and universities; yet
we must note that none of the advocates of new systems
seem to have had any doubt about finding men able to
teach—or at least able to prepare books on—any and all
subjects necessary. Hence, even for the needs of the reformers, these institutions could not have been so unsatisfactory. And where had these reformers themselves been

[15] *Ibid.*, p. 1050, states that there were twenty-two universities; but in the list given there are only twenty-one named as
actually existing in 1789.

[16] A. RAMBAUD, *op. cit.*, Vol. II, p. 272.

[17] F. BUISSON, *op. cit.*, Part I, Tome I, p. 1050.

educated? And where had all the great men who had rendered the seventeenth and eighteenth centuries so illustrious in letters and arts and even in the sciences received their education?

As an actual fact, the chief charges to be found against the curriculum are that the study of the classics was overemphasized; that too much time was spent on the Latin language itself, and too little attention given to the French language and literature; that ancient history alone was taught and practically no modern history; and that the sciences were almost totally neglected; also that too much religion was taught.

In his *Plan of a University for the Russian Government,* Diderot complains chiefly of the lack of scientific study, of the emphasis on the classic literatures and languages, the failure to include modern history, as well as the general methods and objectives of the educational institutions of his day in France. Of the University of Paris, he has not a word of commendation, except for the Faculty of Medicine. This he finds, on the whole, satisfactory enough, though lacking in facilities for clinical instruction. For the sorry picture which he presents of the Faculties of Arts, Theology, and Law, we must refer the reader to the work itself.

Though these charges may possibly be well founded in the case of those colleges that were affiliated with the universities as well as of colleges directed by the Jesuits, they cannot be maintained as universally true. The Oratorians [18]

[18] Congregation of the Oratory; founded in Rome in 1564 by St. Philip Neri, and established in France in 1611 by Cardinal de Bérulle.

had numerous schools in France during the eighteenth century and exerted considerable influence upon the education of the times: let us examine their program of studies. We shall quote from a modern American writer on secondary education in France.[19]

Formed like the other religious orders primarily for the support of the Church, the Oratorians turned their efforts to the recruitment of the priesthood and assumed the responsibility of a teaching body in order the better to attain their primary end. After their formal registration by the Parliament of Paris in 1613, they spread with marvellous rapidity and, all unconsciously, soon became strong rivals of the Jesuits. By 1629 they already had some fifty establishments in various parts of France. Like the Port-Royalists,[20] the Oratorians laid much stress on the vernacular; the first years of the instruction in grammar being entirely in French. Such was the vitality of the Latin, however, that its use was made obligatory from the fourth class up. The history (and at Juilly, their most important college, there was always a special master for that subject) included sacred history in the two lowest classes, Greek and Roman in the next three, and French history in the three most advanced classes. This latter was looked upon as particularly vital, and the instruction from the lowest to the highest class was all in the native tongue. Geography was taught in connection with history, while physics and mathematics (including algebra, geometry, plane and spherical trigonometry, analytical geometry and calculus) were the subjects of special instruction. The Oratorians and the Port-Royalists are equally

[19] F. E. FARRINGTON, *French Secondary Schools,* p. 47, Longmans, Green & Co., New York, 1910.

[20] A congregation of Bernardines which, having embraced Jansenism, was suppressed in 1709.

to be credited with beginning the study of grammar in the vernacular; but for the emphasis placed upon history, mathematics and physics, the Oratorians have to share the honors with none. In fact, in the course in French history, as Rolland bears eloquent witness, the Oratorians were more than a century in advance of the colleges of the university. "The youths who frequent the college know the names of the consuls of Rome, and are often ignorant of those of our kings; they know the great deeds of Themistocles, of Alcibiades . . . they know not those of Du Guesclin, of Bayard, . . . ; in a word the great men who have made our nation illustrious . . . have made no impression on them." [21] Thus we find that the classics have ceased to monopolize the instruction of the colleges, and the courses are being framed more and more with the idea of turning out boys with an all-round equipment, with a liberal education.

The Jesuits continued to place the greatest emphasis upon the study of the classics and upon the Latin language itself in particular. However, in this connection we must remember that, as a teaching order, the Jesuits were chiefly concerned with the education of the upper classes, and, consequently, sought to give rather a cultural education than a practical one. In his *Traité des études,* Rollin, the great chancellor of the University of Paris, defines the aims of university instruction (that is, secondary instruction within the author's meaning) as: (1) the cultivation of the mind; (2) the development of the moral character; and (3) the formation of the Christian man.[22] From the view point of the time, at least, extensive study of the sciences would hardly

[21] May we not have here an example of the "singularly interested testimony of Parliamentarians" to which Duruy refers?

[22] F. E. FARRINGTON, *op. cit.,* p. 51.

14

have been considered as contributing to these aims; rather were they looked upon as forming a part of technical training—an opinion which has not yet been wholly abandoned.

In regard to the large amount of time spent in acquiring the Latin language itself, we must not forget that it was taught as a living language, and that the ability to speak and write correct or even elegant Latin was still considered among the more conservative as a prerequisite to higher scholarship. To say that this was becoming no longer necessary, owing to the increasing tendency to write on all subjects in the vernacular, may well be stating the proposition backwards; for it might just as well be that there was an increasing tendency to write in the vernacular because the ability to use Latin was disappearing. We can easily understand that a conservative and scholarly teaching order, such as the Jesuits, whose chief concern was the preparation of members of the upper classes for scholarly pursuits, would resist to the utmost any such tendency. It is at least permissible to ask ourselves if the loss of this universal language of the institutions of higher learning is, after all, a subject for unalloyed satisfaction. Might it not be well, to-day even, if scholars spoke and wrote one language, so that it would be unnecessary to translate their works, and students as well as teachers could go freely from university to university unhampered by diversity of language? Might it not be at least as worth while to consecrate a good part of the time of those destined to pursue higher studies to the acquisition of such a language as to many of the subjects that are now taught?

The Jesuits in particular and the schools in general are reproached with giving too much time to religious instruction. In this connection, we must, however, bear in mind the fact that religion had for a long time been considered much in the same way as the positive sciences are in our own times; and, though it might indeed be difficult for our self-satisfied generation to entertain such an idea, it may not be wholly impossible that we ourselves may some day be reproached in a similar manner by future generations with having been too much preoccupied with the practical aspects of education—nay, even of life itself. Most men disapprove of what they do not do, and for much the same reason one generation disapproves of preceding ones.

Popular instruction appears to have been of even less concern to the State than secondary—beyond the fact which we have already noted that the schools should be thoroughly orthodox; for in the latter case colleges were needed at least for the education of civil functionaries, and military schools for that of officers.[23] There did not seem to be any need that the lower orders should be forced to receive any instruction other than religious instruction. Both La Chalotais and Diderot complain that too many young people were studying, who ought to have been doing something else; and does not Rousseau say: "The poor man has no need of an education; for his condition of life forces one upon him, and he would not be able to receive any other."[24] Likewise Voltaire enthusiastically declares himself to be of La Chalotais' opinion.[25]

---

[23] A. Rambaud, *op. cit.,* Vol. II, p. 260.

[24] *Œuvres complètes de J.-J. Rousseau,* Tome II, *Émile,* Livre I, p. 20, Hachette, Paris, 1905.

[25] See p. 39.

Turgot and Condorcet, however, are truly concerned with providing universal opportunity for education. Though both of these men are equally solicitous of the welfare of the masses and of their education in order that they may better understand and fulfil their obligations to the State and to society, there is an interesting contrast to be noted in the manner of stating the proposition. Turgot says that his aim is to maintain peace and good order, to impart activity to all useful works, to make the people understand their obligations to society and to the royal authority and the *duties* which these obligations impose. Condorcet represents his aim as being to offer to all men the means of providing for their needs, of assuring their welfare, of knowing and exercising their *rights,* of understanding and fulfilling their obligations. They are both undoubtedly animated by much the same spirit: only, under the old monarchy, it was *duties* upon which the emphasis was laid, whereas, after the Revolution, it was *rights.*

It was the Church which, either under the direct supervision of the parish priests or by means of various religious orders, undertook this work of charity—as it was then considered; for is not "to instruct the ignorant" the very first of the seven spiritual works of mercy? And, if we make due allowance for the fact that religious instruction was, very naturally, considered of paramount importance, we must admit that, generally speaking, the Church did not neglect this duty.

To obtain any precise data on the subject of popular education under the old monarchy has required much painstaking research in diocesan and communal archives, and in parish registers—wherever such are still extant. This has been done by various devoted scholars, and the results of their labors published in sundry articles. The knowledge thus acquired has been collated in a carefully documented work by the Abbé Allain, at that time archivist of the diocese of Bordeaux.[26] We shall quote somewhat extensively from this source.[27]

In regard to the number of schools, Allain reaches the same general conclusion as Duruy, who says without reservation: "It is then certain that the *petites écoles* were numerous in almost all our provinces." [28] Rambaud likewise admits this to be a fact: "France, before 1789, possessed quite a large number of *petites écoles*: this is a fact that is to-day well established by recent works." [29]

Accepting these conclusions as in the main reasonably proven, let us examine in detail, in the light of the results of the studies given by Allain, the general question of popular education in the century preceding the Revolution.

In some cases, we shall have recourse to other authorities to complete the information given by our author.

What was taught in these schools? The curriculum comprised four branches only: religious instruction with sacred history, reading, writing with spelling, and elementary reckoning. To this must be added, in the schools for boys, in certain places only, some notions of vocational training,

[26] Lavisse says of Allain's work that it is the only good one on the subject. See E. LAVISSE, *op. cit.,* Vol. IX, Part I, p. 165, note.

[27] E. ALLAIN, *L'instruction primaire en France avant la Révolution,* Société Bibliographique, Paris, 1881.

[28] A. DURUY, *op. cit.,* p. 13.

[29] F. BUISSON, *op. cit.,* Part I, Tome I, p. 1052 (*Petites écoles,* in article by A. Rambaud).

and, everywhere, in the schools for girls, handiwork.[30] Though such a curriculum would to-day doubtless leave much to be desired, for the time and circumstances it was perhaps as satisfactory as could be expected.

Viewed from the standpoint of to-day, the discipline was somewhat harsh to say the least. Corporal punishments were recognized as being fully justified when deemed necessary; also many other devices, such as making the children kneel, or take the lowest place in the class. On the other hand, there were rewards for merit: exemption from certain tasks, prizes, etc.[31]

By whom were these schools taught? By the members of the twenty teaching congregations and by numbers of lay teachers under the direct authority of the parish priests. Numerous official reports of the parochial visitations of the bishops of various dioceses, which are cited by the Abbé Allain and by Duruy, establish this fact. In certain places, for lack of teachers, the clergy themselves taught. As a general rule, the mistresses of the schools were members of some one of the religious orders devoted to teaching, whereas, in the great majority of cases, the masters were laymen. Instruction given by the religious orders was always free.[32]

What was the financial and social condition of these lay teachers? The Abbé Allain tells us:

As for the financial situation of our former schoolmasters, serious study of public documents during these last years con-

[30] E. ALLAIN, *op. cit.,* p. 163.
[31] F. BUISSON, *op. cit.,* Part I, Tome I, p. 724.
[32] E. LAVISSE, *op. cit.,* Vol. IX, Part I, p. 164.

firmed us in our conviction that, due proportion being maintained, it was about the same as that of our teachers of the present day. . . .[33] One has sometimes made merry, one has even feigned indignation on the subject of our former schoolmasters, who were at the same time teachers, chanters and sacristans. These worthy men looked upon the matter from another point of view. The humble functions which they performed in the church were great in their eyes, and, far from causing them to lose the respect of their pupils and of the parishioners, they added to the consideration with which they were surrounded. It is found quite natural in our day that a schoolmaster should be the secretary of the mayor, our fathers found it just as natural that they should be the sacristan of their parish priest. . . .[34] Let us state, at once, that the opinion which represents to us the former schoolmasters as generally honored has in its favor all the presumptions. They possessed a certain instruction which elevated them very much above the intellectual level of the peasants whom they had to some extent initiated into human knowledge. As obligatory witnesses of the principal religious acts: baptisms, marriages, burials, they entered with a certain prestige into the intimacy of families. They were in constant relations with the village authorities; above all with the parish priest, who had to visit the school assiduously, and to whom they acted in a way as assistants, as well as aids in the ceremonies of the Church and the administration of the Sacraments. The parish priest, according to the ecclesiastical regulations, should give to the schoolmaster the first place in the church after his own. For the General Assembly of the Clergy of France in 1685 had decided that "the schoolmasters clothed in their surplice should be offered the incense in the churches, and should receive the

[33] E. ALLAIN, *op. cit.*, p. 129.
[34] *Ibid.*, p. 132.

20

honors before laymen and the lords of the parish even." . . .[35] In the registers, they are ordinarily qualified as "the honorable man." [36]

The emoluments of the teachers were derived mainly from three sources: a fixed salary and certain payments in kind granted them by the community from its regular revenues, a monthly fee paid by the parents of the pupils, and the revenues from foundations in the case of endowed schools.[37] In any case, some provision for indigent children seems to have been usually made.[38]

How were the schoolmasters chosen and what were their qualifications? This question is answered by the Abbé Allain as follows:

The main principle which established the right of choosing the schoolmaster is indicated by an act of the Parliament of Tournay, dated October 11, 1696, which decrees that "those who pay the salary of a schoolmaster have the right to appoint him." Hence, in case the position of a schoolmaster or mistress became vacant on account of the death, resignation or dismissal of the incumbent, a choice was made, in a general assembly of the inhabitants, of a person of a recognized probity who had the required capacity to be able to teach the children. But if those who founded the schools had reserved to themselves the right of appointing the masters and mistresses, the choice belonged to the founder.[39] The teacher who had been chosen, before assuming his office, was obliged to obtain from

[35] *Ibid.*, p. 143.
[36] *Ibid.*, p. 144.
[37] *Ibid.*, p. 130 *et seq.*
[38] *Ibid.*, p. 184 *et seq.*
[39] *Ibid.*, p. 122.

21

the bishop, the vicar-general, or the rural dean a licence to teach, which was accorded gratis. . . . This episcopal approbation was granted only after a serious examination, although on an elementary program; or, at least, upon the presentation of a certificate of capacity delivered by the priest of the parish where the master had just previously taught. These licences were generally valid for one year only; but they were easily renewed. On the other hand, when the bishops or the archdeacons made the visitation of the parishes, they took great care not to neglect to visit the school and to interrogate the teacher and the pupils. If grave abuses were revealed in the conducting of the school, or if the incapacity of the teacher was recognized, they had the right, according to the existing laws, to dismiss the teacher.[40]

To what extent were the schools frequented? Allain does not attempt to make any very definite statement on the subject; he merely provides us with some rather dry statistics.[41] These statistics refer to different parishes and different dates—of which latter, relatively only a small part deal with the period which we have under consideration. They appear highly inconclusive, and it would seem better to ignore them altogether. The least—or should we say the most? (the writer has no wish to dogmatize)—that we can assume is that, since these schools were more or less voluntarily maintained, they must have been frequented to a sufficient extent to justify their existence. Allain's own statement is: "We believe we have proven the modest thesis which we have proposed: *In many of our old provinces, the schools were generally frequented.*" [42]

[40] *Ibid.,* p. 125.
[41] *Ibid.,* p. 176.
[42] *Ibid.,* p. 183

INTRODUCTION

In regard to the results of popular education in the period just preceding the Revolution, it is Duruy who provides some little data.

As for the results which they (the *petites écoles*) gave, it has been possible, in several departments, to note some of them. . . . In the Department of the Aube, the proportion of the inhabitants, men and women, who, in 1780, knew how to write was about 47 per centum. In the Department of the Nord, from 1750 to 1790, the number of married couples who were able to sign the marriage register was 53.87 per centum for the man, and 32.99 per centum for the woman. . . . In the Haute-Marne, the average of the inhabitants knowing how to read and write,—which to-day (1881) is still only 72 per centum, was already before the Revolution 71.8 per centum (given with the strictest reservations).[43]

What was the material condition of the school buildings?

If, in general, in the towns, scholastic buildings were sufficient and suitable, too often the rural schools were unsatisfactory from the point of view of construction and of hygiene. At times, for lack of a school-house belonging to the community, the classes were held in the home of the schoolmaster, and, as the latter had a tendency to lodge himself as economically as possible, the classes suffered accordingly. In certain cases, school-houses, especially built for the purpose, were nevertheless inconvenient and poor. . . . Sometimes as many as eighty children were assembled in a room with a low ceiling, and of relatively small dimensions.[44]

We may conclude with a brief summary made by the Abbé Allain himself.

[43] A DURUY, *op. cit.,* p. 11.
[44] E. ALLAIN, *op. cit.,* p. 151.

We have the right to assert the existence of primary instruction, before 1789, in our country where thousands of primary schools, unequally distributed, it is true, placed within reach of the children of the people elementary instruction. The movement, begun in the sixteenth century, had greatly developed and widely spread in the two ensuing centuries. A constant and rapid progress continued to manifest itself and remarkable results had been obtained when the Revolution came to brutally tear the Church from its work, to destroy the schools which it had founded, and to make France lose for long years the rank which had been acquired for it by immense sacrifices, generously made [45] to found and develop elementary instruction.[46]

The conclusion reached in judging the school system under the old monarchy would seem to depend much upon the standpoint from which it is judged. Obviously, judged by present-day standards and achievements, it was very defective. If, however, we honestly endeavor to see things from the point of view of the time itself, taking into full consideration the religious, social and philosophical ideas then dominant as well as the material conditions, we reach a decidedly different conclusion. The very efforts of the reformers are open to two interpretations. Certainly they indicate that reforms were desirable and even necessary (are there none to-day?); but, at the same time, they indicate not only a great interest in the subject, but also a conviction that these reforms could and might be effected.

[45] E. Lavisse, *op. cit.,* Vol. IX, Part I, p. 164, represents at twelve million the annual cost of primary instruction during the last year of the old monarchy.

[46] E. Allain, *op. cit.,* p. 119.

INTRODUCTION

Each generation has new ideas and new ideals, to be replaced in turn by those of succeeding ones. Change is a
law of history as well as of Nature. What was adequate for
yesterday is not so for to-day, and what is so to-day probably
will not be so to-morrow. It is, therefore, manifestly un-
fair to judge conditions in the past in relation to the present,
instead of in relation to the time in which they existed.

With due regard then for this primary axiom of historical criticism as well as simple obligation of justice, we do
not hesitate to state that, generally speaking, old France
possessed a reasonably good (for the time) educational
system. That it was indeed susceptible of improvement is
evident and is freely admitted. However, it must also be
admitted that these improvements were being carefully
studied and freely proposed, which is a fact that gives reason to suppose that the schools would have been greatly
benefited, if allowed to continue.

The entire educational system was, with one exception,[47]
destroyed by the Revolution; and, though several attempts
were made to reestablish public instruction, little was actually accomplished. It was Napoleon who provided for this
need: at first by the law of May 1, 1802, creating the *Lycées*
and secondary schools; then by the law of May 10, 1806,
and the decrees of organization which followed.[48]

---

[47] Only the *Collège Louis-le-Grand,* which was called in turn
Institut des Boursiers, Collège Égalité, and *Prytanée Français,*
remained open during the Terror. A.-F. Théry, *Histoire de
l'éducation en France depuis le cinquième siècle jusqu'a nos
jours,* Vol. II, p. 193, Dezobry, E. Magdeleine et Cie., Paris,
1858.

[48] A.-F. Villemain, *op. cit.,* p. 6.

INTRODUCTION

As early as 1791, Talleyrand [49] presented to the Constituent Assembly a bill for the creation and organization of public instruction. This bill was accepted in principle and passed; but, a few days later, the Constituent Assembly made way for the Legislative Assembly, and the law in question became a dead letter.

The following year—in April, 1792—Condorcet presented his famous *Report on the General Organization of Public Instruction,* which concluded with a bill. This bill was even less fortunate than Talleyrand's; for it did not even have the time to become a law before the Convention replaced the Legislative Assembly.

It was Condorcet's task to devise an entirely new educational system: from primary schools to a "National Society of Sciences and Arts," constituted to supervise educational institutions and to further scientific research—a system entirely imbued with new philosophical ideas, and adapted to the political aims of the Revolution. His prime objectives were the inculcation of Republican ideals and the inauguration of a thoroughly practical scheme of education that would increase the material prosperity of the country.

Whether he accomplished this task well or ill is, of necessity, a matter of personal opinion, and must be judged after an impartial examination of the *Report* itself, of which we give a translation. Some of the more salient details will be considered in the introduction to this document.

[49] Charles-Maurice de Talleyrand-Périgord, Bishop of Autun under the old monarchy; President of the National Assembly under the Revolution; Minister of Foreign Affairs under the Directory, the Consulate and the Empire; and delegate to the Congress of Vienna under the Restoration (1754–1838).

I

LOUIS-RENÉ DE CARADEUC DE LA CHALOTAIS

ESSAY ON NATIONAL EDUCATION

Translated from the edition published by Cl. and Ant. Philibert, Geneva, 1763.

LA CHALOTAIS (1701–1785)

and his

ESSAY ON NATIONAL EDUCATION

LOUIS-RENÉ DE CARADEUC DE LA CHALO-
tais, who was for over sixty years connected with
the Parliament of Brittany, was born in Rennes on March
6th, 1701. After completing his studies in law, La Chalotais
was admitted to the Bar, and became first advocate, then
attorney-general of the Provincial Parliament, over which
he exerted for a long time a dominant influence, or, if we
prefer, he was the interpreter of its spirit. At all events, it
supported him in the continuous opposition to the policies
of Church and State which he constantly maintained.

La Chalotais was born out of his time and out of his
place. He would have been admirably adapted to live in
the England of Cromwell's time. The character of a stern
Puritan Roundhead would have suited him to perfection.
He was certainly a magnificent hater, though precisely
what inspired his hatred, it is not so easy to determine. Did
he hate the Jesuits because he considered them the staunch-
est supporters of the dominant ultramontane party in the
Church, or did he hate ultramontanism because it supported the Jesuits? Did he hate the Royal Governor, the
Duke d'Aiguillon [1] because he represented the royal power,

[1] Emmanuel-Armand de Vignerot du Plessis-Richelieu, Duc
d'Aiguillon, Royal Governor of the province of Brittany from
1754 to 1768 (1720–1782).

or did he hate the royal power because it supported the Duke d'Aiguillon? Did he hate the power of Rome because he had Jansenistic tendencies, or did he have Jansenistic tendencies because he hated the power of Rome? That he did have Jansenistic tendencies cannot be denied: it is very evident from the writings which he recommends and the theories concerning religion which he expounds throughout his *Essay on National Education*. Whatever his motive may have been, he certainly fought a valiant fight against the royal power in Brittany in the person of the duke, and against the power of the Church in France in the persons of the Jesuits. The administration of the royal governor afforded the attorney-general of the province ample opportunity to attack him; for it was far from what it should have been, and some of the activities of the Society of Jesus at that time were certainly not above criticism. La Chalotais was not slow in taking full advantage of any lapse on the part of his enemy of the moment, or perhaps we had better say the one that was particularly engaging his attention at the moment.

The first victories in both of the campaigns belonged to the attorney-general. The one over the royal governor was perhaps less important than the one over the Jesuits; but since it rendered the governor ridiculous—and ridicule has always been a very deadly political weapon in France, it may well have had a greater influence upon subsequent events than its trifling nature would seem to justify. In 1756, the English attempted to land troops at Saint-Cast. According to one version of the story, the duke did not, upon this occasion, show either the activity of a general nor the bravery of a soldier. He himself withdrew, with his entire staff, to a mill, and let one of his officers attack without orders, and repulse the English, who left more than three thousand dead or prisoners. Another version has it that d'Aiguillon retired to the mill in question for strategic reasons. At all events, he was in a mill, and it was this fact that gave La Chalotais a chance to indulge his wit at the expense of his enemy; for when it was later said that upon this occasion the governor "had covered himself with glory," the attorney-general replied: "With glory and with flour." This sally was repeated everywhere, much to the discomfiture of the duke.

His first victory over the Jesuits was of a much more important nature. A certain Father de La Valette, who was the Provincial of the Jesuits in the Antilles, had undertaken some great commercial ventures which had come to grief owing to the fact that the English, who were then at war with France, had seized several of his ships. He, therefore, found it impossible to satisfy his creditors in Lyons and Marseilles, to whom he owed large sums, and was obliged to declare bankruptcy. His liabilities were fixed at the enormous sum of five millions of francs, against assets of two million, five hundred thousand. His creditors attempted to recover from the Jesuits in France, who, however, replied that, though they constituted one society as to spiritual matters, each member of the Society was individually responsible for temporalities. The affair rapidly assumed considerable proportions and the scandal was great. This was La Chalotais' opportunity. He rushed into the fray: not to obtain payment for Father de La Valette's creditors; but to attack the entire order, whose doctrine, practices and existence offended him. Under his guidance, the Parliament of Brittany, following the example of the Parliaments of Grenoble and of Toulouse, ordered some of its members to present a report "on the ethical teachings of the priests and scholastics so-called of the Society of Jesus." We can imagine with what satisfaction La Chalotais undertook the task. We know how satisfactorily to himself he achieved it. He presented a striking picture of the theories maintained by the Jesuits, and which he condemned. The Jesuits, who were all-powerful at that time in Rome, caused to be sent by the Pope a series of Bulls, Briefs, Apostolic Letters and Decrees which approved their doctrines and their contentions. La Chalotais adduced these as abuses before his Parliament, which, thereupon, charged him to present another report; this time, "on the books, the ethics and the teachings of the Society." He presented such a report in May, 1762, and, as might be expected, his conclusions were adopted a day or so later by the Parliament, which demanded the suppression of the Jesuits, but was of the opinion that an annual pension of not less than one hundred and twenty and not more than seven hundred francs should be granted each member of the Society by the State. It was suspected that d'Alembert,[2] who was a friend of La Chalotais, was not altogether a stranger to the preparation of this work. However that may be, the attorney-general received the credit—or discredit according to one's personal viewpoint—of provoking the suppression of the Jesuits. La Chalotais was not yet entirely satisfied. The Jesuits were indeed out of the schools; but might not some other "foreign" religious order get control of them?

[2] Jean Le Rond d'Alembert, the associate of Diderot in editing the *Encyclopédie*.

Hence his *Essay on National Education,* which is entirely directed towards the secularization of education. We shall consider this work later.

The Jesuits being completely defeated, the intrepid attorney-general was free to turn his attention towards his other enemy, and in 1763 began the conflict between the Parliament of Brittany and the governor of the province. As the personal enemy of the governor, La Chalotais took the lead in the operation. The Parliament refused to vote the extraordinary imposts demanded by the governor in the name of the King, and forbade by decrees the levy of imposts to which it had not consented. The King annulled these decrees, and all the members of the Parliament, save twelve, resigned. The government considered La Chalotais one of the principal instigators of this little revolt and ordered his arrest with his son, Anne-Jacques de Caradeuc, and four other members of the Parliament. La Chalotais was accused of having written anonymous and insulting letters to the Minister of State, the Count de Saint-Florentin. He was confined in the citadel of Saint-Malo. During his incarceration, he wrote three memorials in his defense—it is said that he wrote with a toothpick and ink made of soot dissolved in wine, upon chocolate wrappers and other scraps of paper—which were secretly printed. A commission of judges was appointed to take charge of the trial, and began their investigations. The whole affair soon became, if it was not so from the beginning, a mere political intrigue on both sides, and the King was obliged to order the matter closed. As a measure of prudence, La Chalotais and his son were both exiled to Saintes. He remained there about ten years, during which he never ceased protesting his innocence. No doubt he was innocent, at least of the charge of writing the letters in question to the Count de Saint-Florentin—if indeed they were ever written at all, except to order. La Chalotais certainly does not appear to have been a man who would have written anonymous letters. The government, however, had no intention of allowing him to raise any more trouble, so he remained in exile until the end of the reign of Louis XV.

One of the first acts of the reign of Louis XVI was the recall of La Chalotais and his son from exile. By order of the King, the sum of one hundred thousand francs as well as a yearly pension of eight thousand francs was granted him, and he was allowed to transmit his office to his son. La Chalotais seems to have been sincerely grateful to the King, and even includes the Queen in his expressions of gratitude. "I arrive in Rennes," he wrote on November 11th, 1775. "Ten years ago to-day, we were arrested. I am going to lead a new life, thanks to the King Louis XVI and to the Queen." He may even have felt some regret for the part he had taken in fostering rebellion, as indeed he ought, if his gratitude to the King were at all sincere; for the opposition to the royal power had gained greatly through this affair, which may be regarded as one of the preludes to the Revolution. He himself, though he had helped to "sow the wind," was spared his own share in "reaping the whirlwind"; for he was fortunate enough to die on July 12, 1785, four years before the Revolution began. Not so, however, with his son, De Caradeuc, who had been so closely associated with him in defying the authority of the Crown. At the outbreak of the Revolution, he fled from Rennes to Dinan; but he was arrested, brought back, condemned and perished on the scaffold January 17, 1795, at the age of sixty-five.

At the time of his death, La Chalotais was engaged in revising his *Essay on National Education.* This work, which is preeminently a book of polemics, appeared in 1763, just one year after Rousseau's *Émile.* The moment was well chosen; for at that time everyone was occupied with the discussion of education, thanks largely to Rousseau's work. Like most of his contemporaries who wrote on the subject, La Chalotais did not possess any special qualifications for drawing up a plan for national education. As a matter of fact, as we understand the term to-day, he can hardly be said to have been interested in the subject. The aim of his essay was entirely political: he wished above all to remove from the influence of the Church, children during their most impressionable years, so that they might be indoctrinated with nationalistic ideals. The last thing that he desired was any increase in educational opportunity for the people in general. In fact, he is almost as bitter against the Christian Brothers as he is against the Jesuits. Thanks to the latter, "even the people can study. Laborers and artisans send their children to the colleges in the smaller cities," and the former "have just appeared to complete the general ruin; they teach people to read and write who ought to learn only to draw, and to handle the plane and the file, but have no disposition to do so. They are the rivals or the successors of the Jesuits." [3] This is one of the most significant passages in the entire work; for it probably explains it. It is ordinarily stated that La Chalotais

[3] See p. 60.

wrote it as a protest against the education and the educational methods of the Jesuits. At the time at which he wrote, he must have felt that, as things then were, he had little to fear from the Society of Jesus, and for a man who had attacked them so viciously elsewhere, he has singularly little to say against them, or even about them, here. He is writing against any sort of education controlled by ecclesiastics, in short against any group of religious that might become the *successors of the Jesuits;* perhaps the Christian Brothers. Hence, this little attack on them. Certain apologists for La Chalotais have pretended that "perhaps he does not so much attack the instruction in itself as the bad way in which it is given." [4] La Chalotais himself, who certainly possessed the courage of his convictions on this point, does not hesitate to make his exact meaning quite clear. Does he not tell us: "The welfare of society requires that the education of the common people should not go beyond its occupations. . . . It is hardly necessary that any of the common people should know how to read and write except those who earn their living by these arts, or whom these arts help to earn their living"? [5] That he wishes vocational training alone to be given to the lower classes is very evident. To place any other interpretation upon his words: "The peasants . . . must not be neglected in a system of instruction," [6] is absurd, in connection with all the rest that he says upon the subject, and the Latin quotation which he uses to illustrate his point.[7]

[4] G. COMPAYRÉ, *History of Pedagogy,* p. 354, translated by Payne, D. C. Heath & Company, Boston, 1897.
[5] See p. 60.
[6] See p. 65.
[7] See p. 60.

La Chalotais possessed a highly trained mind, and was well versed in argumentation. It is with a remorseless logic that he proceeds to establish the foundations of his main contentions.

1. Education should be of the State, by the State and for the State:

I claim the right to demand for the Nation an education that will depend upon the State alone; because it belongs essentially to it, because every nation has an inalienable and imprescriptible right to instruct its members, and finally because the Children of the State should be educated by members of the State.[8]

2. Education should be practical and definitely organized to prepare for certain given functions in the State:

Its aim should be equally that letters should be cultivated and that the fields should be tilled, that all the useful sciences and arts should be perfected, that justice should be rendered and that religion should be taught, that there should be learned and capable generals, magistrates and ecclesiastics, skillful artists and artisans; all in suitable proportion.[9]

3. Morals should be taught independently of religion:

The teaching of the divine law concerns the Church; but the teaching of the moral law belongs to the State, and has always belonged to it.[10]

4. Teachers should be seculars at least, and preferably laymen:

To teach letters and sciences, we must have persons who make of them a profession. The clergy cannot take it in bad

[8] See p. 53.
[9] See p. 65.
[10] See p. 149.

part that we should not, generally speaking, include ecclesiastics in this class. I am not so unjust as to exclude them from it. I acknowledge with pleasure that there are several in the universities and in the Academies who are very learned and very capable of teaching. I shall not omit the Priests of the Oratory, who are free from the prejudices of scholasticism and the cloister, and who are citizens; but I protest against the exclusion of laymen.[11]

At times his style is very involved, so much so in fact that it is often difficult to know just what he means to say. However, as this is true only of premises and never of conclusions—which latter are always admirably clear and to the point—we are almost tempted to ask ourselves if it is not the trained lawyer who is not so interested in justifying as in gaining his case; and we cannot help feeling that in some instances his arguments are less expressions of convictions than bases for assumptions.

Compayré says:

The *Essai* of La Chalotais appeared in 1763, one year after the *Émile*. Coming after the ambitious theories of a philosopher who, scorning polemics and the dissensions of his time, had written only for humanity and the future, this was a modest and opportune work, the effort of a practical man who attempted to respond to the aspirations and needs of his time. Translated into several languages, the *Essai d'éducation nationale* obtained the enthusiastic approval of Diderot, and also of Voltaire, who said: "It is a terrible book against the Jesuits, all the more so because it is written with moderation." Grimm carried his admiration so far as to write: "It would be difficult

[11] See p. 52.

to present in a hundred and fifty pages more reflections that are wise, profound, useful and truly worthy of a magistrate, of a philosopher, of a statesman." Too completely forgotten to-day, this little composition of La Chalotais deserves to be republished. Notwithstanding some prejudices that mar it, it is already wholly penetrated with the spirit of the Revolution.[12]

Certainly, in the four main contentions which we have enumerated, this work embodies much of the spirit that has animated the policies of public instruction in France for the past fifty years or so, and, as for the educational objectives which the author has in mind, almost all the theory of modern education. His aversion to popular education must not be held against him; it was quite usual in his time, even among liberals and reformers. We have already quoted Rousseau on the subject, and we may add that the great liberal, Voltaire, to whom La Chalotais had submitted his manuscript, wrote to him: "I thank you for forbidding laborers to study. I, who cultivate the earth, ask you for workmen, and not for tonsured clerics. Above all, send me some *Ignorantin* [13] Brothers to drive my ploughs or to yoke to them." [14]

[12] G. COMPAYRÉ, *History of Pedagogy,* p. 344, translated by Payne, D. C. Heath & Company, Boston, 1897.

[13] See p. 60.

[14] *Œuvres complètes de Voltaire,* Tome VIII, p. 80, P. Dupont, Paris, 1825.

ESSAY ON NATIONAL EDUCATION OR PLAN OF STUDIES FOR YOUNG PERSONS

Deposited in the record office of the Parliament of Brittany, by Messire Louis-René de Caradeuc de la Chalotais, Attorney-General of the King.

I

Some Preliminary Reflections Concerning the Usefulness of Letters, Bad Means of Teaching Them, and the Qualifications of Teachers

The Sovereign Courts have been occupied for the past year with the means of establishing in our colleges persons capable of teaching the youth of the Nation. It avails little to destroy, if we do not think of rebuilding. We had a system of education which was fit, at the most, to prepare individuals for the study of scholastic philosophy. The public welfare, the honor of the Nation require that we substitute a civil education which will prepare each coming generation to follow successfully the different occupations in the State.

In this memorial, I propose to prove the necessity and indicate the means of doing this. In order to judge adequately, it is perhaps necessary to go further back, and to show the usefulness of the sciences and letters, to what extent a good or a bad education may influence the happiness or the unhappiness of a nation, and to consider at the same time what a nation has the right to exact of its teachers.

Knowledge is necessary to man. If he has duties to fulfil, it is necessary that he should know them: to know them is to possess the most useful of all knowledge; it is to be already well advanced in the course in which useful citizens are trained. Ignorance is good for nothing, and it is harmful to everything. It is impossible for any light to come forth from darkness, and it is not possible to walk in darkness without going astray.

If the apologists of ignorance have the intention of extolling only that kind of ignorance which leads to intelligent and reasonable doubt, and which does not decide because it is aware of itself, they should have called it knowledge; for it is in fact a very real and a very estimable kind of knowledge to know how to doubt and to appreciate one's own inability. But I am speaking now of ignorance, properly called, which is almost always presumptuous, which decides, approves and condemns with the same degree of temerity, and I declare that if we compare its baleful effects with the abuse of knowledge, the question is decided. There is no one who does not agree with me in saying that ignorance is harmful to everything, and who does not desire the reestablishment of good studies in order to diminish as much as possible the abuse of knowledge.

The rudest and the most ignorant centuries have always been the most vicious and the most corrupt. Leave man without culture, ignorant and, consequently, insensible to his duties; he will become timid, superstitious and perhaps cruel. If he is not taught what is good, he will necessarily concern himself with what is bad. The mind and the heart cannot remain empty.

Let us abandon all paradoxes concerning the uselessness or the danger of knowledge; let us separate the thing from the abuse of it; let us direct the studies towards the greatest public benefit; and, while waiting to know whether human society such as it is, whether man such as he is not, could do without it, let us work to impress on the minds of youths the knowledge which they will need to fulfil the duties of their different callings, to work in them for their own happiness, for that of others, and to contribute thereby to the general good of society.

No one fears to assert in general that in the state in which Europe is, there being no need of fearing the invasion of Barbarians, the most enlightened people (all other things being equal, or even not entirely so) will always have the advantage over those that are less so. It will surpass them by its industry, it will subjugate them perhaps by its arms, and, all professions being better exercised, all service better performed, all minds more cultivated and sounder, public and private operations better concerted and better executed, discipline of every kind will be superior and better observed, the interior and exterior administration will be wiser, abuses will be fewer and sooner restrained.

We must apply ourselves in childhood and in youth, otherwise we become incapable of doing so for the rest of our lives. Nature makes a difference between men (no one can doubt this); education makes a greater one perhaps. Talent is a gift of Nature; but there enters into talent well appraised a great deal of what is called acquired art, that is, habit. If it were possible to analyse the talent of a Bossuet, of a Corneille, of a Racine, of a La Fontaine,[1] we should in truth find a richer ground, but perfected by long and continual effort. Cultivation always increases the good quality and the fertility of the soil. Application without talent will make only mediocre men; talent without application will never produce superior men.

To suppose that Nature does everything, that exercise and application add nothing to natural talents is a pernicious maxim which renders good minds listless and increases the discouragement of mediocre ones. We realize from experience that almost all men do not go as far as they could go, if they brought to what they do a greater application. There must be no misapprehension, all who are born to have intelligence do not become men of intelligence. It is to the general advantage that men of all professions should be convinced that it is impossible to know well what has not been learned well. To deny the power of education is to deny in spite of experience the power of habits. What could not an education established by law and guided by examples do! It would change in a few years the customs of an entire nation. Among the Spartans, it conquered Nature itself. There is an art of improving the breed of animals, could not there also be one of perfecting the human race?

---

[1] Jacques-Bénigne Bossuet, Bishop of Meaux, orator and historian, noted chiefly for his sermons (1627–1704). Pierre Corneille, dramatist, the "father of French tragedy" (1606–1684). Jean Racine, tragic poet and dramatist (1639–1699). Jean de la Fontaine, writer, best known for his fables of birds and animals (1621–1695).

If humanity is susceptible of a certain degree of perfection, it is by means of education that it can reach it. The object of the legislator should be to procure for minds the highest possible degree of accuracy and capacity, for characters the highest degree of excellence and of elevation, for bodies the highest degree of strength and health.

We must not hope to attain easily this point of perfection. Too many obstacles oppose themselves especially amongst us; but it must always be our aim. This is the only means of approaching it.

The public morals of a great nation are not always good; too general dissoluteness of youth, too widespread luxury, little love of country and of the public good, the natural restlessness of our spirits, dissipation, forgetfulness of the essential duties of one's profession, a multitude of known causes, oppose themselves to that consideration which is due to merit and to virtue, and which is their most flattering reward. Without self-respect all education will be imperfect, even if the laws should favor it. *Quid leges sine moribus vanæ proficiunt?* [2] said one of the finest and best minds of antiquity. But the government can subjugate even morals. The titles, the honors, the blame which it distributes are as current as its money.

Public education is not directed towards the greatest public usefulness. This is a fact of which the truth has been demonstrated. Fortunately the possibility of reforming it has been as well proved as the necessity thereof. There are a prodigious number of known truths, scattered in an infinite number of books, dispersed in an infinite number of

[2] What is the good of laws in the absence of morals? (Horace).

minds. It is only a matter of collecting them and arranging them, in order to enlighten masters and teachers; but since education is deficient even in principle, it is necessary to rebuild the structure from the very foundations.

I shall not mention here everything defective that has been observed in the ordinary methods. The body of learning has greatly increased in the past two centuries. Thus it is easy to do better than did those who preceded us. However, we should not forget the services which they have rendered humanity. The establishment of the universities and colleges banished gross ignorance, and the plan of study which was adopted was perhaps the best that it was possible to follow then. From the beginning of the last century the university desired a reformation in the curriculum. More fortunate circumstances should to-day make us determine to correct the bad routine of the colleges and to seek a more useful manner of teaching and of learning.

Our education shows everywhere the barbarity of past centuries, of a time when only those who were destined for the priesthood were required to study; when there were no books except those which were copied by the monks, and it was necessary to send to Rome to have the works of Cicero transcribed; when the nobles hardly knew how to read and write; when wars and pillages rendered books rare and studies difficult, and there were schools only at the cathedrals and monasteries. The mother tongue of the French was at that time only a formless and uncertain jargon, and a barbarous Latin had invaded the writs, the charters of kings and the decrees of the sovereign courts. Philosophy was reduced to disputations on the books of Aristotle, and moral philosophy did not teach man his duties. Physics dealt only with chimerical causes and effects which one did not even think of observing. In the place of astronomy and natural history reigned fables which brought about the deliriums of astrology and superstitious practices of medicine. Theology and jurisprudence led only to scholastic disputations or to opinions of doctors; because, for lack of criticism, the texts were abandoned to rely upon summaries or glossaries.

If sublime virtues and eminent talents shine in the midst of these centuries of ignorance, it is through an effort of Nature alone, and of one which she makes but rarely. What great men were Abbot Suger, Bertrand du Guesclin, Barbazan, Bayard, and, in less remote times, the Constable de Montmorency, Colbert, who had not studied! [3] Let no one be astonished; ideas of honor and of virtue predominate in superior souls, and sentiments are far above acquired knowledge. It must appear even more astonishing that great discoveries of the first order were made in those bar-

---

[3] Abbot Suger, abbot of the Monastery of St. Denis, minister of Louis VI and of Louis VII. He was regent of France during the second Crusade, and wrote a *Life of Louis VI* (1081–1151). Bertrand du Guesclin, military hero, fought against the English (*cir.* 1320–1380). Arnauld-Guillaume de Barbazan, general in the armies of Charles VI and Charles VII, was known as *the knight without reproach* (1360–1431). Pierre du Terrail, Chevalier de Bayard, known as *the knight without fear and without reproach,* fought with great valor in the wars of Charles VIII, Louis XII and François I (*cir.* 1473–1524). There were several Constables de Montmorency. The most famous of the family was Anne de Montmorency, who was mortally wounded at St. Denis in a battle against the Calvinists (1493–1567). Jean-Baptiste Colbert, man of humble origin who became minister of Louis XIV (1619–1683). Certainly Suger and Colbert, at least, were not uneducated men.

barous times. They were the products of genius, whose particular characteristic is to pierce the most profound darkness, and even to rise above the most enlightened centuries. The greatest culture of the mind cannot add to genius; but we should at least endeavor to establish a system of education that does not stifle it.

At the revival of letters and sciences, the darkness which had covered Europe for so long disappeared. Printing was invented, colleges were founded, emulation was excited, and people were ashamed of being ignorant; but education was too much confined to the colleges, and it has remained almost entirely scholastic. Letters constitute only a part of the instruction of a nation. Instruction has greater aims. It is for the State what education is for individuals. Its object is to render a nation in every way more enlightened, and consequently more flourishing.

Letters are at the same time the nourishment of the mind, the instruction and the ornament of society. Plato and Cicero, who taught their contemporaries, to-day still enlighten the universe, and the most remote posterity will profit by their lessons. In the State, letters should be considered the source and support of the human and civil virtues. Woe to the nations among which the love of letters would be extinguished!

Letters have received in France the most brilliant testimonials of the patronage of our kings; and the establishments which they have founded to assure every kind of instruction would have been the most solid foundation of public prosperity, if the education of youth had been better directed. The universities, the academies, the chairs of languages, the schools of hydrography: all seemed to concur in producing citizens distinguished in all subjects. The monarch who governs us has encouraged the sciences and has excited emulation by sending explorers to the North, to the Equator, to the Cape of Good Hope, and by founding the Military School; but unfortunately such precious aid is offered only subordinately, if I dare express myself thus. The foremost national instruction has remained the same, and everything has been subjected to it. It is restrained everywhere by the education of the colleges, and this education has been limited to the study of the Latin language. In most of the colleges, absolutely no knowledge of our language is acquired. Only an abstract philosophy is learned: one that is of absolutely no use in the course of life, and which comprises neither the principles of ethics necessary to conduct oneself well in society, nor anything that it is necessary to know as a man. Religion is taught with no more care. Thus, young men leave college having learned hardly anything that can be of use to them in their various occupations.

I appeal to experience and to the testimony of the Nation, of those even who through prejudice would maintain the usual methods. Can the knowledge which is acquired in college be called knowledge? What is known after ten years which are employed either in preparing to enter college or in fatiguing oneself in the course of the different classes? Does one know even the only thing which has been studied: the languages, and which are only the instruments to open the way for the sciences? With the exception of a little Latin—which must be studied anew, if one wishes to make some use of this language—the young men are interested in forgetting, on entering society, almost everything that their pretended teachers have taught them. Is this the fruit that the Nation should obtain from ten years of the most assiduous work?

Out of a thousand students who have completed what is called their course in the Humanities and Philosophy, hardly ten could be found who would be able to explain clearly and with understanding the first elements of religion, who would know how to write a letter, who could habitually distinguish a good reason from a bad one, or a proven from an unproven fact.

The Greeks and the Romans, wiser and more vigilant on a subject so important as education than we are, would not have abandoned it to men who had views and interests different from those of their country.[4] It was directed by legislators or philosophers capable of being such. Solon would never have entrusted to Spartans, and even less to Helots, the education of Athenians, and Lycurgus would not have entrusted to Athenians that of Spartans. When Antipater demanded of the latter a hundred and fifty children as hostages, they replied that they would prefer to give double this number of mature men, for fear lest a foreign education might corrupt their children.

Since education should prepare citizens for the State, it is evident that it should relate to its constitution and its laws. It would be fundamentally bad if it were contrary to them. It is a principle of every good government that each particular family should be regulated according to the plan of the great family which comprises them all. How was it possible to think that men who are not concerned about the

---

[4] The allusion is, of course, to the clergy and the Jesuits in particular.

49

State, who are accustomed to place the head of a religious order above the heads of the State, their order above the Country, their institution and constitutions above the laws, would be capable of bringing up and teaching the youth of a kingdom? The enthusiasm and illusions of devotion delivered the French to such teachers, who were themselves subjected to a foreign master. Thus the education of the entire Nation—that part of legislation which is the basis and the foundation of states—remained under the immediate control of an ultramontane rule, necessarily hostile to our laws.[5] What inconsistency, and what a scandal!

Without entering too deeply into the consequences which result from so enormous an error, should we be astonished if the vice of monasticism has infected all our education? A foreigner, to whom its details had been explained would imagine that France wished to people seminaries, cloisters and Latin colonies. How would it be possible to suppose that the study of a foreign language, and the practices of the cloister could be the means of training soldiers, magistrates and heads of families fitted to follow the different callings which, united, constitute the strength of the State?

We are imbued with monastic ideas which govern us without our knowing it, and without anyone perceiving it. Little devotional practices (and why not dare to say it, since the wise and virtuous Abbé Fleury [6] has said it?) which do not recall the great ideas of religion have taken possession of the Heads of the Churches.

[5] Again, the clergy and Jesuits from a Jansenist viewpoint.
[6] Claude Fleury, tutor of the Princes de Conti, and author of *Traité du choix et de la méthode des études,* 1686 (1640–1725).

Hence these congregations, these confraternities, these conventicles which turn Christians aside from the places where they should learn religion, which prevent pastors from acquiring an instruction sufficiently sound for them to be in a position to instruct others.

When it is a question of schools or colleges, instantly mystic notions take possession of high personages, and only communities of religious or at least of ecclesiastics are mentioned to entrust to them the direction. It is doubted if married professors can teach children. When we recall that in the fifteenth century it required an ordinance—and an ordinance of a Papal Legate in France—to permit physicians to marry, what can we think of the effect of ecclesiastic prejudices? They wish to exclude all except celibates from purely civil positions. What a paradox! It seems that to have children would be an impediment to being able to educate them, and that precautions were being taken to prevent the State from peopling itself, or that it may not people itself too much. The welfare of society manifestly requires a civil education, and if we do not secularize ours, we shall live eternally under the slavery of pedantry.

Why indeed should the colleges be administered by monks or by priests? Under what pretext should the teaching of letters and sciences devolve exclusively upon them? The ecclesiastics will always assign the motive of instructing the children in their religion. It is certain that of all instruction this is the most important; but is it true that only ecclesiastics can teach them the catechism, instruct them in French and Latin, explain to them Horace and Virgil?

There are excellent catechisms printed, and it is not necessary to have been advanced to Holy Orders to read to children those of Bossuet or Fleury; and we may well ask whether it is necessary to be constantly writing new ones, or to revise so often those that have already been written. It is in the bosom of Christian families, and from the instruction given in the parish that the children should learn the elements of Christianity. The churches are the true schools of religion. The Jesuits, who were called approved scholars and who taught it, were not priests, although they wore the habit. Moreover, to employ forty or fifty half-hours a year to explain well or badly the catechism of Canisius [7] is not what learned people would call teaching religion.

A chaplain in each college would suffice for this function, under pretext of which the ecclesiastics claim the administration of the colleges as their exclusive patrimony.

I should not forget an important observation, which is that at present almost all the distinguished men in the sciences and letters are laics. It is constantly being repeated that there are not enough priests to fulfil the sacerdotal functions; why then wish to make of them college professors and tutors?

A crowd of idle priests overruns the cities, while the country districts are deprived of clergy. They no longer wish to live in the country, and thus new places are sought for them in the cities: places which can be accorded as revocable benefices. One of the ills of the State is that everyone wishes to have at his orders troops which are not kept at his expense.

To teach letters and sciences, we must have persons who make of them a profession. The clergy cannot take it in

[7] St. Peter Canisius, Jesuit, author of a *Parvus Catechismus Catholicorum* (1521–1597).

bad part that we should not, generally speaking, include ecclesiastics in this class. I am not so unjust as to exclude them from it. I acknowledge with pleasure that there are several in the universities and in the academies who are very learned and very capable of teaching. I shall not omit the Priests of the Oratory,[8] who are free from the prejudices of scholasticism and the cloister, and who are citizens; but I protest against the exclusion of laymen. I claim the right to demand for the Nation an education that will depend upon the State alone; because it belongs essentially to it, because every nation has an inalienable and imprescriptible right to instruct its members, and finally because the children of the State should be educated by members of the State.

The exclusive right of instructing the youth, which it is desired to grant to regular and secular priests, is not the only disadvantage which results from monastic ideas. Others can be observed even in the details of the education given in the colleges.

Among the regulars, the objective of the exercises is rather to train the teachers than to instruct pupils. In the first years, a young teacher—who himself is only an older student—finishes his own course of studies at the expense of others. He overburdens his pupils with themes which it costs him little trouble to dictate, with long and tiresome lessons. All the trouble and all the work are on the part of the children. During this time, the teacher is occupied with whatever may be useful to him. He makes notes and abstracts. He prepares himself by means of discourses for

[8] Congregation of the Oratory; founded in Rome in 1564 by St. Philip Neri and established in France in 1611.

preaching, or by reading for the direction of consciences. As soon as he is trained and has put himself in a position by means of the knowledge which he has acquired to be useful to others, he abandons teaching, and goes to devote himself to the vocation to which he is destined for the glory and profit of his order.

The management of the classes shows the effects of the uniformity of the cloister. The corrections partake of the nature of cloistral discipline, and seem intended to abase the spirit rather than to elevate it. All of this restraint is dreary and discouraging, and its most ordinary effect is to create a life-long hatred for study. Mature men would hardly resist the constrained and sedentary life to which the children are subjected. It is contrary to Nature that in half a day they should remain seated for five or six hours. Furthermore, there is a monotony in the studies which they are made to pursue, which almost necessarily leads to indolence and distaste for study. Always Latin and themes! Far from inspiring a taste for any sciences, for any art, the tedium and the dreariness which everywhere accompany study produce a repugnance for the elements of all the sciences, for all the arts. Thus nothing is more frequent than to see young people abandon all reading after they leave the colleges. The first fruit of what is called the education of young people is to leave them without anything to which to apply themselves, and at an age when it is most necessary for them to be occupied in order to guard against the multiple dangers of a leisure which is subject to the assaults of the most furious passions.

Let us compare the gloomy darkness of our classrooms with the gaiety of the Portico or the Lyceum of Athens.

Amongst us, a teacher, who is himself still almost a child, returns with his mind impressed by two years of ecstasy and oppressed by despotism, and oppresses other children. Amongst the Greeks, the young people strolled about. They took in these places—if I may use the term—their lessons and their diversions. They conversed with such men as Aristides, Miltiades, Plato, Aristotle, Xenophon, Demosthenes, etc.

In our colleges, there is no amusement for the more frivolous-minded, whom it would be better to entertain by some diversity and by some agreeable studies. The only amusements are enigmas, ballets, dramatic performances, as ridiculously composed as they are acted: exercises only the more contemptible because to loss of time are added examples of the worst possible taste.

Teachers accustomed to scholastic subtilities train young people, who contract the habit of disputing and of cavilling. Some of them seem for the rest of their lives to be always on the school benches.

But the greatest defect of this education, and the most inevitable perhaps as long as it will be entrusted to persons who have renounced the world, and who, far from seeking to know it, should think only of fleeing from it, is the complete lack of instruction in the moral and political virtues. Our education has no relation to our customs, as did that of the ancients. After having endured all the fatigues and the weariness of the colleges, our youths find themselves under the necessity of learning of what consist those duties that are common to all men. They have not been taught any principles by which to judge actions, morals, opinions and customs. They have everything to learn about such important matters. They are inspired with a devotion which is only an imitation of religion, practices to take the place of virtue, and which are only its shadow.

Care of the health, the means of preserving it and physical exercises have been too much overlooked. All that concerns the commonest and most ordinary affairs, what constitutes the support of life and the foundation of civil society, have been neglected. Most young people know neither the world in which they live, nor the earth which nourishes them, nor the men who supply their needs, nor the animals which serve them, nor the workmen and the artisans whom they employ. They have not even the beginnings of knowledge concerning them. No advantage is taken of their natural curiosity in order to increase it. They do not know how to admire either the marvels of Nature or the wonders of the arts. Thus, what is taught them, what is not taught them, the manner of imparting instruction to them and of depriving them of it, all bear the stamp of the monastic spirit.

This spirit, which has for aim only the subjugation of all the faculties of the soul to the observance of a religious rule, could not do other than limit the sciences, and, so to say, place a dividing wall between them. It is not in places where the study of sciences which are of use to the world is purely accessory that it could be thought that all truths are connected, that they are easier to understand when they have points of contact, that it is necessary to bring them nearer to each other in order better to recognize them; since it is ordinarily the characteristic of errors to be isolated and inconsistent.

With a college administration which is similar to the observance of the rule of a religious order, and subjects all the members to an equal constraint, it is not possible to hope to vary the instruction according to the needs of individuals. He who is some day to command armies, or he who is destined for the highest places in the magistracy is educated like the son of a major of the civil militia, or like the son of a village practitioner. I should not complain of a good education being given to the high and the low alike. What I regret is that an equally bad one is given to all.

It is then only by delivering us from this monkish spirit, which for more than two centuries has embarrassed civilized states by all kinds of obstacles, that it will be possible to succeed in establishing a basis for a general education, upon which will rest all special instruction. This basis can be founded only upon a connected system of the different branches of human knowledge—as has been wisely said more than fifteen years ago, by the author of *Considérations sur les mœurs* [9]—since it is indispensable that all branches of instruction should tend to the same end.

II

The Number of Colleges and of Students

Everything holds together in the moral as well as in the physical order. Private education and college education depend upon national education and even upon the constitution of the State.

---

[9] *Considérations sur les mœurs de ce siècle,* 1751, by Charles Pinot Duclos, moralist (1704–1772).

Is it military or commercial? Is it a monarchy, a republic, an aristocracy? Is it a populous state or one with few inhabitants? It is evident that all general policy, all political operations depend upon an exact calculation of the numbers of the different classes: clergy, nobility, military, officials of justice, merchants, laborers, artisans, etc.

For instance, it is asked whether there are too many or too few colleges in France. The answer to this question depends upon knowing whether there are enough laborers, enough soldiers; whether there are not too many professional men, whether there are too many or too few ecclesiastics, too many or too few men of letters. In short, it depends upon the proportion which exists, or ought to exist among the different classes according to their usefulness or their necessity. Without entering into details, which would be useless here, and accepting the proportion which appears to be fixed by the experience of centuries and of nations at a hundredth part for the military, I reply that there are not enough laborers for a country in which there are uncultivated lands, and where the State, rich enough in itself to export its natural products, imports often from foreign countries what it could itself produce.

There is no need to fear an excess in the numbers of a class which nourishes the others, and which is continually producing real values for the State; but it is dangerous in all those classes which, while creating no new values, live on those that create them.

Is there any need, for the instruction of the people and for the welfare of religion, that there be at least two hundred and fifty thousand priests, monks and nuns in the kingdom?

At the time of the Pope St. Cornelius,[10] there were in the city of Rome only forty-six priests, and in all only one hundred and fifty-four clerics, although there was an innumerable population. Now there are several thousands. Either there were not enough then, or there are too many at present. The number of ecclesiastics has increased prodigiously in all Catholic countries. What functions do they exercise to-day which they did not in those flourishing days of religion?

Does the institution of legal proceedings require that unbelievable number of officials and agents of justice who afflict the inhabitants of town and country? Seissel,[11] under Louis XII, counted in France more officials of justice than in all the rest of the kingdoms of Europe together. This calculation was without doubt exaggerated; but to what an extent has not the number increased since then?

Are there not too many writers, too many academies, too many colleges? In former times it was difficult to be learned for lack of books now it is the multitude of books that prevent it. We can say with Tacitus: *Ut multarum rerum, sic litterarum intemperantia laboramus.*[12] There were never so many students in a kingdom where everyone complains of depopulation. Even the common people wish to study; laborers and artisans send their children to the colleges in the smaller towns where it costs little to live, and when they have completed a course of useless studies

[10] Cornelius, Pope and Martyr, reigned *cir.* 251–253.

[11] Claude de Seissel, historian, ambassador from the King of France to the King of England (*cir.* 1450–1520).

[12] We are troubled now by a flood of literature as of many other things.

which have taught them nothing except to disdain the calling of their fathers, they rush into the cloisters, into the priesthood, they become officers of justice, and often subjects that are harmful to society. *Multorum manibus egent res humanæ, paucorum capita sufficiunt.*[13]

The Brothers of the Christian Doctrine, who are called *Ignorantins,*[14] have appeared to complete the ruin of everything. They teach reading and writing to people who ought to learn only to draw and to handle the plane and the file, but who no longer wish to do so. They are the rivals or the successors of the Jesuits. The welfare of society requires that the education of the common people should not go beyond its occupations. Any man who looks beyond his trade will never work at it with courage and patience. It is hardly necessary that any of the common people should know how to read and write except those who earn their living by these arts, or whom these arts help to earn their living.

We know that in a well-organized society the number of those who live at the expense of the others should not be

[13] The hands of many are needed for human affairs; but the heads of few are enough.

[14] This reference is not to the *Congregation of the Christian Doctrine,* which was founded in 1592 by César de Bus for the purpose of teaching the catechism to children and artisans, and which lasted until the Revolution, nor does *Ignorantins* refer to the *Brothers of St. John of God,* who cared for the poor, and in humility called themselves thus. Here is meant the *Brothers of the Christian Schools* (Christian Brothers) founded by St. Jean-Baptiste de la Salle in 1684 for the general instruction of the poor; they were, and still are often called *Brothers of the Christian Doctrine,* and were, more or less contemptuously referred to as *Ignorantins* by their detractors, as they interested themselves only in vernacular schools of the lower grade.

multiplied, and that it is necessary to keep occupations of this nature within the limits of the strictly necessary. It seems, however, that in practice we have adopted a maxim exactly contrary. Soon we shall no longer have among the common people other than wretched artisans, militiamen and students.

Thus it is more advantageous for the State that there be few colleges, provided they be good, and that the course of studies be complete, than to have many mediocre ones. It is better that there be fewer students, provided they be better taught; and they will be more easily taught if they are not in such great numbers.

We live upon systems, inconsistencies and commonplaces. It is said that we must do good, so we cannot then do too much of it, nor do it too often. Colleges are useful and necessary, there cannot then be too many students. It is essential to know our religion, there cannot then be too many convents, and religious orders, nor too many retreats; even for country people, for fathers and mothers of families, whom it is contrary to good order to make leave their homes and their work. And yet, is the world any better? Is society any better regulated? Is not corruption just as great and just as universal? How are we to reconcile these evils which cannot be concealed with the commonplaces which we hear every day about the purer morals of our fathers who knew almost none of these institutions?

On the other hand, it is maintained that the colleges are neither well guided nor well managed, that in them the sciences are badly taught: and to this it is hardly possible not to agree; therefore the colleges should be suppressed, and the sciences should not be taught. Books, it is said, are the scourge of children; from which it is concluded that they should not read any. Thus are formed extreme opinions. The truth is never unreasonable, reason never exaggerates; but there are an infinite number of people who do not distinguish shades of color; for them everything is either black or white.

It is very astonishing that the refinement and the enlightenment of the past century were able, while criticizing it without ceasing, to suffer an education so defective as ours. Habit which controls men, the routine of organizations, a system of education of the sixteenth century, which had never been reformed, and which was unreformable in principle, and, I repeat, monastic ideas would have perpetuated the abuses and the defects. What was done in the beginning to perfect education rendered it a little better then. It is precisely that which has perpetuated its imperfections and deficiencies.

The Jesuits were convinced that the plan of studies (*Ratio studiorum*) drawn up under Acquaviva [15] in the sixteenth century, and the feeble opuscule of Jouvency [16] were masterpieces of literature. Dominated by old prejudices, they were the last to abandon them, and they resisted all reform. They admitted no books except their own, and they began to adopt Cartesianism only when others began to abandon it.

[15] Claudius Acquaviva, fifth general of the Jesuits. According to the *Catholic Encyclopedia,* he was practically the author of the *Ratio Studiorum* (1543–1616).

[16] Joseph de Jouvency, Jesuit (1643–1719). The "feeble opuscule," to which reference is here made, is his *Magistris scholarum inferiorum Societatis Jesu de ratione discendi et docendi,* 1703.

NATIONAL EDUCATION

It is easier to come out of the darkness of ignorance than out of the presumption of false knowledge. In ten years, Russia has made more progress in physics and in the natural sciences than other nations would have made in a hundred. It suffices to examine the memorials of the Academy of Petersburg. Perhaps Portugal, which is entirely reforming its studies, will advance more rapidly in proportion than we shall if we do not think seriously of reforming ours.

During the last centuries, all instruction was directed towards the study of the languages. In the present one, a mania for cleverness has taken possession of the Nation, and has had a bad effect on all professions. Society has perhaps become more agreeable for some individuals; but society in general, the State, has lost by it. Its interest requires that all professions should be exercised by capable men. It is of no importance to an ill person whether or not his physician writes his prescriptions in epigrams. People seek a lawyer who is familiar with the laws, and not a witty man. In a word, the State demands that every man devote himself to his profession, and if the customs do not change, very soon there will be in reality no other professions than the mechanical arts.

The taste for cleverness, having become a fashion, has banished science and true learning, to which we owed so much, on the basis of which our great men had been trained, and which are too much neglected by far, not to say absolutely despised.

It is possible that there be some very able individuals in a nation, and that the mass of the nation be very little learned.

It is the colleges compared with each other that indicate the sum of the knowledge diffused in the minds of the citizens; but it is the memorials of the Academies and the good books that indicate the knowledge of the nation.

If we compare our colleges, of which the methods are defective, with those of Oxford, of Cambridge, of Leyden, of Göttingen, which have better elementary books than ours, we shall see that a German and an Englishman are necessarily better taught than a Frenchman. For the same reason, it is impossible that a well-bred Roman, who was educated by the conversation and in the society of an honorable man, who defended cases, who became an ædile, a prætor, an augur, a consul, who presided over the Senate and commanded armies, was not a man superior to our Englishmen and our Frenchmen; because it is experience alone that can train men.

But if we compare our memorials of the Academy of Sciences with those of London, of Leipzig, etc., our good books with those of foreigners, we shall see that a Frenchman who has been guided in the right way at an early age is as able and perhaps better informed than another, that he has more order, more method and more taste; for we must render justice to the French Nation. It will be all that it wishes to be, all that we wish it to be. It has examples and models of all descriptions to compete with those of antiquity. It has had its Themistocles, its Miltiades and its Pericles, its Demosthenes, its Sophocles and its Aristophanes, and it will have them again when we seriously desire it. It is the State, it is the greater part of the Nation which must be principally kept in mind in education; for twenty million men should be considered more than one million, and the peasants, who are not yet an order in France—as they are in Sweden—must not be neglected in a system of education. Its aim should be equally that letters should be cultivated, and that the fields should be tilled, that all the useful sciences and arts should be perfected, that justice should be rendered and that religion should be taught, that there should be learned and capable generals, magistrates and ecclesiastics, skillful artists and artisans: all in suitable proportion. It is the duty of the government to make each citizen sufficiently happy in his state of life, so that he may not be forced to go out of it.

To attain these various objectives, it will not be necessary for the State to inconvenience individuals nor to restrain the liberty of citizens. It needs only to preside over all, to animate all, to remove obstacles, to provide facilities, and encouragements for an industrious nation, to say what I think, a nation like ours (I speak of the generality of the Nation) needs only to be educated. We have an infinite number of excellent books; but few of them are textbooks or elementary books. Let such books be made for children and for the ignorant; then let genius act. Do not restrict the liberty of minds, inspire love of country and of the public good, and talents will not harm those who possess them if they do not abuse them.

There will be scholars in France when knowledge is honored, and when it is not altogether at the service of a party, of cabal and of intrigue, as we have seen, throughout a century, ecclesiastical learning reduced to what was called the business of the time, or better say, that of the day. There will be professions when there are real apprenticeships, and when application and talents lead to consideration.

It is easy to see that all these great matters depend upon legislation; but it is well to bring them again to the attention of a wise and prudent government, to indicate the extent which should be given to a good education.

Here would be the place to consider at what age children should enter the colleges; but that depends upon the age at which they should leave them in order to begin to prepare for the different professions, and that again is a matter of legislation which deserves careful consideration.

Is it right that children should be inscribed on the rolls of the army or the navy at the age of ten or twelve years, solely in order that they may obtain the recompense for a service which they are incapable of performing? It is a manifest injustice to those who serve in reality.

The ages for receiving Holy Orders and entering the magistracy are fixed by law, and it seems that professional training has been considered only in reference to these professions; as though the others were not equally in need of it.

I think that around ten years might be fixed as the age for entering the colleges, and seventeen for leaving. Seventeen years was the age at which the Romans assumed the *toga virilis*.

A system of education is never discussed without considering the question of public and private education; but if we had good plans of study and elementary books, perhaps we should see that the latter would become as easy as the former, and there would be no comparison to be made. A mother's milk is always better for children than that of hirelings.

A man of great intelligence [17] has said that the greatest service that literary societies could render letters, sciences and arts, would be to prepare methods and indicate means which would spare work and avoid error, and which would lead to truth by the shortest and surest ways.

A young man who is in the right path will know more at the age of twenty-five than another at the age of thirty, if the latter has not been well guided.

Studies are too long and too difficult, because they are encumbered by so much that is useless. This is evident in the case of the colleges, and it is the reason why so much is studied and so little accomplished. When we are not on the right road, the farther we go, the farther we are from our goal. A good guide would spare us much of the distance. It is the useless and false things that are long and prolix. What is true has the additional merit of being more easily understood. It is what is false that is unintelligible.

It seems that in reference to ideas concerning education, there is among the public, in Europe even, a species of fermentation which ought naturally to produce good results. It will certainly produce them amongst us, if it is kept up and utilized, if we do not content ourselves with useless speculations, and if we do not forget within six months what should be put into practice from now on.

It is a question of knowing whether it is possible to obtain better results from our colleges than we have been obtaining. I think that it is easy to prove the affirmative by reasons and by examples. This is what I propose to do in this essay.

[17] Charles Pinot Duclos, in his *Considération sur les mœurs*.

I shall not enter into the details which would be endless, and I exhort teachers to read all the good books on education and on the choice of studies.[18] I shall establish the principles, and present a general formula for a literary education. I shall indicate the principal subjects for study at each age, and note the good elementary books which are lacking. The consequences and the details will present themselves of their own accord.

What is the best plan of studies for the education of youth, and what method should be followed to put this plan into effect?

It may be seen that it is not a question here of a full treatise on education, which would require more extensive views; but simply of a plan of studies that could be substituted for those of the colleges.

I accept throughout this memorial the distinction made by the Abbé Fleury between knowledge which is necessary, useful and agreeable and that which is the most generally useful, according to the needs of different persons.

This distinction is enough, provided we take care to accommodate the studies to the differences in the age of the students, to indicate clearly their aim, not to confuse the means with the end, the words with the things and the

[18] Locke. The Abbé Fleury. The *Dissertation on education* by the Abbé Gédouin. *L'Éducation des Filles,* by M. de Fénelon. The chapter by Montaigne on the teaching of children, which is admirable; and it is very astonishing that, since everyone knows it, we have not profited more by it; this is due to the unfortunate routine. The Abbé de Saint-Pierre, in whose works there are excellent things on the moral and political virtues. M. Nicole, *L'Éducation du Prince.* The miscellaneous works of Crouzas, Bacon, Milton, Du Marsais, Erasmus, Father Lamy: all in general without exception. (Note by La Chalotais.)

instrument with the art itself; provided we indicate exactly in each subject the limits of knowledge beyond which the human mind cannot go: and this seems to me to be the most essential thing in any plan for education.

III

Principles of a Plan of Studies

A plan is the design of an edifice composed of several parts which should harmonize and form a whole. A plan of studies for young people is the order and the arrangement of teaching according to which the knowledge which precedes should serve for acquiring that which follows, and everything should concur in attaining the end according to the aims which have been proposed.

It seems that this method ought not to be a great mystery. The principles to be observed in teaching children should be the same as those by which Nature itself teaches them. Nature is the best of teachers.

It suffices then to observe how the first knowledge enters the minds of children and how grown men themselves acquire it.

Experience—against which it is vain to philosophize—teaches us that we possess at birth only an empty capacity which gradually fills itself, and that there are no other channels than sensation and reflection by which ideas can enter the mind.

It seems certain that man begins to acquire knowledge

only when he begins to make use of his senses: his first sensation is his first knowledge.

Children are no more capable than older people of reflection other than by means of acquired ideas. Abstract ideas presuppose in the mind knowledge with which they may connect; they are called abstract only because they are derived from particular ideas. They must, consequently, be preceded in the order of teaching by particular ideas; just as in the order of Nature. You would never be able to make a person understand that the whole is greater than any part of it, unless he already had an idea of what is a part and what is a whole.

Thus the fundamental principle of every good method is to begin with what is perceptible, and proceed by degrees to what is intellectual; to attain what is complex by means of what is simple, and to make sure of facts before seeking causes.

The surest means of teaching others is to lead them by the way which one himself has been obliged to follow in order to learn. Now everyone can realize from his own experience that ideas are simpler in proportion as they are less abstract, and as they are more closely connected with the senses. Such ideas have the further advantage of being determined by themselves, whereas abstract notions, on the contrary, are vague, and offer the mind nothing fixed. The aim of the philosopher should be to determine his ideas and to fix them.

It is then an invariable rule to inculcate through perceptible and repeated examples the particular knowledge of which general maxims and abstract terms presuppose the possession.

"If we understood the progress of knowledge," says a man who has certainly discovered its origin (Abbé de Condillac [19]), "it would follow in such an order that what each new thing learned would add to what had immediately preceded it would be too simple to need any proofs. In this manner we should reach the most complicated concepts, and we should descend without difficulty from these to the simplest. It would hardly be possible to forget them, or at least if it happened, the connection between them would make it easy to regain them."

"By this means," continues this author, "we should seem rather to discover new truths than to demonstrate those which had already been discovered. Not only would young people be convinced; but they would also be put in a position to render to themselves account of all the progress which they had made, and of making further progress by themselves. They would always know where they stand, whence they come and where they are going. They would be able to judge for themselves the road which their guide had traced for them, and, if they found danger in following it, to take another."

We should study as much to develop ourselves as to inform ourselves. How do men develop themselves and acquire knowledge? It is by seeing different objects, by listening to learned people, by experimenting, by reflecting. He who has seen most, observed most, reflected most, is the most able. He to whom the best models have been shown has the surest taste. This is an advantage which certain children have over others. A greater number of objects have

[19] Étienne de Condillac, philosopher, author of the *Traité des sensations* (1715–1780).

passed before their eyes, there is a greater choice in the objects which have been shown them, they have had better models, more exemplary ideas. A man who had seen only pictures by Raphael and Titian would not be satisfied with mediocre paintings.

It follows from these remarks that any method which begins with abstractions is not suitable for children, and is contrary to the nature of the human mind. This reflection alone banishes abstractions from all elementary books on grammar, rhetoric, philosophy and religion.

When it is a question of building a house, we must first get the materials together. When it is a question of constructing the edifice of human knowledge, it is necessary to have the special ideas which compose this edifice. Facts, observations and experience constitute its foundation; it is therefore to assembling them, to making ourselves familiar with them that we should apply ourselves in the beginning.

Let the children see many objects; let these objects be varied; let them be shown under several aspects and at different times. It is not possible to fill their memory and their imagination with too many useful facts and ideas of which they will be able to make use in the course of their lives. "Variety above all else pleases at this age," says the Abbé Fleury. "Children study more willingly four different subjects during two hours than one subject alone during one hour. One study serves as a relaxation from the other, and the more diverse they are the less it is to be feared that they will be confused with one another." Another great master of the art of teaching ('sGravesande [20])

[20] Jacob 'sGravesande, Dutch scholar and scientist (1688–1742).

says, in Chapter XXX of his book on logic, that those who have acquired the habit of considering only one sort of ideas, however great an ability they may have acquired therein, reason almost always badly about other subjects. He adds that to acquire flexibility and breadth of mind it is necessary to apply oneself to several different things.

All that needs to be known is not contained in books. There are a thousand things about which it is possible to learn by conversation, by usage and by practice; but only minds that are already somewhat trained can profit by this sort of instruction. Man is made for action, and he studies only in order to render himself capable of acting. In society, the spirit of study and of business seem opposed to each other; but a man will not understand business well if he has not studied. The important thing is to acquire the main principles of the more uncommon kinds of knowledge; experience—which is the best teacher—will accomplish the rest. If we do not possess these principles, the best advice to follow is to refrain from judging: of all the precepts of philosophy, this is the one which is the most generally applicable.

Study should be the occupation of our youth and the relaxation of the rest of our lives to fill usefully the intervals of leisure.

Childhood is not the season for harvests; it is the time to sow and to make provisions. The object of study is not that the young people should have, on finishing their early education, complete ideas on all the sciences. This would be a fantastic project, a beautiful dream. It would be easy for them to have some knowledge of the underlying principles, to have acquired a great many material facts and much information, and to possess the art of acquiring more knowledge. This is an invaluable art, and is perhaps superior to knowledge itself.

Almost all our philosophy and education can be expressed in these few words: it is the things themselves that it is important to know. Let us return to the true and the real; for in itself truth is nothing other than what is, what exists, and in our minds it is only the knowledge of existing things.

Such an aim is certainly more correct, and the way to it is straighter than the winding path by which the young people attain only the knowledge of words or of abstractions.

The way to succeed is to excite curiosity, to help intelligence and genius, and to give strength to the mind. This will never be done by means of abstract, dry and wearisome studies. Let what you present to children be agreeable, stimulate their curiosity, flatter their self-esteem, encourage them in the gaiety that is natural at their age, and do not associate with study the idea of labor or trouble. Among the different branches of knowledge, choose those from which the most useful results can be obtained, which have the most bearing on daily life, on morals and on virtue, those which elevate the mind and the spirit. Prefer those activities which are useful in several different ways at the same time. Repeat and investigate the same things throughout the entire course of education, in such a manner that from the beginning to the end it may consist only of the same truths, of the same things more developed.

Experience shows that after leaving college almost everything that has been learned there is forgotten. Why is this? It is because the knowledge which has been acquired is not connected with common notions; because only that which has been often repeated is well retained: and it is only by repeating the same ideas that a deep enough impression can be made for them to be retained a long time. Experience likewise shows that what is impressed on the delicate fibers of the brain in childhood by frequently repeated acts is never forgotten. There is no child who has ever forgotten how to play cards.

It is on these simple principles that is founded the plan which I propose. Every good method should be based upon the nature of the human mind and upon incontestable facts. A brief plan can contain more things than a lengthy one. The longest thing of all is history; however, it can be much abridged. All the knowledge necessary for any man can be comprised in a few volumes.

There is one precaution necessary, and that is that all the work and all the trouble should not be put upon the children. It is in this respect that the usage of the colleges is most faulty; because there are too many pupils in a single class. It is the duty of the teachers to make the children work; but they should take upon themselves the most difficult part of the work; and the State should aid the teachers as much as possible by having elementary textbooks prepared by able people.

IV

EDUCATION FROM THE FIRST YEARS UNTIL ABOUT THE AGE OF TEN

Children are without experience, because they have seen nothing; they are inattentive, because their organs are too weak to permit them to keep their attention fixed for any great length of time on the same subject; they are without judgment, because they do not have enough materials in their minds to compare them; and they lack the experience and strength to seize the details without which all comparison is lacking in accuracy. They have senses which are the doors whereby knowledge enters, and memory which recalls to them the absent things that they have seen; moreover, they have the faculty of reflecting on their sensations, on the inner feeling which never leaves them, any more than it does other people, and on the representations of both, that is to say, on their ideas.

It is only a question of making use of these faculties to fix their attention, to perfect their judgment, and to procure for them the experience which they lack at their age.

I admit that after the inconceivable effort that children have made in learning to talk, what appears to me to be most difficult in all education is to teach them to read. It is difficult for me to understand how it is possible to do this—especially by the method which is used. If we observe all the different combinations, the multitude of operations which this study requires, the number of useless or improper sounds which they are made to articulate, we shall agree that it is not an easy thing, even if it is a common one; and necessarily it must either be almost the effect of a mechanical routine, or their minds are already capable of making an infinite number of combinations when applied to the things which they can perceive.

One thing which would lead us to attribute this capacity to children is the little effort with which they learn games which require very ingenious combinations. But, on the other hand, we can ask if this facility might not come rather from the fact that they have particular ideas concerning what they are doing and are doing with pleasure.

I remark that all that Nature does, however complicated it may be, it does easily. As soon as art appears, difficulty is created; art is long and painful. To learn to talk, to learn a language by usage, is done naturally and easily; to learn to read, to learn a language by rules and by art require several years.

Thus it would be a matter worthy of the investigation of good citizens and of the attention of governments to determine once for all the simplest method of teaching to read and of teaching languages. Such a method would spare children much trouble, and fathers and teachers much worry; it would save time for the acquisition of real knowledge. I believe, after several repeated experiences that the Bureau of Printing is, without comparison, the best that there is for reading.[21]

But supposing that a child already knows how to read and write, and that he knows how to draw—which I con-

[21] Probably means that the Bureau of Printing would be the branch of the government most suited to study the question of a method for teaching reading.

sider necessary—I say that the first subjects with which he should be occupied, from the age of five or six to the age of ten, are history, geography, natural history and physical and mathematical recreations. These are all branches of knowledge that are within his ability; because they all appeal to the senses, because they are the most agreeable, and, consequently, the most suitable occupations for childhood. If it is true that these subjects constitute the basis and the materials of our ideas, the foundation of civil life, of all the sciences and all the arts without exception, it is evident that it is with them that education should begin.

History [22]

Is it necessary to state here that history is within the comprehension of children, and to prove in the eighteenth century a truth that was known two thousand years ago? But the spirit of paradox causes everything to be reduced to a problem; and under pretext of providing children with their own experience, they are to be deprived of the help of the experience of others, as though it were impossible to combine the two.

It is desired that they should have no school but the world, and they are forbidden to see the world. It is desired that they should learn their way only by going astray.

The trouble with these systems of education is not that they are altogether false; it is, on the contrary, in the intermixture of truth that the disadvantage lies.

[22] M. Rousseau excludes history from the education of children. (Note by La Chalotais.)

Nobody can deny the incontestable principle, which is also not new, that the first instruction should begin with things that are perceptible to the senses: with facts, with what is seen, what is touched, what is weighed, what is measured, what is depicted, what is described.

These are facts about Nature, about art and about man. I shall speak in a moment of the first two; at present I am considering only the facts about man, or those of history. The spectacle of what has taken place in the world is, strictly speaking, nothing but the representation of what takes place every day on the public square. If we know how to guide their vision, children can see the one as well as they can see the other, and there is no need of any great intensity of mind. It is well known that they love passionately stories and histories; why then should they be entirely deprived of a pleasure which they feel so keenly?

We do not know what to put in the hands of fathers, mothers and governesses for the instruction of children of a certain age—or rather that they may not be spoiled. Fairy tales are read to them; they are told terrible ones which sometimes leave an impression that lasts as long as they live. Why not seek to teach them while amusing them? If the greater number of histories are beyond their comprehension, is it a reason for not bringing them within their capacity? This would be the fault of the writers. The child who can understand *Hop-o'-my-Thumb* or *Blue Beard* can understand the histories of Romulus and of Clovis. Children know as well as older people that we should do no harm to anyone, nor to the public, which is composed of many persons, and that the wicked, that is to say, those who

79

wrong others, deserve the execration of the public. These quite simple maxims are sufficient to understand almost all histories and to judge them.

Another decisive reason for occupying children with history is that if it is postponed until they have reached a certain age, they will no longer be able to learn it or to retain it; it would become physically impossible. They would find themselves in regard to all history in the same position that we are in regard to the history of China and Japan; which are so difficult to fix in the memory because the names of men, towns and rivers are so unfamiliar to our ears. They would be in the same position as most women, who complain of their lack of memory; because, as they have read little in their childhood, the traces left by new subjects are effaced almost at once. Let anybody try to make a young peasant learn the sequence of our kings since François I, and he will see what should be thought of the proposition which I am combating.

It is then necessary to resolve either to read history to children or to permit them to remain ignorant of it all their lives. There are also tales and stories of fabulous adventures which I should not exclude, if they did not give ideas of imaginary beings or virtues. Novels are harmful in that they describe only the weaknesses of humanity, or because they depict men as they are not. We should see badly if our eyes were like microscopes. These fictitious histories increase, diminish or weaken Nature. Almost all the pictures in novels are of unnatural size.

But let us leave aside all metaphysical paradoxes, and let us not fear to prefer to them maxims taught by all the philosophers of the universe, adopted by all statesmen and consecrated by the practices of all civilized nations. Let us try only to render histories useful to children, and to indicate what they should contain.

I should like to see composed for their use histories of every nation, of every century, and, above all, of the last centuries. I should wish the latter to be more detailed, and that they be read before the histories of more remote ages. I should also wish that the lives of famous men of all sorts be written, of men of all conditions and all professions: heroes, scholars, celebrated women and children, etc., and that vivid pictures be presented of great events, of memorable examples of vice or of virtue, of misfortune or of prosperity, etc.

The lessons in these books should be freely explained, so that almost nothing would be left for the teacher to add, and that he would, so to say, need only read and question. I should desire that questions be placed at the end of each narrative, in order to see what the child has retained, to correct him if he has misunderstood, or if he has not grasped the essentials.

This is the method used by the judicious Abbé Fleury in his *Historical Catechism*.[23] He proves its usefulness in a very philosophic preface, which is very little read; because prefaces are rarely read, above all, those of catechisms.

These books and these histories would serve at the same time to train the hearts and the minds of the children, and it would be possible to teach a moral entirely within their grasp: not by establishing rules concerning right and wrong

[23] *Grand Catéchisme historique,* 1683, written by Fleury for the instruction of his pupil the Count de Vermandois, legitimized son of Louis XIV and Louise de la Vallière.

by means of abstract principles; but by exciting the sentiment of justice which is quite lively with them, and which would be equally so with all men, if it were not stifled by prejudice and self-interest.

Thus, they could be accustomed early to judge men and actions, and they would be inspired with humanity, generosity and beneficence; either by the praises of generous and beneficent men, or by the comparison of great examples of virtue and of vice: of Cicero and Catiline, of Nero and Titus, of Sully and Marshal d'Ancre.[24] Simple questions and short answers would indicate the way. Their minds would open imperceptibly, and would be trained without effort to appreciate what is good and to abhor what is bad. They would learn, by their own examples even, by the judgments which they would be made to pronounce on their private quarrels and on their actions, that we must not do to others what we should not wish others to do to us, that no one is truly great other than by the good which he does to his fellow-men and that we must do to others all the good that we can do.

The morality of children, and even that of grown men, reduces itself almost entirely to these two points.

To what an extent would not the emulation of children be excited by reading the lives of celebrated children? It is astonishing that since Baillet,[25] who wrote a book especially

[24] Maximilien de Béthune, Duc de Sully, able and faithful minister and friend of Henri IV (1559–1641). Concino Concini, known as Marshal d'Ancre, Italian adventurer and favorite of Marie de Medici, who became minister of Louis XIII. He is known chiefly for his rapacity and incapacity (d. 1617).

[25] *Des enfants célèbres,* 1688, by Adrien Baillet (1649–1706).

for this purpose, no one has followed up this idea to inspire them with so precious a love of distinction.

It has been said that among studies we should prefer those which are most useful, that is, those which have the greatest effect on morals, on the conduct of life, on public and private affairs. Now there is no doubt that modern history is more useful in this respect than ancient, that of Europe more than the histories of Egypt and of China, and the history of our own country more than those of foreign countries. This is the opinion of the great Grotius,[26] who spent considerable time in the study of antiquity, and it is also the opinion of all sensible people.

A man of discernment would be able to extract from the books on Egyptian, Greek, Etruscan and Roman antiquities, on the monuments of the French monarchy, from the book of religious ceremonies, from the books on medals, from those which treat of the customs of nations in general and in particular, and from the Dictionary of the Bible, all that would be worth retaining. Also the plans of famous cities, harbors and the finest buildings could be shown as well as some of the works of the best painters, if it were possible, and some engravings. In short a collection could be made of all the most interesting memorials of ancient and modern times, to which could be added a very simple description.

These histories and collections, in order to be useful, should be prepared by philosophers. Philosophy will not be

[26] Huig van Groot, Dutch diplomat and scholar, who wrote, in Latin and under the Latinized form of his name Hugo Grotius, several works on history, law and religion (1583–1645).

degraded by making it speak the language of children; it is the most worthy use that could be made of it. Of what use is it, if not to train the judgment of people of all ages?

The more volumes there would be of well-prepared histories, the more learned society and families would be, and studies the better prepared. They would be of use to mothers, to children and to all generations. Duché [27] made some for use at Saint-Cyr,[28] and the Abbé de Choisy [29] for the Duchess de Bourgogne.[30] They are agreeable, but these authors—like several others of the past century—had little philosophy in their heads.

Let us suppose then that several volumes of such histories, prepared by philosophers, were available.

Children would be made to read them so that they might learn to read well.

They would answer the questions which would be contained in them; and by this means would accustom themselves to judging.

They would be made to relate these same histories in order to teach them to speak fluently.

These are only the materials of history. A chronologic arrangement of facts, the succession of empires, the prin-

[27] Joseph-François Duché de Vancy, obscure dramatic poet, wrote *Histoires édifiantes et poésies sacrées* for use at Saint-Cyr (1668–1704).

[28] Saint-Cyr was at that time a school for girls, which had been founded by Madame de Maintenon.

[29] François-Thimoléon de Choisy, known for his *Lettres* and *Mémoires* (1644–1724).

[30] Duchess de Bourgogne, wife of the grandson of Louis XIV, and mother of Louis XV.

ciples which serve as a foundation of historical certitude and the innumerable uses of history would be reserved for later.

V

GEOGRAPHY

Geography should never be separated from history. It is a matter of sight and of memory, and, consequently, a study well adapted to children. But we should have a geography which would be within their comprehension, which, without entering into dreary and tiresome details (like the Geography of Lenglet [31]), would make them travel agreeably in the different countries, and would make known to them all that is important and curious: the most striking facts, the native places of great men, the sites of famous battles, everything that is remarkable, both in regard to manners and customs as well as to natural products, arts and commerce.

A book of selections from all the works on travel which have been written up to the present could be used. The task of preparing such a work would be neither long nor laborious.

When the children would be more advanced, they would make a second and third voyage by means of historical, political, physical and mathematical geography, as will be said later.

[31] Nicholas Lenglet-Dufresnoy, scholar (1674–1755).

VI

Natural History, Physical and Mathematical Recreations

Other studies that are especially suited to childiren are natural history and physical and mathematical recreations.

Natural history demands of children only eyes, practice and memory. It is one of the most useful branches of knowledge that they can acquire, as it is one of the foundations of economics, of medicine and of politics even. It is also one of the most agreeable and one of the easiest.

It is not a question of reasoning nor of discovering relations and causes. As a great teacher has said, at that age it is only necessary, to see much and to see often. Let children see without design, even without explanation, samples of everything that composes the earth. They should be made familiar with all the objects which the generality of men enjoy without knowing them, and which are so often found in daily use in life.

The principal thing is to show at first the different objects pertaining to natural history just as they appear to the eye. A picture, with a definite and exact description is enough. The descriptions could be rendered less dreary and more interesting by introducing into them some facts concerning the life and the habits of animals, the cultivation and the uses of plants, and the properties and uses of minerals. But in this latter part it is necessary to be sparing, to avoid too great detail, and, above all, to eliminate the fabulous, which naturalists have too often mingled with the true.

In making known at first this multitude of objects, there should be no question of scholarly methods, which would serve only to create confusion. It is enough to restrict ourselves to the first and great division into the three reigns: animal, vegetable and mineral.

For a detailed consideration, we should follow the maxim, which has already been stated several times, of limiting ourselves to those things with which we are most closely associated, which are the most necessary and the most useful.

The preference should be given to domestic animals over wild animals, to those of the country over foreign ones.

Among the plants, those which are used for food or remedies should be preferred. The childern will learn imperceptibly to distinguish the different parts of an animal, of birds and insects, to know how all these living bodies grow, nourish and preserve themselves. But it is essential that the instruction should not go beyond what they can judge by seeing and touching.

It should be the same for fossils, minerals, stones and the different substances found in the earth.

They should be shown one after another the picture and the description. If it is possible to add the object itself, the image will be clearer and more vivid, the impression more durable. If they are presented to the children in order, they will range themselves naturally in their minds according to the same order in which they have been learned. At the same time they will be told of the famous men, of ancient as well as of modern times, who have made discoveries in the sciences relating to these objects, and who, by their labors which were often immense, have perfected these sciences. To render due homage to talent is to honor humanity, and it would inspire the children with veneration for the benefactors of nations. A praiseworthy curiosity would take possession of them, and perhaps it would some day give rise to an ambition to equal and to surpass those who had first served them as guides.

This spectacle, though merely an outline, will elevate their minds, and increase their ideas. A time will come when, after having seen and seen again several times the objects, they will begin to represent them to themselves in general, and to make for themselves divisions. A taste for science will be created, which can then be aided by methods and reflections; but it is necessary to begin always with facts and descriptions which are themselves facts. Drawing would be useful in all this; for children take pleasure in copying what they see.

VII

Astronomical and Physical Observations. Experiments and Mechanics

Under the title of Physical Recreations, I include observations, experiments and the facts of Nature which are the simplest, the most striking and the easiest to retain.

I should foresee here an objection, which it is easy to make, and easier still to turn into a joke. It will be said perhaps that to facilitate study for children, I wish them to learn physics, the mechanical arts and astronomy.

I reply that such an objection could be made only by people who have no knowledge of these sciences. It would be justified if I expected that at this age physicists, astronomers and mechanicians should be prepared; but that is not what I propose. I take as an example natural history, and I claim that in order to learn this science, it is necessary first to distinguish the objects, call them by name, recognize them by their form, their size, their weight, their colors, etc.

This is a necessary preliminary operation, but it does not suffice for the preparation of a naturalist.

To know this science, it is necessary not only to be acquainted with the perceptible qualities, but also to know everything which has to do with the origin, the production, the growth, the development and the use of each object in particular, its detailed history; in a word, all that learned academicians include in their scholarly works on natural history.

It is about the same in mechanical arts, in physics, in astronomy, etc.

I agree that children are not in a state to comprehend these latter operations, nor are they capable of the reasoning which they require; but I maintain that any person who is in possession of his senses is capable of the former, since they consist only in distinguishing objects and their different parts, in weighing them, in measuring them, in observing their colors and in drawing their outlines. Anything that requires only eyes, hands and some very simple reckoning is not beyond the comprehension of the tenderest age.

Nobody intends to attempt to demonstrate to children the divisibility of matter to an infinite degree; but a child seven years old can perceive that a grain of carmine tints perceptibly ten pints of water, and that, consequently, it can be divided into as many particles as there are little drops of the liquid.

He can understand that a grain of gold beaten into leaves can cover a surface of fifty square inches, that a leaf, a square inch in size, can be cut into two hundred little bands, and each little band into two hundred still smaller ones in such a manner that each grain thus divided contains almost innumerable parts.

He can also understand that one leaf of gold covering a cylinder of silver can be flattened, lengthened and drawn out into a wire 444 leagues long; that animals which have been proven geometrically to be twenty-seven million times smaller than a maggot are found in liquids; that these animals have veins, muscles, etc., etc., and, what is still smaller, liquids which circulate in them and maintain their activity (*Histoire de l'Académie des Sciences,* p. 9, 1718).

Nobody expects mechanics to be taught to children; but they cannot be accustomed too soon to observing simple machines which produce and facilitate motion, to noticing the perceptible effects of the lever, of wheels, of pulleys, of the screw, of the wedge and of balances.

Women consider scissors in relation to the material of which they are composed and as a trinket; seamstresses consider them as an instrument for cutting. Would there be any disadvantage in having children consider this instrument as being composed of two levers, united by a rivet which serves as a fulcrum, and the two branches which are sharp on the inside, as two wedges suitable for cutting when subjected to the action of the levers?

Let them be made to observe that the further away the fulcrum is from the power which imparts the motion, the greater is the force exerted, etc., etc.

There is a rather imperfect book which has the title: *Description abrégée des principaux Arts & Métiers, & des instruments qui leur sont propres, le tout détaillé par figures.*[32] The Academy is having printed a description of the arts. It is one of the most beautiful monuments that the present generation could leave to posterity.

Is it beyond the capacity of children to look over these books, to draw some of the figures contained in them? Would it be impossible to have in a college a room in which would be kept some iron or wooden models of machines? If there were in this room some cases containing objects pertaining to natural history, would not the children ask eagerly to see them? They would stroll around, they would be active and they would acquire knowledge at the same time.

Nobody intends to teach astronomy to children; but would it be useless to tell them, for instance, that the sun is about thirty-four or thirty-five million leagues from the earth, that it would take a ball shot from a cannon twenty-five years to reach it?

Would it be useless to tell them that the diameter of the circle which the earth makes around the sun in a year is double the distance of the sun from the earth, that is, seventy million leagues, and that the distance to the stars is incomparably greater?

[32] *Abridged Description of the principal Arts and Trades, and of the instruments belonging to them, the whole illustrated in detail by diagrams.*

Would it be useless for them to know that, supposing the star Sirius, one of the largest and most brilliant and probably the nearest, to be like the sun, it would take a ball shot from a cannon from twenty-seven to twenty-eight million times twenty-five years to reach it?

Would it be useless for them to know that it is possible to count with the naked eye about 1022 stars; but that with a telescope ten or twenty times as many can be discovered, of which each one is probably as far from any other as Sirius is from us?

Would it be useless for them to know that the earth in its journey around the sun goes more than six hundred thousand leagues in an hour, or four hundred and sixteen in a minute; that a ball shot from a cannon would go at the rate of two thousand six hundred leagues in twenty-four hours, and thus the earth goes one hundred and fifty times as fast as a ball shot from a cannon?

Once again I ask, would there be any disadvantage in striking the minds of children with admiration and astonishment by the infinitely great and the infinitely small?

What an idea would this not give of the Being who has created everything! Would it be necessary to ask them, no matter what be their age, *Quis est qui creavit hæc?* [33]

Would it be necessary, after this knowledge had been for a long time inculcated, to prepare them to understand the weight of air, its elasticity, all the phenomena which physical science describes and all those which chemistry discovers? Would there be any danger in showing them that meat upon which flies deposit their eggs becomes wormy,

[33] Who is it that created these things?

whereas that upon which they do not deposit them does not become so?

Would not this fact, which their eyes could witness, lead them to think that everything is organized and has its germ? Would they not naturally conclude that a mushroom is the work of the wisdom of God, just as the world is?

Are there in the books of spiritual exercises reflections more pious than those that result from these observations and these experiments?

It would be desirable that children should early be made familiar with globes, maps, spheres, thermometers and barometers; that they should know how to use the rule and the compass, even if it were only as an amusement; to learn that there is an art of bringing nearer the most distant objects, and of perceiving those which seem imperceptible.

They would see with the aid of a microscope things unsuspected by them on the head of a fly and on the barb of a feather. This instrument would be a new organ which would be added to their eyes and which would make them discover new worlds. They would handle the air-pump and all those instruments invented by genius and used by science to reveal Nature. They would amuse themselves with stereoscopes which place before their eyes the monuments of the four quarters of the world.

They would see the phenomena of electricity which embarrass philosophers, and astonish all men.

They would be made acquainted with the greatest number of things possible; everything will do, provided it be exact. I propose to teach them only facts; facts which the eye can perceive at seven years of age as well as at thirty.

I ask whether these things are difficult studies, or are they useful and agreeable recreations?

I pass to mathematics.

VIII

THE MATHEMATICAL SCIENCES

Common prejudice has attached to these sciences the idea that they are of great difficulty for children; and by whom is this idea exaggerated? By people who put into their hands already at the age of six, grammar, that is to say, the metaphysics of language: a tissue of abstract ideas, in themselves difficult to seize, and rendered almost unintelligible by the manner in which they are presented.

Custom, which rules the multitude, postponed mathematics to the end of the course of studies in order to acquire then a smattering which was soon lost. The enlightenment of this century, the example and the authority of able men have led us back to the opinion of the ancients, of Pythagoras, of Plato, who wished that none should enter the Schools, without having been taught geometry. Socrates advised teaching mathematics at a very early age. (*Plato Rep.*, Dial. 7).

Experience and reason prove that children are capable of applying themselves to these sciences.

Geometry treats of nothing that cannot be seen and felt, nothing to which the senses do not bear witness. Geometricians measure what they see, what they touch, what they traverse. The senses are continuously being exercised, and when the senses do not suffice the memory comes to their aid to preserve the recollection of a first truth, a second, a third, etc. No science is more suited to the curiosity of children, to their character, to their temperament which incites them to be almost always in motion. Nothing flatters their self-esteem more than to believe that they have themselves invented the figures which they construct, or the problems which they solve.

I do not speak of their usefulness in relation to the needs of man, to the perfecting of all the arts, to the aid which they afford all the sciences, above all, physics. The principal motive for teaching them to children is the great advantage which they have of developing the mind.

The first quality of man, the most necessary, the one which affects all his actions, all his occupations, and which, together with righteousness of heart—which it should animate and guide by its enlightenment—constitutes his entire perfection, is rectitude of mind.

To acquire this quality, it is not enough to know the rules which guide to truth; to this must be added the habit of following these rules. This habit is acquired only by the continuous performance of acts which produce it. Now it is evident that by the method which it is necessary to follow in the study of mathematics, the acts which form this habit are continually performed. To learn to reason, it suffices to reason well without ceasing: that is what is done always and necessarily in mathematics.

It is very possible and very common to reason badly in theology, in politics; it is impossible in arithmetic and in geometry; if accuracy of mind is lacking, the rule will supply accuracy and intelligence for those who follow it.

The mathematical sciences accustom us to the spirit of combination and calculation—a spirit which is so necessary in the usages of life. They give aptitude in associating ideas, and this is perhaps the most essential of all abilities; for ordinarily throughout our lives we continue to see things only as we saw them in the beginning.

Furthermore, what comparison is there between the clear ideas of bodies, of a line, of angles—which are perceived by the senses—and the abstract ideas of the verb, of declensions and conjugations, of an accusative, of an ablative, of a subjunctive, of an infinite, etc.? Geometry requires no more application than a game of piquet or of quadrille.

It will be the duty of mathematicians to find a way which has not yet been sufficiently indicated. It would be possible perhaps to begin with mathematical recreation; but those of Ozanam [34] are not so clear as the elements themselves, and are not so instructive.

M. Clairaut [35] has given the elements of geometry and of algebra in the order which their inventors would have followed. He has combined the two advantages of interesting and of enlightening beginners.

Such are the activities which I propose for the earliest years: to learn to read, to write and to draw; dancing and music which ought to enter into the education of all persons above the common people; some history, some lives of illustrious men of all countries, of all centuries and of all professions; geography; physical and mathematical recreations; and the fables of La Fontaine—which, what-

[34] Jacques Ozanam, mathematician (1640–1717).
[35] Alexis-Claude Clairaut. He became a member of the Academy of Sciences at the age of eighteen (1713–1765).

ever may be said to the contrary, should not be taken away from children, but which they should all be made to learn by heart. For the rest, walking, running, gaiety and exercises, and I propose even the studies only as amusements.

IX

The Education of Children over Ten Years of Age

Towards the age of ten years, it would be time to begin the course of French and Latin literature, or the Humanities, and at the same time the activities begun at an earlier age would be continued.

I join together the study of the French and Latin languages. Cicero advised his son to combine the study of Greek and of Latin.

I should add, for those who have a taste for it, the study of Greek, which it would be very useful not to neglect as has been done. Without these two languages, there is no true nor solid learning. I should also advise English, which has become necessary for the sciences, and German for war; but I shall not speak here of these two languages.

We treat the living languages somewhat as we treat our contemporaries, with a profound indifference and almost always disadvantageously. Circumstances and personal inclination should determine the time at which to study them; ordinarily they are postponed until the years which follow formal education.

In the teaching of languages, the preference should be given to the mother tongue. It is the most necessary of all throughout our entire lives. It is therefore unreasonable to neglect it under the pretext that it is always learned sufficiently well by usage.

Experience teaches that it is never perfectly known unless it has been studied; and it is shameful that, in a system of education for France, French literature should be neglected as though we did not have enough models in our language. The Greeks and the Romans cultivated their own languages in preference to foreign ones. Out of a hundred students, there are not fifty to whom Latin would be necessary, and it would hardly be possible to count four or five to whom it might eventually be useful to speak and to write it. There is not one who would have need of speaking or writing Greek, or of composing Latin or Greek verses. It would be then contrary to reason to draw up a plan of education for so small a number of persons.

The languages require application and work, and although they are only a preparation for more serious study, it is necessary to apply oneself to them with ardor during the first years, and to avoid the line of conduct of the greater number of those who devote themselves to literature, and who are obliged, as long as they live, to learn to speak and to write correctly; because they have not given enough time in the beginning to these subjects, or because they have learned them without order and without rules. But it will not be without use to state what I understand by literature; it is what the Romans called Grammar: *Grammatica.* The Abbé Gédoyn [36] says: "At Rome, under this term was un-

[36] Nicholas Gédoyn, translator of Quintilian and Pausanias (1667–1744).

derstood everything that concerns language; that is to say, not only the habit of reading well, a good pronunciation, correct spelling, a pure and regular diction, the etymology of words, the divers changes that the language had undergone, the ancient and the modern usages, the good and the bad usages, the different acceptations of terms, but also the reading and the understanding of all that was good in the mother tongue either in prose or in verse."

Such is the idea that they had in Rome and in Athens of the teachers of grammar or Grammarians, a term which is almost ignoble to-day; but which was then as much in honor as the thing it signified. That is what the children went to school to learn, and what they learned there in fact.

French literature and Latin literature should go side by side. Thus it would be well that the morning hours of school should be, for instance, for French, and those of the afternoon for Latin, until the study of philosophy is begun, which, in spite of the bad custom, should be taught in French. There would be some children who, having no need either of Latin or Greek, would take only the courses in French. I should not consider it undesirable if this custom were introduced.

Are six years necessary to learn two languages? Two or three years for the Humanities would be enough, one year of rhetoric, and two of philosophy. A chair of experimental physics and of mathematics could be added. Perhaps it would be better to finish with rhetoric, or at least not to abandon the study of literature during the two years of philosophy.

To accomplish the purpose of the study of literature, it will be necessary to begin with a general analytic grammar which will contain the foundation of the art of speaking, which will give a clear idea of all the parts of speech, and in which may be seen what is common to all languages, and also the principal differences amongst them.

There is a very good general grammar by Lancelot,[37] with notes by a member of the Academy of which the clearness and accuracy equal the good taste. The author of these notes could more readily than anyone else adapt it to the use of children.

To learn everything according to principles should be counted as a considerable advantage. This practice tends to produce accuracy of mind, and would accustom the children to making use of their reason in the different activities of life—which should be the aim of all studies.

After the work of this first period, upon which too much time should not be spent; because practice is the best teacher in matters pertaining to languages, the reading of great writers should be begun; and the first thing to be done would be to make the children analyse the construction of the phrases of some French book which they understand, according to the notions of general grammar which they had learned, and of French grammar which they would learn at the same time.

This would constitute their first lessons, and the second ones would consist of an abridgement of Latin grammar which would show the differences between it and French grammar. After this, they should begin the explanation of

[37] Claude Lancelot, author of *Jardin des racines grecques* (1615–1695).

the Latin text; for I suppose—as do certain learned persons [38]—that it is with the explanation of texts that the study of languages should begin and continue.

It is natural to think that in order to learn a dead language, we should imitate as much as possible the manner in which children learn their mother tongue, and that in which we learn foreign living languages. That is by usage, practice and habit; however, with this difference: in learning a living language, the ideas of the things which we see associate themselves immediately with the words which we hear pronounced, whereas, in studying a dead language, the association of the words is made only with those of the native language, and not with the things themselves. In the first case, the word is the sign of the thing, in the second, it is the sign of the sign. This is what causes a double mental tension.

In the second, or even in the third year, it would be time, if so desired, to add to the explanation and translation of Latin authors, the method of written exercises. It is necessary to be able to understand before being able to speak. Some author such as Phædrus, Terence, Sallust, or some books of Cicero, which had been translated into French by a man skilled in both languages, should be chosen, and the student should be made to translate into French certain selections from the original text. This translation would then be compared with that of the translator in the French editions. Some time later the student should put the translation back into Latin which would then be corrected from the original text. By this means he would have, for instance,

[38] Scaliger, Tameguy le Fevre (Tanneguy Lefebvre?), M. Rollin, M. de Marsais, etc. (Note by La Chalotais.)

Cicero as teacher of Latin, and the Abbé Mongault[39] as teacher of French. This would be the means of learning perfectly the two languages.

A necessary textbook would be a selection of writings on the present state of our language, taken from the works of Vaugelas, Bouhours, Corneille, Patru, St. Evremont[40] and all those who have written about the language, giving the reasons for their conclusions. This selection would be at least as useful as the *Particules* by Tursellin,[41] and would be of more general application.

We should begin with fables and letters, because the style is less figurative. Care should be taken to make a survey of all kinds of literature in verse and in prose: from epigrams to epics, from letters to public orations, endeavoring as far as possible to join the French and the Latin authors, as Phædrus and La Fontaine, Horace and Boileau, Homer and Virgil with Tasso and the *Henriade*,[42] etc.

The object of these studies would be to inspire the young people with a taste for the beautiful and the good in all

[39] Nicolas-Hubert de Mongault, Oratorian priest, translated Cicero into French (1674–1746).

[40] Claude de Vaugelas, author of *Remarques sur la langue française* (1595–1650). Dominique Bouhours, Jesuit, grammarian (1628–1702). Pierre Corneille, the great writer of tragedies (1606–1684). Olivier Patru, lawyer and man of letters (1604–1681). Charles de Saint-Evremont, author of various literary *Dissertations* (1610–1703).

[41] Horace Tursellin or Torsellino, Italian Jesuit, wrote, among many other things, *De particulis latinæ orationis,* Rome, 1598 (1545–1599).

[42] *Henriade,* by Voltaire, the only epic poem in modern French; its hero is Henri IV. But why Homer and Tasso among Latin and French authors?

kinds of literature, and for the particular beauties of languages; above all of the French language.

Men of letters have proved that it is impossible to appreciate fully the beauties of a dead language; but if it is difficult to perceive all the niceties of the diction of Demosthenes, of Cicero, of Virgil, it is easy to feel the charm of their eloquence, to recognize the noble and grand manner with which they express themselves. It is possible to imitate authors without speaking their language, and we should try to treat the same subjects in our own language in the manner in which they treated them in theirs.

On this subject there is lacking a book of precepts which would guide children and of which they could make constant application, or rather I should say there is such a book, if the teachers knew how to use it and to bring it within the comprehension of children. It is the *Cours de Belles-Lettres,* by M. Batteux,[43] in which the rules are extremely well elucidated by examples.

X

GOOD TASTE; OF WHAT IT CONSISTS, AND THE MEANS OF FORMING IT

The art of speaking was created by observing what persuaded and what hindered persuasion. From these observations a body of precepts and rules has been formulated. However, precepts alone will never create good taste. For

[43] Charles Batteux, philosopher and educationalist (1713–1780).

purposes of instruction, all of them together are not worth a single work of genius; and, as has been said by a very great genius (M. de Voltaire), there is more to be learned from Demosthenes, from Cicero, from Bossuet than from all the rhetorics; for these men were masters of the art. I include among these great models the author of this observation himself, although he is still living. When it is a question of science or literature, contemporary jealousies must remain silent, and we should speak the language of posterity.

The precepts of all the arts are easy and simple; they are derived from Nature and from reason. The important thing is not a knowledge of them, although this is something, but the application of them.

Good taste is a prompt, lively and delicate discernment of the beauties which should enter into a work. It comes from accuracy of mind, and, consequently, it is a gift of Nature; but it can be perfected by study and by practice. It perceives the beauties and the defects, compares them, weighs them and appreciates them by so keen a discernment that it seems to be rather the effect of sentiment and of a species of instinct than of observation.

Good taste can be regarded as a sense; since it functions like the other senses. By means of sight we perceive objects, without knowing how this sensation is produced in us.

It is the same with what is called good taste. We form an opinion concerning what is beautiful, and this opinion is formed in our minds just as if we knew the cause and the origin of the pleasure which we feel, as if we had present before us invariable rules of the beautiful, and, upon all this knowledge, we base a multitude of deductions which would be the result of it.

It is not possible to give the sensation produced by sight to a blind man; but Locke has proved that children learn to see, or rather, to judge by the sense of sight the distance and shape of objects.

Good taste does not differ from the other senses. The organ cannot be acquired. It is, necessarily, very crude in those who have not made frequent use of it; but it can be perfected by exercise.

Taste without rule or reasoning would be a bad guide; reasoning without taste would be a still more fallacious one.

It has often been asked whether a production of the mind should be judged by sentiment or by discussion. This is a question which has caused great disputes, and which may well be only a dispute over words. Sentiment is necessary; for without it, we make for ourselves false rules. Discussion is also necessary, and there must be sentiment in order to discuss well. Thus it seems that these ways converge. All that reasoning can do is to justify the sentiment of taste, as mechanics can demonstrate the movements of a rope-dancer; but mechanics cannot teach how to dance. Exercise, practice and habit are necessary.

The means of acquiring taste is then to examine the principles and the rules, to practice comparing, to read good criticisms, and above all to study the great masters.

If you wish a young man to acquire a taste for epic poetry, let him read Homer, Virgil, Tasso, the *Henriade*. First let him make an analysis of the whole. He should examine the subject of the poem, the construction, the arrangement. He should observe how each part is treated. He should pay particular attention to the poetic style. He should render himself familiar with the subject, the plan, the order and the details. Then let him read some reflections on the epic. Let him do the same thing with all the various forms, and he will infallibly acquire good taste, or he should be declared incapable of possessing it.

The author of the *Henriade* says that the intelligence of young men can be judged by the details which they give of a new play that they have just seen; and he adds he has observed that those who acquitted themselves best in doing this were those who afterwards succeeded best in their callings. "So true it is," says he, "that, in reality, business ability and true literary ability are the same."

This useful practice should be applied to all productions of the mind. After a sermon, a speech before the Bar, a tragedy, a comedy, state in clear terms the subject, the plan, the order, the proofs of the discourse or the plot of the piece; observe what seemed best or least well proved; note the merit or the general defect of the style. This, adds the same writer, is very rare even among men of letters.

One means of judging the beauties and the defects of writers is to compare them with others. The works of Despréaux [44] have been printed with the passages from the ancients which he imitated. In the *Théâtre des Grecs*, [45] one of the small number of works of good taste that have come out of the colleges, some of the modern tragedies

[44] Nicholas Boileau-Despréaux, author of *Satires, L'Art poétique,* etc. (1636–1711).

[45] *Le Théâtre des Grecs,* in 3 vols., 1730, by Pierre Brumoy, S.J. (1688–1742).

have been compared with the ancient. The works of the great writers should be published with these sorts of imitations. They would be the best commentaries; the others are often only scholia of grammarians or of scholars without taste.

When good modern authors have treated the same subjects in prose or in verse, it would be very useful to compare them. These parallels would develop the taste of young people, especially if they were accompanied by comments on each form of literature.

They should be made to read with attention all the good criticisms of great works which have been made. . . .[46]

Young people who have read such works and reflected upon them will notice at a glance all the mistakes in language of the writings which they read, and will not make any themselves. There is no small merit in knowing a language, and it is not possible to neglect diction without being, at the same time, indifferent to the thoughts even.

They must be reminded that to learn a language, three things are necessary: association with cultivated people, reading the works of good writers, and the study of books that treat of grammar.

I shall add a reflection on the taste for letters, independently of languages. This flower of literature is useful to anyone who wishes to cultivate his mind. It can be acquired only in youth, and it is lacking in all those who have not been well educated, who have read badly, or who have not read attentively good models.

[46] A list of works of criticism given by the author has been omitted here; they are probably not of sufficient importance today for the purpose of this study to justify their inclusion.

It is perhaps the *Atticism* of the Greeks, the Roman *Urbanity* and the French *Taste*. Quintilian calls it a tincture of learning extracted from association with educated persons: *Sumptam ex conversatione Doctorum tacitam eruditionem.*[47]

It is easy to discover if a man has a cultivated mind by his manner of expressing himself, of judging, of speaking, of writing. Often an allusion, the quotation of a well-known verse, indicate culture, and we can easily recognize the man who has lived in the company of good authors, just as in the world we can recognize the one who has frequented good society.

After such considerations, is it not intolerable to hear ignorant people or imbeciles ask what could be done with children if they were not occupied morning and evening with themes, particles, prosodies, Latin and Greek verses, development of themes, figures of speech and other questions of rhetoric?

XI

FURTHER STUDIES AND EXERCISES FOR THIS SECOND PERIOD OF EDUCATION

The Studies relating to French and Latin literature for children of this age, besides those which I have indicated, would consist of some compositions such as I shall designate.

But I shall first point out one thing that is essential to, and among the most important in all education. That is

[47] Unvoiced learning derived from association with the learned.

never to make young people write any compositions other than on subjects of which they have already sufficient knowledge. To do otherwise would be to make them work in a void, to accustom them to speak without having any ideas, to make use of commonplaces, to use many words to say a few things; all of which ruins their minds, and corrupts their taste for their entire lives.

Thus, I should like to forbid entirely those puerile dissertations, those heaps of figures of speech made to order, those paraphrases in which is said in ten verses what Horace or Boileau has said in four.

What ideas can be expected of a youth, to whom is assigned as a subject for amplification Cæsar's harangue to his soldiers on the fields of Pharsalia? He knows nothing about Cæsar, Pompey, the Romans, the interests, the strength nor the weakness of the two parties. A teacher who dares to put himself in Cæsar's place, or to attribute sentiments to him knows no more. A ground so badly prepared can produce only bad and tasteless fruit.

It is most important that the young people should be fully convinced that before learning to write, it is necessary to learn to think; that one errs more frequently by saying too much than by saying too little; that the only means of speaking well on a subject is to understand it well; that when all that should be said on a subject has been said, whatever is added is tiresome, displeasing and noxious. It is well that they should know by experience that it is insufferable to read or hear empty phrases and commonplaces. *Scribendi recte sapere est principium et fons.*[48]

[48] Understanding is the source and beginning of correct composition.

They should make epitomes and analyses. They should write the eulogies of great men, and letters—not fulsome epistles about facts or subjects of which they are ignorant—but letters about what has actually happened to them, their occupations, their amusements, their troubles. They should write an account of a ceremony, of an entertainment at which they have been present. This is something more difficult than might be supposed. To realize the difficulty, it suffices to have attempted it.

They should practice making definitions. This is an extremely useful exercise, both for training the mind, and for teaching to speak and write with accuracy and precision.

Ask the generality of men what they understand by a certain word. They will have such difficulty in answering, or they will do so in such a vague manner, that you will perceive that they have no definite notion about it. Their language is like their ideas. They use expressions devoid of sense, commonplaces, and circumlocutions only because they are ignorant of the signification of terms.

Philosophers (e. g., the Abbé de Condillac [49]) have investigated the relation between the intelligence and the language of men, and by very subtle arguments they claim to have proved that the progress of talent kept pace with the progress of language.

The definitions of the Dictionary of the Academy [50] are exact. This is one of the principal merits of this work which is so estimable in every respect.

[49] Étienne de Condillac, author of a *Traité des sensations,* and of a celebrated theory concerning language (1715–1780).
[50] *Dictionnaire de l'Académie,* first edition published in 1694.

By the term definitions, I understand the descriptions of things; for it is impossible to define otherwise than by describing. In the beginning, it suffices to describe in such a manner as to distinguish the object in question from every other object.

I should prefer that a young man should know how to give a clear description of a flower, of a plant, or of the manufacture of a pot which he has seen turned; that he should know how to describe a machine, a plough, a mill, a clock, etc., than that he should know how to write all those college dissertations and other similar absurdities. It would be more useful to him throughout life.

Another exercise which could be added to that of giving definitions is to compare the words which appear to be synonyms, to note the differences between them, as the Abbé Girard [51] has done in his book on French synonyms, and as Laurentius Valla [52] had done before him on Latin synonyms in his book entitled *Elegantiæ latini sermonis*. It would also be well to note the true antonyms when it is possible. These exercises, if carefully done, would be of an inestimable utility in training the mind to be exact.

Accuracy is preferable to all else; but it is sometimes a question of giving warmth to a cold imagination, and of rendering sterile minds fertile. An almost infallible means would be, for instance, to analyse an act of a play by Racine,[53] and to reduce it, so to say, to a theme, just as

[51] Gabriel Girard, grammarian (1677–1748).

[52] Laurentius Valla, Canon of St. John Lateran in Rome; his *Elegancies of the Latin Language* was the first critical study of the Latin language since classic times (1405–1457).

[53] Jean Racine, the great tragic poet and dramatist (1639–1699).

the author might have conceived it before his genius developed it, to make a sketch of it, like the one that has been preserved which Racine himself made of a tragedy of *Iphegenia in Aulis,* and which he never finished; to indicate how this great genius was able to animate this bare skeleton, to clothe it with living flesh and with natural colors.

XII

Continuation of the Studies of the First and Second Periods. Natural History, Physical and Mathematical Recreations, Mechanics, etc.

I am, perhaps, passing too rapidly over what concerns French and Latin literature; but learned persons will supply what I fail to say. I return to the occupations of the first period of education, which I have already indicated, and which should continue until the end. To learn to read, to write and to handle the pencil is the occupation of the first period; to learn to read well, to pronounce well, to write well and to define well is that of the second. I include always music, history, geography, mathematics, natural history and literature.

It is then that should be begun the study of Nature from Nature itself, and the study of the arts and manufactures in the workshops. It is then that to the facts of history which were learned in early childhood, should be added the general history of nations, and, what is no less useful, the history of the sciences and, above all, of the arts which are most closely connected with our needs.

To initiate the young people into the knowledge of these precious arts, it would be enough to show them the simplest machines, which it would afford them great pleasure to take apart and put together again. I am convinced that in proceeding by degrees it would be possible to succeed in making a child of twelve put together all the works of a clock or the springs of any other machine, and, consequently, make him understand its mechanism. Most of them require only eyes and a plan together with some knowledge of geometry. Several articles on the arts, in the *Encyclopédie* [54] are masterpieces, and what there is about physics and the arts in the *Spectacle de la Nature* [55] is excellent, but the dialogue is often poor. It would be desirable that some able members of the Academy should assume the task of preparing the elementary books which would be needed, and I guarantee that children from twelve to fourteen years of age who had been prepared by mathematical and physical recreations would understand them with more ease than they do the rudiments that are taught them; for such things are truths which they could perceive.

Does anyone think that it would be very difficult to teach them the principles and practices of surveying, of measuring plots of ground, and that it would not be a great pleasure for them to measure a garden, a field, a plain, to see and

[54] *L'Encyclopédie,* the immense publication directed by Jean Le Rond d'Alembert and Denis Diderot, published from 1751 to 1772, and of which a number of volumes had appeared at the time of La Chalotais' writing.

[55] *Spectacle de la Nature, ou Entretiens sur l'histoire naturelle et les sciences,* in nine volumes, published 1732, by Noël-Antoine Pluche (1688–1761).

draw fortifications, to construct them for themselves with cardboard?

And finally, since in the opinion of everybody such branches of knowledge constitute the foundations of human life, why not teach them in preference to those which all agree in considering useless, difficult and tiresome?

XIII

GEOGRAPHY AND HISTORY

I shall pass on to what concerns geography and history. There is need of a second volume of geography: one which would combine ancient and modern geography, the ancient and the modern worlds; which would give the exact divisions of empires according to the most recent treaties, the descriptions of countries—not tiresome details concerning cities, towns, bailiwicks, or administrative districts, but interesting facts about their situation, the quality, fertility and products of their soil, their population, the customs of their inhabitants, their government, their religion, their laws, their strength, their land and sea forces, their riches, their commerce, etc. It would be possible to introduce reflections on politics, on the interest of princes, in a word, things easy to learn, and useful to retain, and not details which one almost never needs to know, and, when they are needed, can readily be found on maps and in dictionaries.

Instead of learning such details, let a young man learn how the multitude of men who compose society live, how and by what means they subsist; what kind of bread a laborer, an artisan, a journeyman eats; upon what sort of bed he sleeps; the details concerning the different occupations and with what they are concerned. He will see eventually how the bread which they have earned so painfully is taken away from them, and how one portion of humanity lives at the expense of the other.

XIV

HISTORY

As for the study of history, the way having been prepared since the first years of study by stories about the lives of great men who have been of importance in the world, of famous scholars, and of celebrated artists, by pictures of great events and of great revolutions; the young people should be given histories in which the moral would be made clearer, the reflections would be more profound, the maxims of the rights of individuals, the principles of right and wrong, and those of good government more thoroughly established by dwelling longer, as has been suggested, on modern history. Is there anyone who doubts that a collection of the lives of the famous men of France would be a monument very precious to the Nation, and very useful for maintaining and increasing its honor and susceptibility? Let a French Plutarch arise, and from the ashes of the heroes whose memory he celebrates, will arise men who will do honor to their families, to their century and to humanity.

According to the Abbé Fleury, when the children are about ten or eleven years old, it would be time to arrange these histories in order, without, however, bothering about an exact chronology which it is impossible to fix, or forcing them to retain dates which tax the memory too much. I should content myself with explaining to them the fine historical chart [56] which divides the time before and after Christ, coming forward and going backward, without entering into more exact chronological details which are useless.

I should repeat to them some general observations which would render the study of history briefer and more useful. I should tell them, as the Abbé Fleury does, that "we do not possess the histories of all times nor of all countries. There have always been an infinite number of ignorant nations, and of those which have written there are few of which we know the books.

"All the histories of the ancient Orientals, of the Egyptians, of the Syrians, of the Chaldeans and of the Persians have been lost, and the most ancient that remains to us, besides that of the Chosen People, is the history written by Herodotus, who wrote about four hundred years before Christ. We have, up to that time only the Greek and Roman books, which contain hardly any history worthy of belief more ancient than the foundation of Rome. After Christ, during nearly five hundred years, there is only one history to be studied, and that is the Roman; but since the fall of the Western Empire, Spain, France, Italy and England have each been making its own history. To these must be added,

[56] Published, with the approbation of the Academy of Inscriptions, in 1740.

as they begin, those of Germany, Hungary, Sweden and Denmark.

"This is the whole series of histories that are known to us; unless we wish to add Byzantine history, which we have known for the last two centuries. As for that of the Mussulmans, which comprises all that has taken place during the last thousand years in Egypt, in Syria, in Persia, in Africa and in the other countries to which the religion of Mohammed has extended, we have remained ignorant of it up to the present. We know also that the Chinese have a very long history of which a sample has been given us in Latin. The Hindoos have a very ancient tradition written in a special language. Something is known about Mexico and the Incas, but it does not go very far back, and we have had during the last two hundred years a great number of narratives and travels.

"This is all that we know about history. It can be seen how little it is in comparison with all the extent of the earth and all the succession of centuries. It is in this study especially that we should make selections and limit ourselves."

The study of history is the one in which there is the greatest need of a guide. What is most ordinarily lacking, both to those who write it and those who read it, is a philosophic mind.

We read to divert ourselves, without aim and without principle. We heap up in our memories facts, without discernment and without examination, and, after reading much history, we have no knowledge of men, of customs, of laws, of the arts and sciences, of the world at present, of the world in the past, nor of the relation between the one and the other.

The important thing would be to give the young people principles and rules, so that they may read history with profit. In the first place, in order that they may know what use to make of it, what aim they should have in view. In the second, that they may be able to distinguish between proven and unproven facts; and may not become the dupes of ignorance, of prejudice and of superstition. In the third, in order that they may be capable of recognizing the historians in whom they may have some confidence, and the centuries upon which it is possible to throw some light.

XV

The Use of History

Concerning the use of history, there is a little book by the Abbé de Saint-Réal [57] which is good; but what is incomparably better is what M. de Voltaire has said in the seventh volume, edition of 1757, of his *Philosophical, Historical and Literary Miscellanies,* chapters 60 and 61, and what he has inserted in some of his prefaces. When he proves facts, no one proves them better nor presents them so well; and as it is impossible to repeat what he has said without lessening its forcefulness, I content myself, in regard to this part of the subject, with referring teachers to him.

[57] César de Saint-Réal, historian and man of letters (1639–1692).

XVI

Principles of Historical Certitude, or Criticism

It is necessary to establish principles concerning historical certitude, and to know upon what it is founded.

We are certain of facts which we see and hear. We know by narration those which others see and hear. Testimony is one of the most general means of obtaining human knowledge; but in order to convince, it must put us in the place of those who have themselves seen and heard.

This is the viewpoint from which historians must see events in order that their readers may do the same. Facts that are based upon this foundation are of a certitude that excludes the slightest doubt.

This is the most general principle of historical certitude, and from it are derived all the others.

Thus, when we wish to examine a fact, we must first know its nature. Does it conform to the common experience and to the ordinary course of events, or is it contrary to them? This examination requires some particular reflections: By whom is it attested? By one or by several? Did these historians live in or near the time at which the event took place? Can they be said to have immediate or first-hand knowledge of it? Do they give their authorities? Have either the ones or the others of them the qualifications necessary to bear witness? We should weigh their testimony and consider their statements, just as is done in the case of witnesses in a court of justice. If there are other historians, we should see if they state the contrary. We should read all that is written for and against the statement. We should consider the motive of the writers: why and on what occasion they wrote. We should ascertain whether their testimony has come down to us in all its integrity, or whether it has not been corrupted. After all this has been done, we may pronounce judgment, either by affirming, if there are sufficient proofs, or by denying or doubting, if the proofs are lacking or insufficient; for between believing and disbelieving, there are degrees of difference which have not even any particular name.

XVII

THE EPOCHS TO WHICH IT IS POSSIBLE TO GO BACK IN HISTORY

As for the epochs to which we can go back, and the histories to which we can give credence, the surest rule is to hold as doubtful all that preceded the times when each nation acquired the use of letters. Another principle, which is equally certain, is that when there are interruptions or great lacunæ in a history, all that preceded them is false or dubious.

Thus, nothing is more uncertain than all ancient history of which the writers relate events which happened long before their time. In the subsequent centuries, and even in those which are nearest to our own, we find the same uncertainty, when the memoirs of contemporaries are lacking or are defective. This excludes from certitude almost all the history of Egypt and of the Orient—of which only a few vestiges have been preserved—all that preceded the Olympiads among the Greeks, and up to about the time of the second Punic War among the Romans. In a word, the origins of all the nations, except of the Jewish people, of which the trace has never been lost.

We may place in the same rank the greater part of the history of the Middle Ages. Not because of a lack of contemporary writers; but their memoirs are so defective, and the lacunæ so great that it is not possible to fill them. Nothing could be more correct nor more ingenious than what M. de Fontenelle says about ancient history in his eulogy of M. Bianchini.[58]

"If scattered over a vast extent of ground, we should find the remains of a great palace which has fallen into ruin, and even though we could be sure that none of them were lacking, it would be a prodigious task to assemble them all, or at least without assembling them, to form a correct idea, by examining them, of the entire structure of this palace; but if any of the remains were lacking, the task of imagining this structure would be still greater, and the more of the remains that were lacking, the greater would be the task. Thus it would be possible to make of this palace different reconstructions which would have nothing in common with each other. Such is the state in which we find the history of the most ancient times. The works of a multitude of writers have been lost, and those which remain to us

[58] Bernard Le Bovier de Fontenelle, nephew of Corneille, perpetual secretary of the Academy of Sciences, noted for his eulogies of deceased members (1657–1757). Francesco Bianchini, Italian astronomer, member of the Academy of Sciences of Paris (1662–1729).

are only rarely complete. A great many little fragments which could be useful are scattered here and there in places very distant from the ordinary routes of travel, where no one thinks of going to unearth them; but what is worse, and which would not happen to material remains, those of ancient history often contradict each other, and it is necessary to find the secret of reconciling them, or resolve to make a choice which can always be suspected of being arbitrary. All that the most original scholars of the first order have given us on this subject is different combinations of these materials of antiquity, and there is still room for new combinations; either because all the materials have not been used, or because it is possible to assemble them better, or merely to assemble them otherwise."

XVIII

CRITICISM

The principles and rules which should serve as guides in reading history constitute what is called criticism. I do not mean by this the art which stops at restoring passages and at verifying the variants of a text; but the one which teaches how to judge facts, to examine the proofs of them, to distinguish actual facts from supposititious or doubtful ones, certain facts from those which are only probable; in short the art which weighs the different degrees of certitude, and determines—if it be permitted to express it thus—the different shades of truth and of likelihood. This is an art of the greatest usefulness and of the widest application.

It is, properly speaking, a logic of facts, which is as necessary for guiding the judgment in the belief in events, as logic is for guiding the reason in the search for truth. The two united render a man judicious and rational. They are both the foundation of knowledge of all kinds and the instruments for other studies.

XIX

CRITICISM AND LOGIC

An accurate mind; a mind that is capable of governing states and directing private affairs: such a mind as those which guided Sully, Turenne and Catinat; [59] which dictated the *Consultations* of Charles Dumoulin, the *Essays* of Locke, of Nicole, and the *Discourses* of Fleury; [60] which inspired Themistocles, Polybius, d'Ossat, Richelieu and Charles de Lorraine [61] in their conjectures concerning fu-

[59] Maximilien de Béthune, Duc de Sully, minister of Henri IV (1559–1641). Henri de la Tour d'Auvergne, Vicomte de Turenne, Marshal of France and a great general (1611–1675). Nicholas de Catinat, Marshal of France, one of the foremost military leaders of his time (1637–1712).

[60] Charles Dumoulin, jurisconsult (1500–1566). John Locke, the English philosopher (1632–1704). Pierre Nicole, moralist and theologian (1628–1695). Claude Fleury, educator (1640–1725).

[61] Polybius, Greek historian (*cir.* 210–125 B.C.). Arnaud d'Ossat, Cardinal and diplomat (1537–1604). Armand-Charles du Plessis, Cardinal de Richelieu, statesman, minister of Louis XII, founder of the Académie Française (1585–1642). Charles de Guise, Cardinal de Lorraine (1525–1574).

ture events. Such a mind, I maintain, is only a solid judgment which grasps the state of questions, the true point of view of affairs, and recognizes in everything the decisive factors. It is that good sense which is so useful in the world, while what is called intellect serves often only to ravage it. It is as estimable when it dictates a good administration of justice and of finances as when it traces the plan of a campaign.

Intelligent men of all times have known the principles and the rules. When Scipio conversed with Polybius, and while exhausting the science of government, they prophesied changes in the Roman Republic; when from the remotest part of Macedonia, Philip roused all Greece; when Cæsar took such proper measures to subjugate the Gauls, or to destroy Pompey's party; when Richelieu concerned himself with the means of humbling the reigning house of Austria; did all these great men base their conclusions upon any other foundation than an accurate knowledge of persons, exact notions of things, circumstantial facts or faithful reports? Did they thoughtlessly accept all that was said, all popular rumors?

Good sense is the rule of all the virtues and of all the good qualities. It distinguishes a reasonable man from an unreasonable one, a true scholar from one who has only a confused knowledge, knowledge from superstition, a great man from one who is only a hero. With this faculty in addition to those they already possessed, the Emperor Julian and Charles XII [62] would have been perhaps the greatest men in the world.

[62] Julian the Apostate (reigned 361–363). Charles XII, King of Sweden (1682–1718).

Good sense is always useful to learning, because it makes one limit himself to things that are within his comprehension. Knowledge without good sense is often pernicious and always ridiculous.

There are certain primitive notions which serve as a basis for all certitude, and which it is impossible to refuse to accept without renouncing common sense. Of such is, in matters of testimony, the notoriety or the evidence of a generally accepted matter of fact which is the result of a multitude of sense perceptions; of such is, in matters of reasoning, the immediate perception resulting from a simple mental view or inner sentiment.

But the limits of reason are not fixed, and nobody has the right to propose his reason as the measure of that of others. Reason having then no common well-defined measure, principles and rules are necessary to guide it, to aid it in discriminating between the true and the false in matters of reasoning as in matters of fact. This is what is called logic and criticism.

Is it true that there is an art of thinking and reasoning which is taught in five or six months to our young people in the colleges of Europe? It is not taught to women nor to children who are not made to study. However, in the end it is found that the latter reason about as well as the former, and often those who teach this art reason the worst. It is not astonishing that this spreads doubt concerning the usefulness of the rules, or at least concerning that of the method which is used to teach them.

The teaching of logic to children is begun only towards the end of their studies, and they are taught nothing about criticism. It is customary to wait almost until their minds have become warped before righting them. The different branches of knowledge are considered as so many different countries in which the young people are made to travel successively.

All the general rules, all the precepts of any art whatsoever are of no use unless they are applied. Properly speaking, we retain only those things of which we have made use, and with which we have had experience. The rules of poesy and of painting are better known and more perfect than at the times of Homer and Virgil, of Raphael and of Titian. Have we better poets and better painters? Have we better minds than had Hippocrates, Aristotle and Plato?

I am aware of the usefulness of rules and even of the necessity for them. They serve to prevent the causes of bad reasoning, and to reveal sophisms; but alone, they have never advanced human knowledge very far. After the natural character of the mind, it is application, experience and the knowledge of facts which make one man reason better than another.

The advantage which we have over the ancients is that our knowledge is more exact and more extensive. We have a greater experience of facts and of things. We are undeceived in regard to some prejudices and some errors which they had adopted.

When they reasoned concerning only what was within their comprehension, they judged as well as we do. In matters of politics, civil morality and laws, I do not believe that it is possible to contest this.

Why and in what does our century surpass the preceding ones? Because, during the last two hundred and fifty years or so, an infinite number of discoveries of all kinds have been made; the languages have been studied; the texts of the ancient writers have been verified; the true books have been distinguished from the supposititious ones; sacred and profane history, geography, chronology, criticism, fable, medals, inscriptions, etc., all have been made clear and explained; the limits of mathematics have been almost discovered.

Since the time of Galileo and Bacon all bodies have been observed with care; they have been examined under all circumstances; they have been made to undergo all imaginable changes by the great natural agents, air, water and fire; by means of the telescope and the microscope, those which were imperceptible have become visible, extremes have approached each other, bodies situated at an immense distance and those which are near to us have become objects of curiosity, of research and sources of knowledge.

Voyages to all parts of the world have increased the number of observers and multiplied the observations. The invention of printing and the establishment of academies have served to publish and to preserve discoveries and to guarantee their certainty. In spite of reverses and hindrances of all sort, persevering industry and diligent work have overcome the greatest obstacles. It is these which have perfected our art of thinking, and if the result is not all it should be, it is to the systems of philosophy, the abuse of abstract ideas and theological disputes that this should be imputed.

One man acquires superiority over other men by the same means that one century becomes superior to another. It seems then reasonable to employ in learning and in teaching the same principles and the same rules. We should avoid in particular the defects which in general have arrested the progress of knowledge.

XX

RULES OF LOGIC AND OF CRITICISM

One of the principal rules, and at the same time one which would remedy one of these defects, is to reject the suppositions of all systems of philosophy which are employed to explain things for which it would otherwise be impossible to account; to pronounce judgment only concerning things which are within our comprehension, concerning which we possess acquired knowledge, positive elements. When we do not possess these elements, or not enough of them to judge, reason requires that we suspend judgment.

The second rule, which is equally important to prevent the abuse of abstractions, is to fix and determine the ideas. The means of doing this is to reduce abstract and complex ideas to particular and simple ones, or to the elements which compose them. This is what is called to define; for definition is only the enumeration of the simple ideas comprised in a complex and abstract idea.

Strictly speaking, simple ideas are indefinable. They can be fixed only by reflecting on the manner in which they have been acquired. Thus, they are ordinarily defined only by rendering them by equivalents or synonyms. The generality of men have no fixed and determined notions, because they almost never trace them back to their origins. However, they boldly decide the most obscure and complicated questions. I need no other examples than the equivocal use that is made every day of the words *religion, truth, glory, honor, justice, duty, piety, devotion,* etc.

To define exactly a term which indicates a complex idea, it suffices to find in the language the words which signify the simple and characteristic ideas of which it is composed. It is in the common speech that we should seek these words; for we should deviate from the ordinary language as little as possible.

By definition, I mean the description of natural things which can be defined only by describing them; for it is impossible to explain by definitions the essence and even the nature of things. It is only by giving exact descriptions of objects, by seeking carefully all their properties, by distinguishing what is proper to them and what is only accidental, that it is possible to acquire knowledge.

The third rule is to make sure of facts before seeking causes, if we do not wish, as has often been said, to expose ourselves to ridicule by finding the reason for what does not exist.

If the facts were assured, if the terms were exactly defined, if the objects were described with precision, the greater number of questions would be closed. From this can be seen the usefulness of definitions, and, what is still more useful, the manner of making them. However, such a philosophic dictionary should be made by philosophers.

The fourth rule is to apply to each subject the proper proof. Much progress has already been made when we know what kinds of proof we should employ in matters of reasoning, of fact, of observation and of experience. All that can be said and written on the subject reduces itself to this:

good reasons, irreproachable evidence, assured experience constitute the most certain means of not confusing things and proofs, of not employing reasoning when it is a question of facts, and facts or authorities when it is a question of reasoning, of not demanding a proof of fact when it is possible only to obtain one of likelihood, and not to be satisfied with likelihood when it is possible to have a proof of fact.

I am not speaking of theological disputes. They are a reproach to religion and to reason, the scourge of states, of letters and of good studies. What would not such men as Arnauld, Nicole and Lancelot [63] have done for learning, if meddlers, unfortunately too powerful, such as Annat, Ferrier and La Chaise [64] had not persecuted them cruelly, and forced them to occupy themselves with such disputes and such sacred trifles!

The principles and rules which have just been established, besides their importance in what are called logic and criticism, serve to prove the maxim which has been followed in this plan of education, and which is that the basis of any method of teaching and learning is to associate knowledge with sense perceptions, with immediate impressions, with simple ideas. It is like proving one rule of arithmetic

[63] Antoine Arnauld, theologian, defended the Jansenists against the Jesuits (1612–1694). Pierre Nicole, moralist, theologian, collaborated with Arnauld (cir. 1628–1695). Claude Lancelot, Jansenist, grammarian (1615–1695).

[64] François Annat, Jesuit, theologian, opponent of Jansenism (1590–1670). François d'Aix de La Chaise, Jesuit, confessor of Louis XIV (1624–1709). Probably Jérémie Ferrier, Protestant clergyman who was converted to Catholicism, after which he wrote much in defense of the Church against all heresies including Jansenism (d. 1626).

by another. When we have reached this point, we can go no farther, and the examination is finished.

We should conclude from this that it is to acquiring these notions that children should apply themselves, to furnishing their minds with useful facts, to procuring through practice the experience which they lack, to forming their characters and their minds, to applying the simple and sure rules of logic and criticism, and not to discussing them minutely.

A good method is the continual application of the rules of dialectics to all sorts of subjects.

Any well-made book will serve to teach logic. Any exercise which accustoms the young people to adding order and clearness to their thoughts: a good grammar, for instance, which would teach them to arrange in order the subjects of their discourse, to perceive clearly the simple and natural reason for the rules, would be more useful for teaching them dialectics than any artifice of the syllogism.

That is why the elements of geometry, when attentively studied, constitute the best of all logics.

It is by reading good criticisms: the works of such men as Grotius, Pétau, Sirmond, Valois and Saumaise [65] that the art of criticism can be learned.

The most perfect physical art, the art of performing experiments, is found in the memorials of the Academies.

Up to now, books on logic have been written for philosophers or theologians, works on criticism for scholars; meta-

[65] Huig van Groot (Hugo Grotius), diplomat and writer (1583–1645). Denis Pétau, theologian, librarian of the *Bibliothèque Royale* (1583–1652). Jacques Sirmond, Jesuit, confessor of Louis XII, preacher and writer (1559–1651). Henri Valois, philologist (1603–1676). Claude de Saumaise, scholar (1588–1653).

physical systems have been created. It was useful that able men should elucidate these subjects. However, at present, when so much has been written on all sorts of matters, we must have methods that can be applied to the ordinary affairs of life; for everyone needs to reason correctly, not only about matters pertaining to the sciences and learning, but also about those pertaining to civil life, and at every age and in every profession.

These methods are the foundation of what is called learning, knowledge, erudition, reasoning. To be acquainted with such methods, to know how to apply them properly is to be a philosopher and a scholar.

XXI

METAPHYSICS

Logic and criticism are instruments for learning to think. Metaphysics is the science of principles. It teaches us about the aims to which the faculties of man are directed, about their extent, their limitations and their use. It pertains to this science alone to determine what is truth, in what error consists, and what are the means of avoiding the latter. It shows by experience that everything reduces itself to sense perceptions, to immediate knowledge. With logic, it teaches us to discover truths, to deduce them from their veritable principles, to arrange them in order. In short it is the basis of all knowledge, of which it contains the germ and the outline.

It demonstrates the existence of God and His attributes, and it justifies His providence. It establishes human liberty, natural laws and the immortality of the soul.

It reveals the weakness of the human mind; but it appreciates its strength. It proves that their reason is the sole natural means that the Author of their being has given to men to guide them, that all that is intelligible is in its province, that nothing is foreign to it but that which is incomprehensible, that it pertains to it to determine the nature and limits of authority, and, consequently, to indicate the cases and matters for submission, to weigh the motives for belief. It proves that to believe is to judge that reason obliges us to recognize, on the strength of external proofs, the existence or the properties of a being or an object, that thus it is its function to regulate the limits between itself and faith; because it precedes, accompanies and follows always a rational submission.

One part of this science, and not the least useful, is that which teaches how far it is possible to go in matters of reasoning, and where investigation must stop. This negative knowledge—if it be permitted to express oneself thus—would be of as great value as the positive knowledge which it teaches.

It is a great service to mankind to fix the limits beyond which it cannot go without going astray.

Plutarch, in his life of Theseus, says that just as geographers, when they have indicated on maps inhabited and discovered countries, put *beyond are unknown lands and coasts and inaccessible seas,* so should historians do for remote, unknown and fabulous epochs. This is what I have tried to do in the preceding reflections on history.

It would be still more useful to mark the limits of knowledge in reasoning, and to indicate how far it is possible to go or not to go. This would be the most valuable result of a good method. To make known its limitations is to extend the human intelligence. Not to employ them uselessly is to spare its forces. A river which is confined to its channel flows but the more rapidly.

The principle of sound metaphysics, that irrefutable evidence and certainty are attached only to immediate perceptions, proves manifestly the uncertainty in the sciences of reasoning of all systems of philosophy.

When immediate perception is lacking it is necessary to suspend judgment. This is the true rule of the epoch which the followers of Pyrrho [66] applied so badly. By this same rule the majority of systems of philosophy are refuted or banished to the realm of phantasy.

Those opinions which cause so much discussion in one century, and in the following century are forgotten, are shown to be false or uncertain for the sole reason that they are not founded upon the principles of knowledge.

Immediate perception is lacking in all questions into which enters the idea of the infinite, such as space, void, full infinity, immensity, eternity, creation, foreknowledge, physical premotion, concursus, divine decrees, with the exception of clearly revealed facts; in those which concern the nature or the essence of existing things, of beings or of qualities; whenever the question transcends experience, such as the union of the soul and the body, occasional causes, preestablished harmony, monads, etc. It is lacking in those con-

[66] Pyrrho, Greek philosopher of the fourth century B. C. who denied the possibility of arriving at truth in general.

cerning which we possess no assured elements, such as judicial astronomy, systems of ancient and modern divination, the imaginations of the Cabala, etc.; in all physics that is of pure reasoning and can be only conjectural; in what concerns the realm of possibility, such as to know whether there are several worlds, and the nature of their inhabitants; almost all that concerns the future life—with the exception of what God has formally revealed, or what is a necessary consequence of His revelation; in short, in all kinds of vague abstractions of which we have only ideal or confused knowledge, such as Spinoza's [67] ideas about the unique substance, Malebranche's [68] ideas about being in general, the intelligible world, the Beatific Vision, etc.

XXII

The Logic of Probabilities

Almost all that has been said up to now should be understood as applying only to what is necessarily true or the necessary consequences of positive facts, beyond which logic and ordinary criticism have not yet gone.

M. de Leibnitz [69] who understood so well the strength and the weakness of philosophy, who had perceived the limits of knowledge, and who was so well qualified to direct

[67] Baruch de Spinoza, Dutch Jewish philosopher (1632–1677).

[68] Nicolas de Malebranche, metaphysician (1638–1715).

[69] Gottfried Wilhelm Leibnitz, German philosopher (1646–1716): the de is probably an eighteenth century courtesy on the part of La Chalotais.

or to extend it, has already remarked that one part of the science was lacking: that part which would serve to estimate the importance of probability, which would weigh the appearances of true and false.

Such a logic is above all necessary in dealing with ethical and practical matters, in which men, not being always sure of discovering the truth, are often obliged to regulate their conduct by indications or probabilities of it, or what is called in law *presumptions*. These are of different degrees of importance.

XXIII

The Spirit of Philosophy

From the continual practice of an exact logic and a good criticism founded upon the solid principles of an enlightened metaphysics, would result a spirit of philosophy.

This spirit of enlightenment is useful in everything, applicable to everything, and derives everything from its principles independently of opinions and customs.

The spirit of philosophy is different from philosophy, and is as superior to it as the spirit of geometry is to geometry or as the spirit of the laws is above the knowledge of the laws. It is the product and the aim of philosophy, which recognizes and discusses particular truths; whereas the spirit of philosophy appreciates them all.

Philosophy is a science; the spirit of philosophy comprises all the sciences.

If it is a question of history, it shows the usages and the

purpose; it brings together the different times and ages in order to compare them; looking down from above, it sees at a glance distant relationships, from which it deduces singular resemblances or striking contrasts.

If it is a matter of philosophy, it knows which are the recognized truths, their uses and their relations; what is lacking to knowledge at present, and what can be added to it. It perceives not only principles, but the extent of these principles, the strength or the weakness of the proofs upon which they are based.

It observes the progress and the delays of the mind and the reason in the speculative and practical sciences, in the morals of men in the different centuries.

The spirit of philosophy is a real science, and it is the result of comparing different sciences. That is why it ordinarily follows them. The sixteenth century was that of science and learning, the seventeenth that of talent, and the characteristic of the eighteenth century is philosophy. Cujas and Dumoulin [70] could probably not have written *L'Esprit des Lois;* but perhaps M. de Montesquieu [71] could not have done it either if Cujas and Dumoulin had not prepared the way of jurisprudence.

Usserius and Pétau [72] prepared annals giving the results

[70] Jacques Cujas, interpreter of the spirit of Roman law (1522–1590). Charles Dumoulin, interpreter of the spirit of French law (1500–1566).

[71] Charles de Secondat, Baron de Montesquieu, lawyer and philosopher (1689–1755).

[72] James Usher or Ussher (Latinized Usserius), Anglican Bishop, compiler of the Biblical chronology which appears in the King James version of the Bible (1580–1656). Denis Pétau, theologian, librarian of the *Bibliothèque Royale,* wrote against Arlaud, Grotius, Saumaise, *et al.*

of the most careful research. M. Bossuet [73] wrote a most eloquent general history. M. de Voltaire erected upon these foundations a philosophical history. These are all masterpieces of erudition, eloquence and philosophy.

This spirit of philosophy, developed to an eminent degree, has just produced elements of philosophy, to which nothing is lacking except greater extensiveness.

The spirit of philosophy cannot be too highly recommended. It should preside over all knowledge, even literature. But man must always guard against extremes. It is to be feared lest in history, while perceiving more distant things, it may fail to distinguish so clearly the intervening ones; lest in philosophy it wish to go too far back, and penetrate to first principles which will always be enveloped in dense clouds; lest in literature it incline too much to an analysis which would chill sentiment. Finally, it would bring upon itself too much reproach if it attacked religion, and if it abandoned science and erudition, upon which it should be founded, and which have served it as a stepping-stone—if one may so express oneself.

XXIV

The Art of Invention

Beyond philosophy and above the spirit of philosophy, rises, not an art properly speaking; for it is not a method

[73] Jacques-Bénigne Bossuet, Bishop of Meaux, sacred orator, scholar (1627–1704).

of doing something according to certain rules, not a science; for it is not the knowledge of things in which one is learned: but an art superior to rules and instructions, the art of inventing: the creative genius which is the sublime of reason, and, if I may express it thus, the ultimate of philosophy, which is granted only to privileged spirits; for in the annals of nations, the celebrated inventors can be counted. I do not speak only of those who have made discoveries in the sciences, of which mathematics offers the most numerous and the most illustrious examples; but in all the arts and in all things that can be useful to mankind.

It has been said that he who in rude times invented the plough would have been an Archimedes in later ages.

There are certain political problems which require more skill, more combinations than the most difficult problems of algebra.

Granted the illness, to find the remedy. This is the problem of medicine.

From given facts, to conclude what should happen. This is the problem of politics.

This art of judging the future in advance, which Themistocles possessed in a superior degree (*futura callidissime prospiciebat* [74]), is parallel with invention. There are geniuses to whom God seems to have granted a share of His foreknowledge. It is a gift of Nature alone, and all human art is unable to attain it; but as there is no faculty of the mind which does not owe its perfection to art and practice, every operation which bears upon known elements presupposes that the thing is not impossible to discover and that the problem can be solved.

[74] He was most ingenious in foreseeing the future.

If there is a means of developing this precious germ in the eminent geniuses in whom Nature has placed it, it is that of a good education directed according to the principles of an exact philosophy.

If there can be an art of inventing, it consists in the habit and in the practice of inventing. Instead of solving problems, let one accustom oneself to guessing them. This is why I prefer the *Elements of Geometry and of Algebra,* by M. Clairaut [75] which is too much neglected by teachers, and which would lead the children by the way which Nature itself has indicated.

In regard to the conduct of life and of affairs, experience is the first and the greatest teacher, perhaps the only one; but aids and assistance must not be neglected. They can be found only in examples. A good moral philosophy and a knowledge of history prepare the way. Let him who wishes to instruct himself in the art of conducting great affairs read, for example, the letters of Cardinal d'Ossat, of President Jeannin.[76] Let him observe the subject of their negotiations, their aim, the means of succeeding and the obstacles that were foreseen. He will see that the obstacles have always come from the direction from which they had been expected, and likewise the means of succeeding. He will not fail to admire the prophetic genius of these men who seem to have been inspired. Let him read afterwards the result of the discussion of Scipio with Polybius on the constitution of Rome, the Epistles of Cicero to Atticus, the let-

[75] Alexis-Claude Clairaut, mathematician (1713–1765).

[76] Arnaud d'Ossat, Cardinal, diplomat, ambassador of Henri IV in Rome (1537–1604). Pierre Jeannin, called President Jeannin, minister of Henri IV (1540–1623).

ter of Marshal de Saxe to Folard [77] on the blockade of Prague and the affairs of Bohemia. He will realize that the art of these great men consisted in seeing clearly, in not adding anything to the facts, of having present, without omitting any of them, all the elements necessary to foresee the future. A single circumstance overlooked might have caused a dangerous paralogism.

Such reading would be a training in prudence, and would always be useful; even if it were only in order to recognize the style of these great men, and, if we desire to compare style with style, the letters of d'Ossat and Duperron,[78] in which they render account of the same transaction, of the same event, can be studied. It will be seen, as someone ingeniously said of Racine and Pradon,[79] that these two are never so different as when they are saying the same things.

The inventive mind is the same as the mind which debates; but the former passes over, by knowledge and as though by instinct, greater intervals. It sees at a glance more objects at the same time, and it perceives the connection between several theorems very far apart: they are always the same truths considered in the same manner.

This is without doubt too much about something to which no rules are applicable, and which can only be the product of genius; but it is not entirely useless to propose perfection

[77] Maurice de Saxe, Marshal of France, great general of Louis XV (1696–1750). Jean-Charles, Chevalier de Folard, military tactitian (1669–1752).

[78] Jacques Davy, Cardinal Duperron, theologian, moralist, instrumental in the conversion of Henri IV (1556–1618).

[79] Jean Racine, tragic poet and dramatist (1639–1699), author of *Phèdre,* a tragedy, which was copied by Nicholas Pradon, poet and dramatist of less ability (1632–1698).

to men. They will never go very far without an ardent desire to excel themselves and to surpass their fellow-men.

XXV

MORAL PHILOSOPHY

Logic and criticism have for aim the training of the mind and the prevention or correction of errors. The object of moral philosophy is the training of the heart and the combating of vices. However, as all vices are founded upon false opinions and errors, logic and criticism are of great use even to moral philosophy.

It is true that man does not invariably follow his principles; but he who is without principles or has bad ones will surely nearly always do wrong. He who possesses sound knowledge will not always do the good that he sees; but he will do it more frequently, he will return to it more easily. It is a state of violence to be always in contradiction with oneself. Enlightenment leads ordinarily to truth; darkness and ignorance lead to vice.

On many subjects, it is possible to reason correctly without having a true heart; but in all cases into which interest or the passions can enter, that is to say, in almost all the affairs of life, rectitude of mind and righteousness of heart are inseparable, and, just as the mind is often the dupe of the heart, so also is the heart sometimes the dupe of the mind. Thus, to work to attain rectitude of mind is, at the same time, to work to attain righteousness of heart. Hence, it may be that virtue has been well defined (by M. de

Formey [80]) as rectitude of mind applied to the conduct of life and morals.

Men's actions are usually a consequence of their principles, and principles implanted in the mind early produce sooner or later their effect. As long as the soul governs the body, men's ideas will influence their conduct. Their influence acts always, although it may not always impel, it will act more or less to the same extent that the ideas are more or less deeply rooted. They will lead to good or to evil, according to whether they are good or bad.

Men's ideas moderate to a certain extent the course of their passions. We must agree that this world is habitable and that human society maintains itself only by dominating ideas—though often confused—of order, virtue and duty.

In the schools, moral philosophy is deferred until after the other branches of philosophy, and it has been reduced to a few useless questions of scholastic philosophy. It has been forgotten that of all the sciences, it is the most important, and that it is as susceptible of demonstration as any other.

Rules of conduct have their origin either in sound reason or in divine or human laws. The former dictates natural laws, or ethics properly called, which are equally divine and immutable; for the existence of a Divine Law-giver is no less necessary to moral philosophy than the existence of a Divine Creator is to natural philosophy. But the laws of ethics take precedence over all positive laws, both divine

[80] Johann Heinrich Samuel Formey, German philosopher, of French (Huguenot) descent, professor of oratory at the French College in Berlin and perpetual secretary of the Berlin Academy (1711–1797). The *de* was added by La Chalotais.

and human, and would, consequently, subsist even if these laws had never been declared.

It was true before Moses, and even among all the peoples who were deprived of the light of the Revelation, that we should do as much good and as little evil as possible to our fellow-men. It was true that Cain ought not to have done violence to his brother, that Sichem [81] ought not to have taken by force the daughter of Jacob, that the brothers of Joseph committed an injustice against him when they deprived him of his freedom, that Pharaoh acted like a tyrant in oppressing the Hebrews and in massacring their children.

It is not the written law which has revealed to men the turpitude and the terrible injustice of these deeds. It is, at the same time, a natural as well as a divine law which is written in all hearts, and to which the conscience bears witness, says the Apostle. It is of all centuries, of all countries, of all nations, and, so to say, of all worlds. It is of this law that Cicero says: "It is born with us. We have not received it from our fathers, nor learned it from our teachers, nor read it in our books. We have taken it, derived it, imbibed it from Nature itself. It is a law of which we are not merely aware, but with which we are, so to say, penetrated and imbued."

Would it then be useless to recommend to men moral virtues that even pagans have so highly recommended?

Can there not be, and is there not in fact, a communion of morals even between peoples who differ most in religion? What is it that a Catholic, a Protestant, a Jew and a Mo-

[81] Sichem, Vulgate and Douay: Sheshem, King James Version, Gen., ch. 34.

hammedan, who deal and traffic with each other, exact of each other reciprocally? And in religion even, it is not by means of these principles that it is possible to maintain the probity and humanity so necessary among those who have the misfortune not to be sufficiently amenable to higher motives?

The second part constitutes the positive divine law, civil law and international law: different kinds of law, each of which entails particular obligations.

The difficulty of treating these different kinds of law comes from the fact that the different precepts from which they are derived have been continually confused. Some adduce reasons to prove facts, others facts in proof of reasons; which is equally contrary to good sense and the precepts of sound dialectics. For instance, in regard to marriage, theologians, philosophers, and jurisconsults are constantly confusing the natural and the divine laws with the civil and ecclesiastic laws.

A great philosopher, in considering moral philosophy in relation to duties, divided it into what men owe to themselves as members of society in general, and what particular societies owe to their members. These divisions comprise: (1) The natural law, or the ethics of humanity; (2) the ethics of legislators, or political law; (3) the ethics of states, or the law of nations; (4) the ethics of the citizen, or positive law.

He adds a fifth branch of ethics, those of the philosopher, which treats only of ourselves.

It is not a question of going deeply into all of these sciences in youth; and I have no intention of giving lessons to the teachers of mankind; but it is important that young people should be acquainted with the principles of natural law, of ethics and of politics. . . .[82]

I shall not dwell any longer on this part of education, although it is the most important of all. It suffices to indicate the sources as follows: history will serve as the school of ethics; experience and reading will develop the principles, and aid in drawing conclusions. They will teach us to know men: a knowledge which is the foundation of ethics and of politics.

In ethics, we shall perhaps never go beyond the innate principles of justice and virtue, nor the natural feeling for them which conscience has graven in the hearts of all men; just as in metaphysics we shall not go beyond immediate perceptions, and in physics beyond perceptible qualities.

XXVI

Continuation of the Studies of the Last Period

Here is the place, and now is the time to perfect the knowledge of physical geography—which is beginning to be a science, and of which Varenius [83] gave, a hundred years ago, a model which has not been sufficiently imitated—and also of mathematics. Courses in experimental physics and in botany are beginning to be introduced in the provinces. This is one of the most notable results of an education which is better than that of the colleges.

[82] La Chalotais here gives a list of books which may be read on the subject, and which has been omitted.

[83] Bernhard Varen (Latinized Varenius), Dutch geographer, author of *Geographia Generalis,* 1664 (*cir.* 1610–1680).

The young people will read some day the Natural History by M. de Buffon.[84] They will see the arts in the manufacturies and shops, and, on the earth itself, agriculture, the first of all arts. They will learn anatomy and the elements of physiology, or the structure and functions of the different parts of the human body.

I presume that they will keep up the acquaintance which they have made with the good Latin and French authors— of which several ought to have been learned by heart—and that they will continue to exercise themselves in the activities of the first and second periods of study. I shall not enter into details; they are well known or easy to supply.

XXVII

The Care of Health, Business Affairs and Religion

There are three essential matters which must not be overlooked in an education: care of health, business affairs and religion.

In regard to health, for the sake of brevity, I refer my readers to the judicious observations of the Abbé Fleury on this subject, see chap. 20 of his *Choix des Études*.[85] Physical education ought not to be inconsistent with moral education; for it is the entire man that it is a question of training.

[84] *Histoire Naturelle* (pub. from 1749 to 1789) remarkable work by Georges-Louis Leclerc de Buffon (1707–1788).
[85] *Traité du choix et de la méthode des études,* by Claude Fleury, Paris, 1686.

I add that in order to uproot the prejudices of governesses and mothers who inspire, without reason, children with an adversion for certain remedies, such, for example, as blood-letting, quinine, etc., it would be apposite to translate that part of the Institutes of Medicine by the celebrated Boerhaave,[86] which is entitled *Hygiene,* and which treats of the preservation of health. We shall always make fewer mistakes if we have a good knowledge of physic and experience for guides.

A sensible education for a nation such as ours would indeed require a practical course of gymnastics, or physical exercises like those of the Greeks. Tilting and tourneys—though more agreeable than our games of chance—did not have the same aim nor the same utility.

In regard to a knowledge of business affairs, I likewise refer the reader to the chapters on economy and jurisprudence by the Abbé Fleury. I shall remark only that to facilitate the study of the system of public law in France, if there be one, the state of France should be shown in detail; the differences between the orders in the kingdom, the division of offices, the competence of the different jurisdictions: civil, military and ecclesiastic, of which the limits are so well known in theory and so little respected in practice. All these are matters which are easy enough to determine, but which are most frequently settled only by the law of the strongest or by the manœuvres of the greatest intriguer.

Every Frenchman should have a knowledge of the liberties of the Gallican Church.[87] It is an important part of the

---

[86] Herman Boerhaave, Dutch physician and chemist (1668–1738).

[87] That is, the canonical privileges of the Church in France.

public law of France. We possess on this subject a book which is within the comprehension of children, and which should be taught in all the schools. It is entitled *Exposition des Libertés de l'Église Gallicane,* and is by M. Dumarsais.[88]

After examining all that contributes in any way to the formation of taste or the training of the mind, we should seek with still greater care what concerns morals, what constitutes virtue and religion.

I have spoken of the moral law which precedes all positive laws, both divine and human. The teaching of the divine law concerns the Church; but the teaching of the moral law belongs to the State, and has always belonged to it. It existed before it was revealed, and, consequently, it does not depend upon Revelation, although it acquires its greatest force and its most powerful motives from its confirmation by Revelation.

Revelation is a fact. The moral law is based entirely upon right.

The distinction between virtue and vice, between right and wrong, as has been said, is derived from reason and from the very nature of things. Love of order cannot be absolutely extinguished in the heart of man, because it is not possible to renounce reason entirely.

Revelation adds supernatural motives. It promises rewards, and it foretells punishments. But even if it foretold

[88] César Chesneau Dumarsais, the famous grammarian, wrote a book entitled *Exposition de la doctrine gallicane par rapport aux prétentions de la cour de Rome. Les libertés de l'Église gallicane,* Paris, 1594, was by Pierre Pithou (1539–1596). La Chalotais, who, certainly, was familiar with both works, probably confused them.

neither punishments nor rewards, moral obligation would nevertheless subsist. It would exist even in the false hypothesis of unbelief. Saint Paul and Saint Augustine have said: *The faith and the prophesies will pass away, the intelligence will remain eternally* (I Corinth., ch. 13, v. 8.) [89]

It follows thence (according to the Abbé Gédoyn) [90] that morals have been made to depend too much upon Revelation. "Whatever care we may take," says he, "to inspire children with religious sentiments, there comes a time when the ardor of the passions, the taste for pleasure, the transports of impetuous youth stifle these sentiments. If they had been told that morals are common to every country and to every religion; that by this word is understood the moral virtues which Nature has impressed deep in our hearts: justice, truth, honesty, humanity, kindness, decency; that these qualities are as essential to men as reason itself, of which they are only an emanation; a young man, when shaking off, perhaps, the yoke of religion, or when making for himself one after his own manner, would preserve at least the moral virtues, which might subsequently lead him back to the Christian virtues. But, since only an austere gospel has been preached to him, when religion fails everything fails."

Experience proves the truth of these remarks. In these

[89] St. Paul is not correctly quoted; in fact he says quite the contrary. The Douay version gives: "Charity never falleth away: whether prophesies shall be made void, or tongues shall cease, or knowledge shall be destroyed." The King James version has: "Charity never faileth: but whether there be prophesies, they shall fail; whether there be tongues, they shall cease, whether there be knowledge, it shall vanish away."

[90] Nicolas Gédoyn, translator of Quintilian, and author of various works (1667–1744).

times of an evident spiritual ferment, during the twilight of a light which is dawning—shall I say?—or one which is fading, religion is being attacked. It lacks defenders;—for vague condemnations prove nothing and have never convinced anyone. It is compromised by interminable questions and futile controversies which it has been wished to make seem essential to religion.

At the age of which the Abbé Gédoyn speaks, any learning acquired by a young man from the religious orders or in retreats succumbs to the first specious objection raised by an unbeliever, and unfortunately the entire edifice of a badly grounded morality collapses. Young people yield with a sort of security to passions which cause them life-long unhappiness. They consider themselves freed from all obligations; everything is confused in their minds with little devotional practices of which they are ashamed, and which they have come to despise.

I speak only according to facts. I am expressing here the opinion of almost all fathers of families, who are irreproachable witnesses and better judges than men who are strangers to society.

I dare to affirm that the ancients, the pagans even, appear to have been more religious than we. Their legislation was based wholly upon the fear of the gods. This can be seen from the laws of Zaleucus, of Minos, those of the Twelve Tables,[91] etc. Plato, in his speculations on laws, makes re-

---

[91] Zaleucus, philosopher and legislator of the Italic city Locri (seventh century B.C.). Minos, a legendary king of Crete, and a wise legislator who was made judge of the infernal regions. *Law of the Twelve Tables,* first written legislation of the Romans, 450 B.C., written on twelve tables.

ligion their principal foundation. He refers to the Divinity on every page of his works.

Cicero, in defining the principles of laws in his first book, *De Legibus,* establishes as a basis the existence of the gods and their providence.

Among the pagans, it was the legislators and the philosophers who preached virtue. The priests did not teach the rules of morality. The Scribes and the Pharisees among the Jews corrupted these rules by their traditions and their attachment to vain observances.

The philosopher Panætius taught virtue and duty, while the augur Scævola [92] ordered the sacrifices and ceremonies of religion. We have a priesthood and pontiffs who should teach all goodness, justice and truth, what is well pleasing to God,[93] with all humility and mildness with patience, supporting one another in charity; [94] and whatsoever things are true, whatsoever modest, whatsoever just, whatsoever holy, whatsoever lovely, whatsoever of good fame.[95]

Moreover both states and individuals have everything to lose by the destruction of religion. Eh! let anyone say what advantage can it be to mankind to weaken among citizens the principles of virtue, and the motives for good deeds. Would it not be to authorize vice and crime which can never be sufficiently restrained, and which already the most powerful motives cannot stop?

I ask whether history offers a single example of a people

[92] Panætius, Greek stoic philosopher (*cir.* 180–111 B.C.) Q. Mucius Scævola, pontifex maximus, Roman jurist (d. 82 B.C.).
[93] Eph., ch. 5, v. 9 and 10.
[94] Eph., ch. 4, v. 2.
[95] Philip., ch. 4, v. 8.

whose national religion contained all natural religion?—all I say, and has not Christianity alone made it known to the world? Are not the modern philosophers indebted to the advantage that they have of having been born in the Christian religion for their knowledge of the most important points of natural religion? Would they have been, by the light of reason alone, less vacillating and more positive in regard to points which they now establish with so much more truth and forcibleness than Socrates, Cicero and the greatest geniuses of antiquity?

Furthermore, I ask, is it possible to make a purely philosophic religion a national religion? Would not a religion without worship soon destroy itself? Would it not infallibly lead the multitude to idolatry?

When unbelievers have answered these questions satisfactorily, we can reply to objections which have been offered fifteen centuries too late; objections of which men like Porphyry, Celsus and Julian [96] were unaware, and which they could have made avail without reply, if they could have destroyed beforehand three or four facts concerning the establishment of the Christian religion, which was not very distant from their time.

The method of studying religion, like that of studying

[96] Porphyry, philosopher of the School of Alexandria, who wrote against Christianity (*cir.* 232–304). Celsus, philosopher who lived in Rome during the third century A. D. and author of a treatise against Christianity, called *The True Discourse,* of which the major part is preserved in the reply *Contra Celum* which Origen made to it. Julian the Apostate, Roman Emperor from 361 to 363, who, though he had been brought up in the Christian religion, renounced it and attempted to reestablish paganism.

the sciences, is derived from the general method of study. It is not necessary to be a physician in order to be acquainted with the means of learning medicine; and without usurping the right to teach religion, which is reserved to ecclesiastics, it is possible to affirm that it is very badly taught in most of the colleges.

During the first years, a simple explanation of the Decalogue, the Lord's Prayer and the Creed would suffice, together with the Catechism of Fleury or of Bossuet, the abridgment of the Old Testament by M. Mésengui,[97] in which he has preserved, as far as possible, the words of the Scriptures and which was printed in Paris in 1732, the Gospels and the Acts of the Apostles.

The spectacle of Nature, such as it is represented by Fénelon and by Derham,[98] and Nature itself, with which the young people would have some acquaintance, would have already proved to them the existence of a God whom His works make manifest on earth.

I presume that they would have acquired some just notions of the Divine Attributes and of Providence. Toward the end of these studies, it would be time to make them apply to the facts of the Christian religion the principles of the art of criticism, and, without involving them in discus-

[97] François-Philippe Mésengui, author of numerous works, most of which were for the propagation of Jansenism; among them was an *Abrégé de l'histoire et de la morale de l'ancien testament,* 1728 (1677–1763).

[98] François de Salignac de La Mothe-Fénelon, Archbishop of Cambrai, author of the famous *Télémaque* which he wrote for the instruction of his pupil the Duke of Bourgogne, grandson of Louis XIV (1651–1715). William Derham, English clergyman and philosopher (1657–1735).

sions beyond their comprehension, they could be made to read the treatise on the truth of the Christian religion by Grotius, or the one which has been taken in part from Turretin,[99] translated by Vernet, revised and corrected by a Catholic theologian, which was printed in Paris in 1753, in two volumes, by Garnier.

A young man who had read these books attentively would be better grounded in his religion, and better prepared against the attacks of unbelievers than by ten years of spiritual exercises. The spectacle of Nature, the knowledge of the existence of God and of His attributes are the first treatise of all good theology. He would be prepared to read some day the excellent books written on religion.

XXVIII

OBSERVATIONS CONCERNING TWO ABUSES EXISTING IN THE COLLEGES

The object of a good method should be as much to uproot abuses as to indicate and clear the way.

I shall say a few words about the abuse of the note-books of philosophy and of rhetoric which are dictated in the colleges. Besides being miserable lessons which are intended rather to afford practice to the teachers than to teach the children, there is a considerable amount of time lost in writing them. Not a student writes them entirely, and, in a thousand, there is not a single one who keeps them two

[99] Benedict Turretin, or Turretini, Swiss protestant theologian (1588–1631).

years, or who ever makes any use of them during the rest of his life. I appeal to experience.

Another is the abuse of memory work. Children are made to learn by heart rudiments, particles, etc., as well as rules which it would suffice to note and understand. They are annoyed and wearied by long and disagreeable lessons, and they lose time which they could employ agreeably and usefully in learning the most beautiful passages of French and Latin literature. All of these passages joined together would not amount to the half of the lessons that the children are obliged to learn daily from the lowest class up to the class in rhetoric.[100]

Children should be made to learn by heart only what they ought to retain, what they can use as a model. Are there not enough fine passages in the works of the great authors for them to learn instead of wearying them in learning what they must forget?

XXIX

Advantages of This Plan of Studies

Such is the outline of a plan of studies for a primary education: studies which constitute only the elements of the education of a nation; the consideration of the whole of which would call for more profound views, and would re-

[100] The author must mean the aggregate of the daily memory tasks that are learned from the time the pupil enters the lowest class to when he enters the highest, or class in rhetoric. His style is so involved at times that it is impossible to accept his statements as conveying his meaning.

quire men more able and more enlightened than I. The organization of this education is reserved to a wise and prudent monarch whose intentions are righteous and pure; an earthly image of God who can create minds and fashion hearts.

He will not leave imperfect a work which can contribute so much to his glory and to the welfare of his subjects. He will consult his universities, his academies and even the faculty of medicine, so that from their united knowledge may result a new education, or a regeneration, that is so necessary in letters and perhaps elsewhere.

I am convinced that this plan is correct, because it is founded upon the nature of the mind and upon the principles of human knowledge. I believe that a young man who had been thus educated would be better prepared to receive the secondary education that would be necessary for the profession which he would embrace; and if there were plans of instruction and catalogues of analytic books for each particular profession, as in Germany, he would be spared much trouble and much time which is now completely wasted. He would have as clear and accurate a mind as it is possible to have at seventeen or eighteen years of age. He would be familiar with a great many subjects. He would have taste and some knowledge; and what is worth more perhaps than knowledge itself, he would possess the art of acquiring it. He would be able to open a way for himself, and to judge the one which he would be made to follow. He would know how to occupy himself—knowledge that is so useful and so rare at this and any other age. He would be able to frequent society with advantage, to read untranslated books and to travel profitably.

The lives of illustrious men which he had read would serve to reveal his inclinations and his talents. It is impossible that in the course of studies, in which several things are placed before the eyes of young people, there should not appear, in those who possess genius, some sparks of that fire which manifests itself of its own accord, and which made Pascal a geometrician without knowing it, Descartes a philosopher, Tournefort [101] a botanist, etc.

Natural inclinations will be shown by what is most pleasing to the taste. When Ulysses, at the court of Lycomedes, offered to Achilles, disguised as a girl, arms and women's ornaments, Achilles' interest in the former betrayed him and revealed the bravest of the Greeks, the one who was to be the conqueror of the Trojans.

We know that the triumphs of Miltiades robbed Themistocles of sleep, and how much Carracci,[102] while still a child, was impressed by what he heard about Raphael. The life of Homer and his works seized the imagination of Virgil in his childhood, and Charles XII [103] was transported with enthusiasm on reading the life of Alexander the Great.

It will be possible to distinguish the children who possess genius and taste from those who have none. The latter will remain cold and unmoved by narrations that will move the former profoundly. On completing their studies, they will occupy themselves according to their inclinations. They will be in a position to choose a profession with understand-

[101] Joseph de Tournefort, botanist (1656–1708).
[102] Anibale Carracci, Italian painter (1560–1609).
[103] Charles XII, King of Sweden, subject of Voltaire's famous history (1682–1718).

ing, and they will succeed better in one which will be according to their taste and their choice.

What an advantage this would be to society in general and to all the professions!

Sound and cultivated minds would not be occupied with games and trifles. Young nobles would not go to the capital to dissipate their fathers' patrimony; instead they would devote themselves to rendering it more useful, and make it yield the quadruple. They would say with Horace:

> *Beatus ille qui procul negotiis*
> *Paterna rura bobus exercet suis.*[104]

They would add with Virgil:

> *Me vero primum dulces ante omnia musæ*
> *Accipiant. . . .*[105]

They would cultivate in the midst of peace and plenty the arts and sciences which had nourished their childhood.

It is inconceivable that the education of women should have been so neglected in France. Almost all the instruction that is given in the vernacular could be adapted to their use. If they were better educated and more learned, they would educate and train their children better. Perhaps they would aspire some day to the glory of imitating such women as Cornelia, the daughter of Scipio and the mother of the Gracchi, as Aurelia, the mother of Julius Cæsar, and as Attia, the mother of Augustus; all of whom contributed so

[104] Blessed is he who, far removed from business,
Tills ancestral acres with his own cattle.
[105] But may the muses, above all beloved,
Receive me first. . . .

greatly to the training of the minds of these famous men.

With more cultivated minds, they would be only the more amiable, and they would know how to occupy themselves. If they were familiar with some of the usual and approved remedies, they would distribute them gratuitously, and would save the lives of a multitude of unfortunates.

The lord of the manor would settle lawsuits, he would become the benefactor of his vassals, and would maintain the bond of benevolence which the law has placed between them and him: a bond which is nearly worn out and almost without strength.

The man who lives upon the income from invested capital would imitate the nobles, he would disdain mean chicanery, and not be disposed to oppress the wretched.

He who is destined for war would look upon military service as an occupation; whereas now the greater number of the young men who enlist are most frequently seeking only idleness and dissipation.

He would have acquired, through his knowledge of mathematics, an aptitude in matters concerning fortifications. The reading of the lives and memoirs of great commanders would have rendered him able to profit by their campaigns and their expeditions. He would know that Alexander and Cæsar were scholars, that Cæsar wrote commentaries, that Henri de Ronan, Turenne and Montecuculli wrote memoirs, and that Feuquières [106] gave precepts on military science.

[106] Henri, Duc de Ronan, general and chief of the Calvinists under Louis XIII (1579–1638). Henri de La Tour d'Auvergne, Vicomte de Turenne, Marshal of France (1611–1675). Ray-

He would learn military law, of which his need would become greater as he advanced in rank.

The magistrate would have acquired during a sound education habits of attention and diligence. From the study of philosophy, he would have acquired judgment and reasonableness; from literature, the ability to treat subjects with order, clearness and force.

From the lives of great magistrates, such as Chancellor de l'Hospital, De Thou, Molé, Servin, Talon, Bignon,[107] etc., he would have seen that there is a courage of soul which is as great as courage in war. *Sunt domesticæ fortitudines non inferiores militaribus*,[108] says Cicero.

He would seek the spirit of the laws in the principles of the natural law and of true ethics and wise politics, and, although he would be charged only with the execution of the laws, he would render himself capable of being a lawmaker. Pythagoras furnished the laws for all Greece, Plato for some republics, Locke the constitution of Carolina.[109]

---

mond Montecuculli, Austrian general (1608–1681). Antoine de Feuquières, French general, author of *Mémoires sur la guerre* (1648–1711).

[107] Michel de l'Hospital, Counselor of the parliament of Paris, ambassador to the Council of Trent, Superintendent of finances, and finally Chancellor of France (1507–1573). Jacques-Auguste de Thou, magistrate and historian (1553–1617). Matthieu de Molé, president of Parliament, keeper of the seals (1584–1656). Louis Servin, magistrate and scholar (*cir.* 1555–1626). Jérôme Bignon, attorney-general of the Parliament of Paris (1589–1656).

[108] Acts of courage in civic matters are in no way inferior to those in war.

[109] John Locke, the English philosopher, drew up, in 1669, a constitution for the colonists of Carolina.

It was philosophy that produced the Code Frederick.[110]

Merchants or traders would carry to, and bring back from distant countries useful knowledge. The Royal Society of London gives navigators information about the natural history of the countries to which they are going. Educated and well-informed men will see with advantage what others fail to see although it be before their eyes; intention, which is so useful in everything, is of still greater use to them under these circumstances.

In what can the ministers of the religion be more useful to the world? By what means have our missionaries penetrated to the most distant countries? It was not by the help of the dead languages, nor of their controversies (those which they have had in foreign countries have only delayed the fruits of their labors). It was by means of teaching knowledge that was useful to society. They have overcome all obstacles only by teaching men those things that were beneficial to humanity.

I think I may venture to say that a parish priest who would teach his parishioners their religious observances—which are very brief and very simple as far as the laity are concerned, their most ordinary, and hence most essential, duties; who would acquaint them with the simplest means of avoiding and curing the illnesses that are common in the country and of cultivating better their fields; who, knowing something of the principles of the laws and legal customs of the country, would adjust and prevent lawsuits; and who would know a little about physics, the usual medicine and surveying, would contribute more to the happiness of

[110] Code Frederick, codification of the laws of Prussia, made by Frederick the Great in 1751.

men than all the priests can do with their bad Latin, useless scholasticism and theological quarrels.

It would be well that all the orders of the State and all the members of each order should know that esteem is gained by doing good and by being useful to others, that the observance of religion consists in doing good, that to be good is the principal means of imitating the supremely good Being and Him who went about doing good: *Pertransibat benefaciendo.*[111]

A man who would seek to fulfil the duties of a calling which he had chosen according to his taste, or who would occupy himself with the natural sciences or the exact sciences, and who would know the limits of reason and those of authority would never be a dissenter, a factionist nor an intriguer. He would not let himself be troubled by, and he would not trouble others with the frenzies of superstition— that epidemic disease, nor by the various forms of fanaticism which attack the tranquillity of innocent souls. He would never persecute his brothers. "Do not fear similar misfortunes," says the Abbé de Saint-Pierre,[112] "from such men as Descartes, Liebnitz, Newton and Derham."

XXX

Manner of Putting This Plan into Effect

The objections will be raised perhaps that the education which I propose is not possible, that we have neither the

[111] Acts, ch. 10, v. 38.

[112] Charles-Irénée de Saint-Pierre, author of a curious work entitled *Projet de paix perpétuelle* (1658–1743).

teachers nor the books which would be necessary, that young people could not learn in their early years all that is comprised in this plan.

I shall reply that the education of the Greeks and Romans was much more difficult, that very sensible people have considered possible what I propose here, and that one must guard against condemning, because of prejudice, the opinions of such great men as Fleury, Locke and Nicole. What names! and who is the man who would dare raise his voice against their united authority? I declare that in this memorial I have done nothing more than comment upon them.

Finally, every sensible project must be based upon facts, and I agree that there is nothing morally worse than what is physically impossible.

To create a system of education, it is necessary to have either teachers or books; apparently, it is necessary to have both. It is proposed to train teachers; this is a work of long duration, and it would not dispense with the need of having books already prepared. I ask for books that would be easy to write, and which would perhaps dispense with the necessity of having teachers. I say that all these books are easy to write, or rather that almost all of them have already been written. For the greater part, it is only a question of sensible and reasonable compilations which would be made; not by men who do not think, and who have never imagined anything; but by persons who would themselves be capable of writing the books which they would compile, of finding new ways, of perfecting those that are already known, of imagining methods and of judging with a philosophic mind the various branches of knowledge.

In regard to the pretended impossibility of teaching these subjects to young people, I shall remark that in the first place they are taught—in truth, badly—things that are more difficult. Furthermore, I am supposing an education that will extend over a period of at least ten years, that is, from the age of six or seven to the age of seventeen or eighteen. What would it not be possible to learn in ten years, if well guided, and if there were good elementary books?

There is not a child who, in college or while preparing to enter, does not work eight and a half or nine hours a day.

I ask only four or five hours of classes, in which the work would be done chiefly by the teachers, who would make the children work in their presence; and during which the more advanced students would give demonstrations to the younger and less advanced; [113] and books in which everything would be clearly explained: an education, which would require in the beginning only eyes and memory.

During the first three or four years, there would be no study out of class except agreeable lessons worth retaining, which could be learned while walking. The hardest part would be writing, drawing and learning a little geometry.

Learned persons will easily arrange and apply this plan, if it has the good fortune to meet with the approbation of the Sovereign and of the Nation.

I repeat, that in order to put into effect a good plan for a literary education, all that is needed is books that will serve for instruction and as methods of instruction, and that these

[113] It is quite interesting to note that La Chalotais is not only absolutely modern in planning that "the work would be done chiefly by the teachers"; but likewise seems to have advocated the monitorial system to a certain extent.

books are easy to prepare. The King needs only to order it. Let him speak and all will be done, and then education will be easy. Nothing more would be required of teachers, tutors and governesses than that they be religious, of good conduct and able to read well. This would bring us back to education at home, which is the most favorable to morality and the best for society.

I have conducted the young people to the gates of knowledge; it is reserved to wiser men to introduce them into the sanctuary.

Postscript

After having finished this memorial, there came into my hands a pamphlet entitled *De l'Éducation publique*.[114] On the important point of determining the subjects of study I found myself in agreement with a man who seems to have an extensive acquaintance with the *Encyclopedia of Sciences,* and who knows how to establish lines of communication between the different branches of learning.

My first idea was to suppress my memorial, as being perhaps unnecessary. It is not worth while to read the same things twice; but as I am of an opinion which differs from that of this author concerning the qualifications of teachers and some other essential details, I have been advised to submit this work to the public. Matters that are clearly stated before this tribunal will always be well judged.

I believe, moreover, that our plan is good, and that it can be useful. I say our plan; for the two are almost identical.

[114] *De l'Éducation publique,* by Jean-Baptiste Crévier (1693–1765), published anonymously in Amsterdam in 1763.

We differ only in its application, and in the fact that the author excludes seculars whom I should wish to admit, and that he admits many schools which I should exclude.

The most essential article of a plan for colleges is to fix the subjects of study; for if they are badly chosen—as I believe I have shown they are—it is necessary to substitute others for them. The author of *De l'Éducation publique* and I are in agreement on this point. We even agree concerning the subjects that should be substituted. It is on this subject that it is absolutely necessary, if it be desired to reform studies, that the government should pronounce. In the first place, because it pertains to the King to regulate the education of the Nation; in the second, because it is expedient that this education should be uniform in the entire kingdom, and because it is essential that it should not be optional.

Let His Majesty have the kindness to appoint a committee of five or six persons to examine these two projects, or such others as may be presented. The first task of this committee would be to determine the subjects of study for all the colleges.

It seems necessary to say that this committee should be composed principally of statesmen and men of letters, and that the adherents of any special faction should not be included in it.

The second point, and the one that is perhaps the most important to-day, is a method of teaching in order to carry out the plan which would be approved by His Majesty.

To succeed, we must have teachers. Some speak of secular communities, others want celibates, still others propose married people, and there are some who would admit both without distinction. Moreover, it is a question of finding a great number of teachers who are already trained, or of the means of training them in a short time. If we stop to reflect, we shall see that it is impossible to recruit all at once so great a number in the kingdom; and if it is desired to decide the question of the qualifications of teachers, the door will be open to difficulties without number, into which the spirit of partisanship, rights and privileges will necessarily enter, and, which, consequently, will become interminable. Each group will protest, party spirit will be rife, the strongest will triumph, and the State will be no better served nor the Nation any more enlightened.

I think that if the subjects of study were once determined, His Majesty could have elementary textbooks prepared, in which all the instruction would be adapted to the comprehension of children between the ages of six or seven and seventeen or eighteen.

These books would constitute the best instruction that the teachers could give, and would replace every other method. It is not possible to do without new books, whatever decision is made. If these books were well made, there would be no need of trained teachers, and there would no longer be any reason for disputing about their qualifications; whether they should be priests, married or celibates. All would be good, provided they be religious, of good conduct and know how to read well; they would soon train themselves by training the children.

It would be then only a matter of having books, and I say that this is the easiest thing of all at present. A word from His Majesty would be enough. There are in the republic of letters many more books than would be necessary to compile within two years all that would be needed, and there are in the Academies more men of letters than would be necessary to prepare these works. There is not one of these men who would not consider it a duty and an honor to further the views of His Majesty and the general welfare of the kingdom.

Another very simple means would be to propose such books as subjects for prizes to all the Academies. This would produce in a short time excellent essays, which men of literary ability could be commissioned to edit. The Government will be able to do everything when it is willing to make use of the genius and the industry of the Nation.

These works could be printed in one of the Royal Printing Establishments, without any expense to the King, and the books would cost the families little, provided the printing were not a commercial enterprise, and did not become a source of revenue.

II

ANNE-ROBERT-JACQUES TURGOT, BARON DE L'AULNE

THE MANNER OF PREPARING INDIVIDUALS AND FAMILIES
TO PARTICIPATE PROPERLY IN A GOOD SOCIAL ORGANIZATION

(Contained in a memorial on the *Organization of Municipalities,* presented to the King, probably in 1775.)

Translated from the text published in *Les Œuvres de Turgot,* Vol. II, p. 506, Guillaumin, Paris, 1844.

TURGOT (1727–1781)

and his

MANNER OF PREPARING INDIVIDUALS AND FAMILIES TO PARTICIPATE PROPERLY IN A GOOD SOCIAL ORGANIZATION

ANNE-ROBERT-JACQUES TURGOT, Baron de l'Aulne, was born in Paris on May 10, 1727. He was the son of Michel-Étienne Turgot, Provost of the Merchants of Paris, and was descended from an ancient noble family of Normandy. His great-great-grandfather was president of the nobility of the province at the Estates General of 1614.

Turgot received his earlier education at the *Collège Louis-le-Grand,* and later at the *Collège du Plessis.* Upon the completion of the Humanities, he entered the Seminary of Saint-Sulpice with the intention of becoming a priest. In 1749, he went to the University of the Sorbonne, of which he was elected prior. However, conscientious scruples caused him to renounce the ecclesiastical career which would, according to all appearances, have assured him a brilliant future, and, as he had, while making his theological studies, also studied law to a certain extent, he decided to enter the magistracy. He was first appointed assistant to the attorney-general, then counselor of the Parliament of Paris and member of the Council of State (*mâitre des requêtes*). This new position was more in conformity with Turgot's desires, as he had entered the magistracy in reality only in order to open the way to an office of state, which seemed to him to offer the greatest opportunity to serve, at the same time, the country, justice and truth.

In 1761, he was named intendant of the district of Limoges. On this occasion, Voltaire wrote to him: "One of your colleagues has just written me that an intendant is fit only to do harm; I hope that you will prove that one of them can do much good." [1] Never was a hope more completely realized; for the success of Turgot's administration was such that it was said that the province which he governed was like a very happy little state within a vast and wretched empire: and certainly this condition was the result of his efforts, as he had found everything in a deplorable confusion when he assumed the intendancy. This success prepared for him a favorable reception when he later became Minister of the Marine.

In the year 1764, the long and, at least towards the end, unfortunate reign of Louis XV came to an end. With Louis XVI, ascended the throne the old Count de Maurepas, a crafty statesman of the old school whom an epigram on Madame de Pompadour had kept in exile for the past twenty-five years; and from this day the feudal monarchy, which had received its death-blow from Richelieu, entered upon the final period of its dissolution. Even if the new King had not been imbued with principles entirely different from those of his grandfather and predecessor, a general reorganization of the entire ministry which had become odious to the Nation was necessary. It was on account of

[1] *Notice historique sur Turgot, Œuvres de Turgot,* Vol. I, p. XL, Guillaumin, Paris, 1844.

this necessity that Turgot was called to the Ministry of the Marine. We must not, however, think that this choice was dictated by public opinion. In the first place, this was not the way things happened; and, in the second, though he was famous in his province, and highly esteemed in Paris by philosophers, men of letters and several members of the government, the Intendant of Limoges was, and necessarily by the nature of things, unknown to the city and the court. His appointment was really due to the influence which the Abbé de Véry—one of his former colleagues at the Sorbonne—exerted over the Countess de Maurepas, who persuaded her husband to appoint Turgot.

Turgot had been only a short time at the Ministry of the Marine when the King gave him the post of Comptroller General of Finances. If his first appointment to the ministry had been due to a little intrigue, not so with this one. It was entirely due to the perspicacity of the King, who saw in Turgot the man destined to work with him at those reforms which were so needed and which he so sincerely desired. Indeed, no two men were ever more fitted to understand each other and work together for the welfare of the Nation than Louis XVI and Turgot, in spite of, or maybe even precisely on account of, certain fundamental differences of character. They seemed to supplement each other.

In a letter which he wrote to the King immediately after the audience in which he had received his nomination, the new comptroller general resumed in a few words the program which he intended to follow: "No bankruptcy, no increase in taxes, no government loan," [2] and the means for carrying out this policy was to be in reducing by the strict-

[2] *Op. cit.,* Vol. II, p. 165.

est economy government expenditure to an amount less than the income of the State: this he proceeded to do. Naturally, no measures could have been more unpopular with the all-controlling and, for a great part, sinecure-holding bureaucracy. We cannot even mention the various reforms inaugurated or proposed by Turgot during his period of office, nor the endless succession of intrigues against him; we must hasten to the final outcome.

In 1774, he had established free trade in corn; but as the harvest had been bad, there was a great scarcity of grain and prices were in consequence very high. The people became excited against him, and there were uprisings in Paris and in some other parts of the kingdom. These outbreaks were quelled; but Turgot had lost his popularity. As well may be understood, his enemies did not fail to make use of the fact that there had been popular manifestations against the comptroller general, which it had been necessary to suppress by force, to endeavor to prejudice the mind of the King against him. Louis XVI, who wanted peace above all and had such an adversion to any repressive measures against his people that he later lost his crown and his life rather than employ them, could not fail to be impressed, at least by what was told him about riots and bloodshed, and, although he still continued to believe in the soundness of Turgot's theories and the purity of his motives, and did not cease saying, as he had so often said before: *"Il n'y a que Monsieur de Turgot et moi qui aimions le peuple,"* [3] he grew more and more timid in regard to trusting Turgot's judgment concerning the opportuneness of the measures he proposed, as well as more willing to listen to criticism of him.

[3] There are only M. de Turgot and I who love the people.

Many others, who, like the King, sincerely desired the welfare of the people, began to lose confidence in Turgot, so that in January 1776, when he presented to the Council of State a project for six important reforms, all of which affected more or less the privileges of the governing classes, it was easy for intrigue to prevail against him. The King withdrew his support, and Turgot was forced out of office in May 1776.

Another thing which had done Turgot no good in the minds of some who had wished him well was the fact that Voltaire had written much in his praise. As usual with Voltaire, this praise was mixed with condemnation of things that he should have respected, so that the general effect was bad.

After his retirement, Turgot ceased entirely to interest himself in public affairs, and dedicated himself exclusively to the study of the sciences until his death on March 20, 1781. Fortunately for him, he was able to end his days in peace before the great disaster, which he had so clearly foreseen and so valiantly tried to forestall, overtook France.

Turgot was perhaps the only man of his time who was both willing and able to aid Louis XVI in his sincere efforts to bring about reforms which might well have abolished the most crying abuses and thus gradually led to a complete reorganization of the monarchy.

Turgot's task was primarily to bring about order in the state of the finances of the kingdom. In the first place this was the great necessity, in the second, it was the subject which he had studied above all, and, as Comptroller General of Finances, it was his particular province. Nevertheless he interested himself in all that would improve the condition of the people and correct abuses of power. It is in this spirit that, in 1775 probably, he presented to the King a memorial on the organization of municipalities, in which there was a subdivision entitled: *On the Manner of preparing Individuals and Families to participate properly in a good Social Organization.* It is with this subdivision that we are immediately concerned.

In a very few pages, one may almost say in a very few words, Turgot proves the need and proposes a means of remedying the greatest defect in public education at the time: the lack of equality of educational opportunity. He does not write pages on the subject of what is to be taught, how it is to be taught and by whom it is to be taught, as most educational reformers have done. Turgot has the insight to know that no one man can or should determine all of these details, so he merely calls attention to the need of a civic education within reach of all, and recommends the creation of a Royal Council of Public Instruction; in other words, nothing less than a Ministry of Education: a living perpetual body, qualified and authorized to deal with details and supply needs as they present themselves; and above all to make such changes and innovations as might seem necessary at any given moment.

THE MANNER OF PREPARING INDIVIDUALS AND FAMILIES TO PARTICIPATE PROPERLY IN A GOOD SOCIAL ORGANIZATION

The first and the most important of all the institutions which I should consider necessary, the one which seems to me to be most suited to immortalize the reign of Your Majesty, and which ought to have the greatest effect on the entire kingdom is, Sire, the creation of a Council of National Education; under the direction of which would be placed the academies, the universities, the colleges and the primary schools. Manners and customs constitute the strongest bond in a nation; the basis of these manners and customs is the instruction received in childhood on the social duties of man. It is astonishing that this science should be so little advanced. There are methods and establishments for training geometricians, physicists and painters. There are none for training citizens. There would be one if national education were directed in the public interest, and according to uniform principles by one of your Councils. This Council would not need to be very numerous; for it would be desirable that it should be animated by one spirit. In this spirit, it would have textbooks prepared according to a progressive plan; in such a manner that one would lead to another, and that the study of the duties of a citizen and of a member of a family and of the State would be the foundation of all other studies, which would be arranged in the order of their utility to the country.

This Council would watch over the whole educational policy, and it could make use of all the literary societies. At present, their efforts tend only to train scholars, men of intelligence and of good taste. Those who are unable to reach this goal are neglected and of no importance. A new system of education—which can be established only by all the authority of Your Majesty, seconded by a very well-chosen Council—would serve to train, in all classes of society, virtuous and useful men—just in spirit and pure in heart, zealous citizens. Those among them who later would be able and would wish to devote themselves especially to the sciences or to letters, having been turned away from frivolous things by the importance of the first principles which they have acquired, would show in their work a more virile and more regular character. Taste even would gain by it—as well as the national tone—it would become more severe and more elevated; but, above all, attracted to more worthy things. This would be the result of the uniformity of patriotic ideals which the Council of Education would cause to be spread by all the instruction that would be given to youth.

At present, there is only one kind of instruction that is to some degree uniform; that is, religious instruction. And yet, this uniformity is not complete. The textbooks on religion vary from one diocese to another; the catechism of Paris is not the same as that of Montpellier, and neither the one nor the other is the same as that of Besançon. It is impossible to avoid this diversity of textbooks with an education which is under the direction of several heads who are independent of each other. The education which would be provided by your Council would not have this disadvantage. It would be but the more necessary since religious instruction is particularly restricted to the things of Heaven. The proof that it does not suffice for the ethical code necessary in the relations between citizens, and, above all, between different associations of citizens, is in the multitude of questions which arise every day, in which Your Majesty sees one part of your subjects desirous of vexing another part of them by demanding exclusive privileges; so that Your Majesty's Council is obliged to curb these demands, and to proscribe as unjust the pretexts upon which they are based. Your kingdom, Sire, is of this world; and it is over the conduct of your subjects in their relations with each other and with the State that Your Majesty is obliged to watch, for the sake of your conscience and in the interest of your Crown. Without placing any obstacle (indeed, quite the contrary) in the way of any education which has a higher objective, and which already has its rules and its teachers, I believe that I can propose to you nothing more advantageous for your people, more apt to maintain peace and good order, to impart activity to all useful works, to make your authority cherished, and to attach to you more and more each day the hearts of your subjects, than to give them an education which will make them clearly understand their obligations to society and to your authority which protects it, the duties which these obligations impose upon them and the interest which they have in fulfilling these duties, both for the public welfare and for their own. This moral and social instruction requires books specially prepared with great care and selected by means of a competition, as well as a schoolmaster in every parish, who will impart it to the children, together with the art of reading, writing, counting, measuring and the principles of mechanics. A more scholarly education, that would comprise progressively the knowledge necessary for citizens of whom the State demands a more extensive enlightenment, would be given in the colleges; but always in conformity with the same principles, which would be more developed according to the functions which the rank of the students fits them to fulfil in society.

If Your Majesty approves of this plan, Sire, I shall submit to you the details relating to it in a special Memorial.[1] But I dare to guarantee that within ten years your Nation would no longer be recognizable, and that for education, good conduct and enlightened zeal for your service and for that of the country it would be infinitely above all other peoples. The children who are at present ten years old would then be men of twenty, prepared for the service of the State, devoted to their country, submissive to authority— not through fear, but through reason—helpful to their fellow-citizens, and accustomed to recognize and to respect justice, which is the first foundation of every society. Such men will fulfil all the duties to their families which Nature imposes upon them, and will without doubt create families that will comport themselves well in the villages to which they belong. It is, however, not necessary to await the results of this good education before interesting existing families in public affairs and in the service of Your Majesty; and nothing prevents using them just as they are to form regular

[1] Such a Memorial seems never to have been presented; probably because Turgot was removed from office within a few months.

villages which will be something more than an assemblage of houses or cottages and of no less passive inhabitants. It might even be a good means of rendering education still more profitable and of exciting the emulation of fathers and of students, to offer to a worthy ambition an objective, and to merit an employment, in the part which the more distinguished subjects will naturally take, in time, in the ordering of the affairs of the place where their families are domiciled.

III

DENIS DIDEROT

PLAN OF A UNIVERSITY FOR THE RUSSIAN GOVERNMENT

Translated from the text published in *Les œuvres complètes de Diderot,* Vol. III, Garnier Frères, Paris, 1875.

DIDEROT (1713–1784)

and his

PLAN FOR A RUSSIAN UNIVERSITY

DENIS DIDEROT was born on October 5, 1713, at Langres (near Chaumont) where the Diderot family had been cutlers from father to son for some two hundred years. His father, however, decided to break with this tradition, at least so far as this his first-born son was concerned, and determined, when the child was still quite young, that he should become a priest. He appears to have been influenced by the fact that there was an uncle, a certain Canon Vigneron, who could dispose at his death of an ecclesiastical benefice which he possessed. To this end, young Diderot was placed, at the age of nine, in the Jesuit college of his native town. As might be expected, he gave evidence of unusual ability, and, consequently, was sent to Paris to continue his studies in the *Collège d'Harcourt* (later *Lycée Saint-Louis*). The circumstances of his going to Paris are somewhat variously related. One of his biographers [1] tells us a highly dramatic story about the Jesuits of Langres having determined to kidnap the child, so that he might later adorn their order; whereupon, his father, who had learned of the plan, took him to Paris and placed him in the college there. However,

[1] F. GÉNIN, *Œuvres choisies de Diderot précédées de sa vie*, Firman Didot, Paris, 1869.

as this would certainly not have removed him from the influence of the Jesuits, it would probably be better to accept the more commonplace version, which is that it was upon the advice of his professors at Langres, that he went to the *Collège d'Harcourt*.

On leaving college, Diderot entered the office of a solicitor, Clément de Ris, in order to study law. He remained there about two years: during which time, he seems to have studied almost everything except law. This was obviously not what De Ris expected of him, and he inquired of his pupil just what he did expect to become. Upon young Diderot's reply that he really wished to become nothing at all, that he liked to study, and was very happy as he was, the connection ended, and his father was informed. When his father learned of his son's views concerning a career, naturally he was not altogether content, and ordered him either to choose some more regular profession or return home. Diderot did neither; with the immediate result that his father discontinued his allowance, and he was obliged to give lessons in order to earn some sort of livelihood. At one time it appeared as though he had found a place that would suit him as tutor to the children of a wealthy financier, whose name is given in some accounts as Randon d'Hannecourt, and in others as Randon de Boisset. This was, however, only another disappointment. A few months of close and continual contact with children seems to have driven the poor young man nearly insane and, at the same time, given him the jaundice. In order to regain his health and retain his reason, he was obliged to give up his post.

As his father continued to remain obdurate, Diderot lived chiefly by doing any kind of writing that came his way—

even, it is said, composing sermons for a missionary—and partly by his wits. Having begun the translation of *Chambers' Encyclopedia,* he conceived the idea of an entirely new work, which he persuaded a publisher to agree to accept. This was the origin of the famous *Encyclopédie* or *Dictionnaire des sciences, des arts et des métiers* which Diderot edited in collaboration with d'Alembert (for the mathematical part), and to which many famous writers contributed: among them were Voltaire, Montesquieu and Rousseau.

The *Encyclopédie* was from its inception not only a scientific work, but a polemic organ which all the innovators and free-thinkers who wished to reform society from the political and religious standpoints used for the elaboration of new principles and the destruction of the beliefs of the past. The first volume appeared in 1751, and at once obtained a great success: a success which likewise created for its editors many enemies. Opposition to the work was very powerful, and its publication was suspended in 1752 and in 1759. D'Alembert grew discouraged and withdrew, leaving Diderot to continue editing the work alone. This he did, and the last volume appeared in 1772.

Although the *Encyclopédie* contributed greatly to Diderot's fame, it does not appear to have brought him much in the way of a financial return. Indeed, both from it and from his other writings together he seems to have obtained no more than a rather uncertain livelihood. At all events, when the time came for his daughter to marry, he was unable to provide her with a suitable dowry, other than by selling his library; which he resolved to do. When Prince Galitzin, the Russian ambassador, heard of Diderot's plight, he informed the Empress Catherine, who, with a truly regal generosity, ordered that it be purchased in her name for the sum of fifteen thousand francs; stipulating that Diderot should retain possession of it, and act as her librarian at a yearly salary of one thousand francs. Two years later, upon learning that this salary had not been paid—and probably purposely—the Empress, under the pretext of avoiding the repetition of such an occurrence, commanded he be given fifty thousand francs as salary in advance for fifty years.

A few years later, in 1773, Diderot went to Russia to thank his imperial benefactress for her generosity. His success with the Empress was instantaneous and complete; she accorded him access to her study any day between the hours of three and five. During these audiences, the conversation of this strangely assorted pair seems to have ranged from philosophy and politics to platitudes and personalities. Diderot expended himself in projects for reform and utopias, which, however, could not have impressed his imperial patroness overmuch; as—apparently—she placed them in her desk [2] . . . and left them there. Somewhat the same must have been the fate of the plan of a university, which Diderot tells us he made at the request of the Empress; for it remained many years undisturbed in the library of the Hermitage.

Whether Her Majesty really seriously considered establishing any such institution, or whether she was merely prompted by a generous and delicate thought in asking Diderot to prepare the plan, as she had been in the matter of the purchase of his library, and wished to afford him the opportunity of thinking that he was rendering her an important service, it is impossible to say. At all events, she made no use of it when she did have it. Diderot certainly indicates

[2] See p. 276.

that he was pleased to be able to show his gratitude for Catherine's benefactions. It is hard to believe that the devoted, humble and grateful servant of Her Imperial Majesty (so many times so!) could ever have been suspected of being the author of the couplet which, even though he may not have written it, must have sounded quite like his known sentiments, or else his contemporaries would not have attributed it to him:

> *Et des boyaux du dernier prêtre*
> *Serrons le cou du dernier roi.*[3]

Perhaps he made a mental reservation and excepted "the female of the species." In any case, it was fortunate for him that this unpleasant operation had not been performed before the Empress had paid his salary for fifty years in advance and entertained him so lavishly at her court.

Much has been written about Diderot's attitude to religion. After all, is it very important, and if it be, does he not express himself clearly enough on the subject, at least by implication, in the parts of his plan which concern the study of metaphysics and ethics and the faculty of theology, to satisfy those who have not read his *Lettre sur les aveugles à l'usage de ceux qui voient,* which is, in reality, only an exposition of atheistic and materialistic doctrines? He too, though, when he came to die, made some sort of peace with the Church.

Diderot returned to Paris in 1774, where he remained until his death in 1784. It was during these ten years that he wrote,

[3] And with the entrails of the last priest
Let us strangle the last king.
(Also attributed to Voltaire.)

among other less important works, *Le Neveu de Rameau,* and *Essai sur les règnes de Claude et de Néron;* which, the one fiction and the other an historical study, may perhaps be taken as the best examples of his work in these two different kinds of literature. It was, however, from his association with the *Encyclopédie* that his reputation as a writer was chiefly derived.

Diderot had a slight attack of apoplexy in February 1784. His faithful and sympathetic biographer Génin,[4] who seems to have obtained his information from Diderot's daughter, Madame de Vandeul, affirms that the rector of the church of St. Sulpice came several times to visit his parishioner (Diderot had lived for the past thirty years in this parish) and that the latter welcomed him cordially, but was never willing to write any recantation. More striking events were held in store by the irony of fate.

The apartment which Diderot occupied at the corner of the *Rue Saint-Benoît* was situated on the fourth floor, his library was on the fifth, to which he was no longer able to mount without danger. When his generous friend and patroness the Empress Catherine learned of this, she gave orders that a magnificent apartment should be taken for him in the *Rue de Richelieu,* to which he was moved just twelve days before he died. Now this new dwelling was in that part of the *Rue de Richelieu* which was comprised in the parish of St. Roch. A short time before his death, which occurred on the 30th or 31st of July, Diderot was visited by the rector of his new parish, St. Roch. Whether he was called, whether it was of his own initiative or whether at the instigation of the parish priest of St. Sulpice, we do not

[4] F. Génin, *op. cit.,* p. lxii.

know, nor do we know what transpired at this interview. All we do know is that the Archbishop felt himself justified in permitting the rector of St. Roch not only to celebrate Diderot's obsequies in his parish church, but even to grant him sepulture therein. It is precisely the vicar of St. Roch,[5] of whom Diderot speaks so disparagingly in that part of his plan of a university in which he discusses the faculty of theology, who visits him on his death-bed, does whatsoever is needful to obtain for him honorable sepulture, celebrates his funeral and grants to his remains a final resting place in the Lady chapel of his own church where they still lie!

It was after his return to Paris from Russia that Diderot prepared the plan of a university; probably in 1775 and 1776. It was sent to his patroness; but there is no record of any attempt to carry it out in Russia. We are told that Jacques-André Naigeon, who was an intimate friend of Diderot and who published an edition of his works, gave a summary of it, which, however, contained only some insignificant fragments—four or five pages; and, it was not until much later that anything like the whole plan became known.[6]

In 1813, the original manuscript came into the hands of François Guizot, who was at that time editor of *Les Annales de l'Éducation*. Guizot published a large part of it in this journal in November and December, 1813, and January, 1814. This manuscript, which consisted of one hundred and seventy pages entirely in the handwriting of Diderot, was

[5] See p. 279.

[6] *Œuvres complètes de Diderot,* Vol. III, p. 411, Garnier Frères, Paris, 1875.

covered with erasures and corrections; which gave reason to suppose that it was only a first draft of the plan. That part of the manuscript which had been published by Guizot was subsequently included in an edition of the works of Diderot; but it was not until much later that a complete edition was published. This edition was prepared from a transcript made in 1856 by Léon Godard from the definitive copy of the manuscript which had been forwarded to the Empress, and which was preserved in the library of the Palace of the Hermitage in St. Petersburg. It is from this edition, as published by Garnier Frères, Paris, 1875, that the present translation has been made.[7]

Guizot published only those parts of the plan which dealt with the faculty of arts, and, for reasons of prudence, he omitted here and there a great deal of these. This so greatly damaged the whole that it did not represent Diderot or his ideas, and it is probable that this mutilated edition is responsible for some misunderstanding of what the author of the plan had in mind.

Compayré says of Diderot's plan: "His Russian university resembles, detail for detail, and forty years beforehand, the Imperial University of 1808. It will have for its head a statesman, a grand master of public instruction, etc." [8] Is this statement exact, and did Diderot have in mind the creation of a general school system for the entire country, or did he merely contemplate something in the nature of what is called a State University in the United States: a university

[7] *Ibid.,* pp. 411, 427.

[8] G. Compayré, *Histoire critique des doctrines de l'éducation en France depuis le seizième siècle,* Vol. II, p. 178, Hachette, Paris, 1898.

comprising the undergraduate or collegiate department as well as the graduate or professional schools? The answer, if there be one, will have to be found in the document itself.[9] In the first place, Diderot himself asks the question: "What is a university?" To this question, he replies: "A university is a school of which the door is open without distinction to all the children of a nation, etc." Just so could we define a State University in this country to-day. Before this, he has already stated what he understands the Empress wants: "Her Imperial Majesty . . . demands a plan for a university or public school of all the sciences." On another occasion, he says: "If the university were composed of several colleges, etc." If he had in mind a state system, he would hardly consider the possibility of there not being several colleges. The writer, while not venturing to make a positive assertion, believes that the plan was for a great university to be established in St. Petersburg under the immediate patronage of the Empress, and which could eventually have branches elsewhere.

Certainly Diderot was in no way specially qualified to undertake the preparation of this plan. He had never, apparently, frequented any institution of learning of higher grade than the *Collège d'Harcourt,* and his teaching experience was limited to only some few months, which made him ill and nearly drove him mad. We are not told the effect it had on his pupils; but if he made any such demands upon them as he proposed to make upon the students in the university that he had in mind, they must have been in a worse state than he. He, of course, thought he was quite capable of any undertaking. It was the common idea of the

[9] See pp. 200, 204, 291, 304.

time that the well-trained mind, the philosophic mind could deal adequately with any problem which presented itself. Most of the theories concerning everything under the sun which were being formulated about then were the result of this idea.

Diderot tells us that before beginning to write, he had read all that the most enlightened men of his nation had published concerning the subject, in previous times as well as his own time; but later he asserts that he was indebted to no one for his ideas. This too was characteristic of men of his period. Nothing good had preceded them; all good was to follow them. However that may be, he certainly had a number of ideas in common with La Chalotais.

In refutation of an imaginary aim of education which he attributes to Rollin: that of producing priests and monks alone, Diderot states his own objective: "It is a question of providing for the sovereign zealous and faithful servants; for the empire useful citizens; for society learned, honest and even amiable individuals; for the family good husbands and good fathers; for the republic of letters some few men of great ability; for religion edifying, enlightened and peaceable ministers." [10] All of this he proposes to do almost entirely by means of teaching a great deal of science, a little history, less philosophy and almost no language at all. His attitude to the classics is probably unique in the annals of pedagogy. He provides in one class alone for the study of Latin and Greek, and simultaneously. At the most it can be only two years; for he tells us that no student should remain more than two years in the same class, and then, when he comes to discuss the department of theology, he says that

[10] See p. 202.

if the candidate for the priesthood has completed the entire course in arts, he will know Latin and Greek!

This restriction on the length of time that a student would be permitted to remain in a class must, of necessity, apply only to the classes of what Diderot calls the first course of studies, and which are eight in number. In the second course of studies there are only two classes; and in the third course but one. As both of these courses are to be parallel with the first and to continue for the same length of time, it is obviously impossible that a similar restriction could apply to them.

In the main, the general internal organization of the school was copied from that of the Jesuit schools of the time; though Diderot introduced what we call to-day departmental teaching much earlier than was the custom. If he desired—and we have every reason to believe that he did—to render the clergy unpopular, to say the least, with the rising generation, he could hardly have found a more effective means of doing so than that of making of the school chaplain a sort of official public scold as he proposed to do.

The daily program of a student will seem appalling to those who are accustomed only to the school requirements of the present day; however it is probably not very different from that to which Diderot had been accustomed in the *Collège d'Harcourt*. Indeed, those of us who were students in a French boarding school of some forty years ago can recall something very similar.

Though we may find much to criticize in the plan for the faculty of arts, or undergraduate department, we are obliged to admire unreservedly the thoroughness of the courses proposed for the two professional schools: the faculty of law and the faculty of medicine. Unfortunately it is not possible to say the same in the case of the faculty of theology. In the first place, it is perfectly evident that Diderot had no desire that the clergy should ever occupy anything but a subordinate place in the State, and priests were to be educated in such a manner that they would be fit for nothing else, and would, consequently, starve if deprived of their benefices; as they would certainly be in his scheme of things, if they were not absolutely submissive. This he did not hesitate to tell us. In the second place, Diderot was totally unfamiliar with the needs, traditions, and customs of the Russian Church; so he merely drew up his plan as though it were a question of a seminary to be established somewhere in France.

However at fault Diderot may have been as a pedagogue, as a writer he was certainly most able. No one can expound one's ideas more forcibly nor more persuasively than he could. Let the reader then turn to the plan itself; it is certain that he will not fail to see all that is good in it.

The lists of textbooks which were indicated for use in each class and for each subject have been omitted.

PLAN OF A UNIVERSITY FOR THE RUSSIAN GOVERNMENT SUBMITTED TO HER IMPERIAL MAJESTY CATHERINE II

EDUCATION

To educate a nation is to civilize it. To suppress learning within its borders is to bring it back to its primitive state of barbarity. Greece was barbarous; it acquired learning and became flourishing. What is it to-day? Ignorant and barbarous. Italy was barbarous; it acquired learning and became flourishing. What happened when the arts and sciences abandoned it? It became barbarous. Such was also the fate of Africa and of Egypt, and such will be the destiny of all empires in all the countries of the earth and in all the centuries to come.

Ignorance is the portion of the slave and of the savage. Education gives dignity to man. With it, the slave is not long in feeling that he was not born for servitude and the savage loses that fierceness of the forest which recognizes no master, and assumes in its place a reasoned docility which makes him submit to laws made for his happiness. Under a good sovereign, he is the best of subjects; and the most patient under an unwise one.

After the needs of the body, which brought men together to struggle against Nature—their common mother and indefatigable enemy—nothing draws them nearer to each other and unites them more closely than the needs of the spirit. Education mollifies dispositions, makes duties clear, subtilizes faults, eradicates or conceals them, inspires love of order, of justice and of the virtues, engenders good taste in all things in life.

Savages make long journeys together without speaking to each other, because they are ignorant. Educated men seek each other; they like to see each other and to converse. Learning awakens a desire for consideration. Men like to be pointed out, and to have people say: *There he is, that is he.* From this desire arise the ideas of honor and glory, and these two sentiments, which elevate and magnify the spirit, diffuse at the same time a tint of delicacy over morals, customs and conversation. I should dare to affirm that the purity of morals has followed the progress of clothing from the skin of the beast to the stuff of silk.

Of how many delicate virtues the savage and the slave are ignorant! If anybody thinks that these virtues—the fruits of time and of knowledge—are mere conventions, he is mistaken; they are to the science of morals what the leaf is to the tree that it embellishes.

Her Majesty, being convinced of these truths, demands a plan for a university or public school of all the sciences. The subject is of the greatest importance, the task of an extent perhaps beyond my ability; but zeal, which sometimes makes up for lack of talent, has always served to excuse the defects of a work. Therefore I obey.

I shall be brief. A few lines, but clear; a few ideas, but fruitful, if possible. I shall endeavor to establish general principles or reach important conclusions and neglect exceptions. Above all, there will be nothing systematic.[1] The best of plans—under all circumstances, but especially under the present—is the one which combines the greatest number of advantages with the least number of disadvantages. An objection signifies nothing, for against what cannot objections be raised? Several objections could be of no more importance, since it is not impossible that the plan which would meet with the most objections might still be the best.

WRITERS ON PUBLIC EDUCATION

In order to obey Her Majesty's commands and to deserve as much as I can the confidence with which she honors me, I have begun by informing myself concerning what the most enlightened men of my nation have published, in former times as well as recently, on this subject. All of them have recognized well enough the defects of our public education, but not one of them has indicated the means of reforming it. They have made no distinction between what everybody ought to know and what ought to be taught to a few only. They have paid no attention either to the more or less general utility of the various branches of knowledge or to the order of studies that should be determined by their relative importance. Everywhere the essential connections of the sciences have been either unknown or neglected. They have not had the least suspicion that some of them, which have only a slight and distinct connection with others, are

[1] Probably means according to no special system of philosophy.

necessary to all conditions of society and, consequently, seem to require and do require a separate but parallel course. Rollin,[2] the celebrated Rollin, has no other aim than to produce priests or monks, poets or orators. It is indeed that of which it is a question!

—And of what then is it a question?

—Eagle of the University of Paris, I shall tell you. It is a question of providing for the sovereign zealous and faithful servants; for the empire useful citizens; for society learned, honest and even amiable individuals; for the family good husbands and good fathers; for the republic of letters some few men of great ability; for religion edifying, enlightened and peaceable ministers. This is not an unimportant objective.

There can be nothing optional in the teaching or the order of duties and studies, and their duration is not the affair of a day. Neither the teacher nor the pupils have an easy task. It can be made easier without doubt, but I do not believe in the least that it can be made an amusement. We should laugh at the simplicity of those good people who claimed to be able to educate honest and able citizens, useful and even great men, by walking, chatting and joking with them; to be able to accustom young people to the enlightened practice of the virtues, and initiate them into the sciences by way of a pastime. Yes, certainly, we should laugh at them if we did not respect too much their kindness of heart and their tender compassion for the innocent years of our lives.

[2] Charles Rollin, humanist and historian, Rector of the University of Paris and author of *Un Traité des Études* (1661–1741).

PLAN OF A UNIVERSITY

Let us not subject man to useless torment, but let us also not seek to remove all the thorns from the way that leads to knowledge, to virtue and to glory; for we shall not succeed.

The temple of Glory is situated beside the temple of Science on the summit of a steep rock. The way which leads to virtue and to happiness is narrow and painful. Work shortens and smooths it by the right method. Let us seek this method. We must not conceal from ourselves nor from our pupils that their progress can be the fruit of persistence alone. Let the teachers console themselves with the importance of the service which they are rendering their country, and let the students be encouraged by the hope of the reward which awaits them; which is public esteem.

Objection and Reply

But some will claim that the diversity of characters is such that, to certain ones, the difficulty must be represented as greater, to others, as less than it really is. This may be true; but, for the greater number, the exact truth, which is almost always without regrettable consequences, is to be preferred to dissimulation. So let them see the distance that they have to go, but, at the same time, let them be convinced that you desire to help them and are able to do so. Then say to them on every occasion: Do you want to be ignorant and stupid? . . . You answer no? . . . Very well! then be diligent and docile.

After having closed all these fine books on public education, the first thought that came into my mind was that there would have been as many different solutions of the

203

problem as there would have been learned men to whom Her Majesty had submitted it. The theologian would have considered everything in its relation to God, the physician in its relation to health, the lawyer in its relation to legislation, the soldier in its relation to war, the geometrician in its relation to mathematics, the man of letters in its relation to literature; and each one would have been the counterpart of the dancing-master Marcel, who believed that an empire could not be well governed unless everybody in it danced the minuet perfectly.

As I am sufficiently versed in all the sciences to appreciate their value, and not profoundly enough learned in any one of them to have a professional preference, I shall assign to them their due order without partiality.

What Is a University?

A university is a school of which the door is open without distinction to all the children of a nation, and where teachers paid by the State initiate them into elementary knowledge of all the sciences.

I say *without distinction,* because it would be as cruel as it would be absurd to condemn to ignorance the lower classes of society. For all classes, there are certain kinds of knowledge of which they could not be deprived without disadvantage. Since the number of cottages and other small houses is to that of palaces in the ratio of ten thousand to one, there are ten thousand chances to one that genius, talents and virtue will come rather from a cottage than from a palace.

—Virtue?

—Yes, virtue, because more understanding, more enlightenment, more will power are necessary to be a truly worthy man than is commonly supposed. Is it possible to be a worthy man without being just, and is it possible to be just without being enlightened?

The less wealth there is around the cradle of a new-born child, the better his parents realize the necessity of education, and the sooner and the more seriously the child is made to apply himself to study. As he is accustomed to the sight of a laborious life, the fatigue of study appears to him less disagreeable. The parents of a child born in poverty obtain from him by means of an unsparing reprimand what the caresses of a wealthy father or the tears of a mother could not obtain from a child spoiled by the assurance of a great fortune.

The efforts of the former are maintained by the severity with which his negligence or laziness is punished. Being incessantly warned of the fate which awaits him if he does not profit by his time and his teachers, a repeated threat stimulates him. He himself is not slow in realizing instinctively that there is nothing better to do for his happiness than to excell in the career which he is following, and that he has everything to hope from his progress and nothing from favor. This is a lesson which is only too frequently and too forcibly inculcated by the vile and baleful preference of teachers for the children of the rich, and by their beneficial severity towards the children of the poor.

Properly speaking, a public school is instituted only for the children of fathers whose modest means would not be sufficient for the expense of a private education, and whose daily occupations would prevent them from supervising it. These constitute the greater part of the Nation.

PUBLIC EDUCATION

But laws suitable to the generality of minds cannot be particular laws; and, as they are useful to the greater number, there will necessarily be some individuals who will suffer from them.

The capacity or the incapacity of a person remarkable either for his intelligence or for his stupidity will determine the nature and the extent of the education which suits him. The ordinary range of the human mind is the rule for a public education.

The manner of educating a hundred students in a school is precisely the inverse of the manner of teaching a single one alone.

But if the subjects taught and the extent of the curriculum ought to be adapted to the needs of the majority, it follows that genius, which advances with great strides, will sometimes be sacrificed to the herd that strolls or lags behind.

But is it ever possible to educate genius? Is it not enough if a public education does not stifle it?

WHAT IS OUR UNIVERSITY?

What was France under Charlemagne, England under Alfred? The latter founded the schools of Oxford and of Cambridge, which have continued to perfect themselves; but which are far from being what they might be.

PLAN OF A UNIVERSITY

The stupidity or the self-interest of the great Constantine, who relinquished almost all of the important functions of the State to the Christian priests, has left traces so deep that they will perhaps never be effaced.

Charlemagne, who was born at a time when the ability to read, write and stammer some bad Latin was not a common accomplishment, founded our poor university. He founded a Gothic institution, and such it has remained. But, in spite of its monstrous defects, against which the learned men of the past two centuries have not ceased to protest, and which still exist, to it is due everything good that has been accomplished since its origin until the present time.

A scholar of the twelfth and thirteenth centuries was only a wretched quibbler, and insufferably impertinent in every sense of the word, but, even so, he was highly esteemed. The general admiration which he received without deserving it maintained the desire for knowledge. The taste for scholastic futilities passed, that for true learning appeared, and all the great men of the following centuries came from around the chairs which had been occupied formerly by Thomas Aquinas, Albertus Magnus, Abelard and Johannes Scotus, and which are still occupied by teachers who are almost their contemporaries in studies.

Our Faculty of Arts

It is in the same schools that are still studied to-day, under the name of literature, two dead languages which are useful to only a small number of citizens, and which are studied for five or six years without being learned. It is there that, under the name of rhetoric, is taught the art of speaking before teaching the art of thinking; and that of good expression before the students have any ideas to express. It is there that, under the name of logic, heads are filled with the subtilities of Aristotle, and with his very sublime and very useless theory of the syllogism. What could be clearly stated in four pages is there drawn out to fill a hundred obscure pages. I do not know what is taught there under the name of ethics, but I do know that not a word is said about the qualities of the mind or those of the heart, about the passions, vices, virtues, duties, laws or contracts, and that, if a student were asked, on coming out of class, what virtue is, he would not know what to answer to a question that would perhaps embarrass the teacher. There, under the name of metaphysics, is a great to-do about time and space, being in general, possibility, essence, existence, the distinction between the two substances; all theses which are as futile as they are thorny, and are the first elements of skepticism and fanaticism, the germ of that unfortunate readiness to answer any question, as well as of that still more unfortunate conviction that the most formidable difficulties have been solved by some indefinite and indefinable words, without realizing that they were devoid of sense. There, under the name of physics, are wearisome disputations about the elements of matter and the terrestrial systems; but not a word about natural history nor good chemistry, very little about the motion and fall of bodies, very few experiments, still less anatomy and no geography. With the exception of the first principles of arithmetic, of algebra and of geometry —of which the teaching is due to one of my former teachers —there is almost nothing that is worth being retained, and which could not be better learned in a quarter of the time.

PLAN OF A UNIVERSITY

The only advantage that is derived from our schools is one that was never intended; that is the habit of application, of continuous application to futile but difficult things. This habit gives a marvelous aptitude for subjects that are of greater importance for all the functions of society. It is a habit that particularly distinguishes one man from another, especially if the usages of society cure him of the tendency to cavil; which, however, does not always happen.

This is the result of seven years of hard work and continuous imprisonment.

At the end of this long and barren avenue, which is called the *Faculty of Arts,* and along which seven or eight tedious, wearying and fruitless years are spent, open three vestibules which lead to the *Faculty of Theology,* the *Faculty of Law* and the *Faculty of Medicine.*

Questions and Replies

—But do all those who have followed this Avenue of the Arts to the end enter one of the schools of these three faculties?

—No.

—Then, what becomes of them?

—As they are lazy, ignorant and too old to begin to learn some mechanical art, they become actors, soldiers, pickpockets, gamblers, rogues, swindlers and vagabonds.

—And those who quit along the way?

—Though they know absolutely nothing that can be of use to them, still they have lost less time and are not incapable of following some useful calling. This is their resource.

Without doubt it is not the intention of her Imperial Majesty that her university should be copied from this model. May she permit me to add that neither is it mine.

Our Faculty of Law

Our Faculty of Law is wretched. Not a word of French law is read; no more of international law than if there were none at all; nothing about our civil or criminal codes, our legal procedures, our laws, our statutes, the constitutions of the State, the rights of sovereigns, those of subjects; nothing about liberty or property, and no more about obligations and contracts.

—What is done there then?

—Roman law is studied in all its branches. A Law which has almost no relation to ours. Thus, he who has just been decorated with the cap of a Doctor of Laws is about as helpless, if someone seduces his daughter, abducts his wife or disputes his right to his field, as the least of the citizens. All this fine knowledge would be of great use to him if he were called Mœvius or Sempronius, and if we returned to the times of Honorius or of Arcadius. Then he would plead his case magnificently. Under Louis XVI, he is as stupid as a villager from Chaillot or a peasant from lower Normandy. The Faculty of Law no longer occupies an old Gothic building, but it continues, nevertheless, to speak Gothic under the superb arcade of the modern edifice erected for it.

Our Faculty of Theology

The Faculty of Theology has regulated its studies according to the present circumstances. They are all directed towards the controversies with Protestants, Lutherans, Socinians, deists and the host of modern unbelievers. It is, itself, an excellent school of unbelief, and there are few Sorbonists who do not conceal under their furred robes either deism or atheism. They are only the more intolerant and interfering, either by disposition, or through ambition, self-interest or hypocrisy. They are the least useful, the most intractable and the most dangerous subjects of the State. They and their adherents, priests or monks, have often abused the right of addressing public assemblies. If I were a sovereign, and I thought that, on every holy day and every Sunday, between eleven o'clock and noon, a hundred and fifty thousand of my subjects say to all the others and make them believe, in the name of God, all that suits the demon of fanaticism and pride which possesses them, I should shudder with terror.

Her Imperial Majesty certainly does not wish any of this kind of people, and, if she must have priests, she will without doubt demand that they be edifying, enlightened and peaceable.

Our Faculty of Medicine

Our Faculty of Medicine is the best of the four. There is little that needs to be rectified. Anatomy, surgery, the treatment of diseases in all its branches, the elements of natural history, botany, chemistry and pharmacy are all taught. There is need only of fixing the order and the duration of these studies. Besides, there is no practical experience, which is a great defect. How many things there are pertaining to the science of healing that cannot be learned either from books or lectures! Can the discourse of a professor teach how to recognize whether a pulse is strong or weak, slow or rapid, regular or irregular, normal or abnormal? What description can be accurate enough to give a precise notion of certain wounds, discharges, fractures, etc.? A young physician then makes his first experiments on us, and he becomes skillful only through murder.

We have flayed the centaur to the knees, but the old beast still walks and drags his skin after him.

THE ESTABLISHMENT OF A NEW UNIVERSITY

In all that concerns public education, there is nothing variable, nothing that may depend essentially on circumstances. The objective will be the same in all centuries: to make men virtuous and enlightened.

The order of duties and instruction is as inalterable as the relations of the different branches of knowledge to each other. We must proceed from the easy thing to the difficult thing, go from the first step to the last, from what is most useful to what is least so, from what is necessary to everyone to what is necessary to a few only. We must spare time and fatigue, by adapting the teaching to the age of the students, and the lessons to the average capacity of their minds.

AN IMPORTANT PRECAUTION

If the general plan is beyond the resources of the moment, a time more favorable to its complete and perfect realization should be awaited, but nothing should be left to the caprice of the future. The same should be done for an establishment for public education as is done by an intelligent architect, when he is building for an owner whose means are limited. If the owner is unable to provide at once the sum necessary for the entire building, the architect digs the foundations, lays the first stones and builds that wing of the house which must be built first. When he is forced to suspend the work, he leaves, on the part which he has built, and to which is to be added, some projecting stones that can be seen. He also leaves in the hands of the owner a general plan, to which, when the building is resumed, it will be necessary to conform, or else run the risk of having only a confused group of rooms, ugly or beautiful, as the case may be, but which do not harmonize, and form an unsatisfactory whole.

A Singular Phenomenon

Is it not an astonishing phenomenon that barbarous and Gothic schools for public education should subsist with all their defects, in the midst of an enlightened nation, beside three famous Academies, after the expulsion of those bad teachers known by the name of Jesuits, in spite of the protests of all the orders in the State, to the detriment of the Nation, to its shame, to the prejudice of all the youth of the kingdom and in contempt of a multitude of excellent works, at least in contempt of that part of them wherein an attempt has been made to show the defects of this education?

The Reasons for This Phenomenon

It is because nothing struggles so obstinately against public interest as private interest, nothing resists reason more forcibly than inveterate abuse. It is because the doors of

societies and communities are closed to the general enlightenment that has long been making useless efforts
against barriers which have existed for centuries. It is because the spirit of institutions remains the same while
everything changes around them; and because bad students
become themselves bad teachers who, in turn, make of their
pupils teachers who resemble them, there has been established a sort of perpetuity of traditional ignorance, which
is consecrated by old institutions. While knowledge shines
on all sides, the dark shadows of ignorance continue to
hover over these asylums of futility and noisy disputes.

The time of serfs has passed, but feudal jurisprudence remains. Scholasticism maintains itself proudly in the midst of
the Sorbonne. It is Roman jurisprudence that is taught in
our law schools. Hence the necessity for arranging things
not for the present time, but for the entire duration of an
empire.

The Times of Charlemagne and of Alfred

Charlemagne in France and Alfred in England did about
the best they could. All Europe was in a state of barbarity,
and there were neither sciences nor arts. All that had existed
formerly was concealed in ancient books which were not
understood. What was to be done under the circumstances?
Teach the science of words, the key of these old sanctuaries
of learning which had been closed for so many centuries.
But now that the riches which they contained have been
withdrawn, now that the arts and sciences have made such
immense progress, and science has begun to speak in the
vernacular, so that the ancient languages are no longer of

use except in certain special cases, the order and the nature of the teaching should be altogether different. It would be very singular, to say nothing more, if a public school, a school to which all the subjects of an empire would be admitted, should begin its course with a study which is of use to only the smallest part of them. To these reasons, I shall add others no less peremptory for postponing the study of Greek and Latin until almost the end of a university course.

THE ADVANTAGEOUS POSITION OF HER IMPERIAL MAJESTY

I shall content myself here with remarking that the time Her Imperial Majesty has chosen for forming the project of a university is very favorable. The human mind seems to have outgrown its childishness, the futility of scholastic studies is recognized, the mania for systems has ceased, and there is no longer any question of Aristotelianism, of Cartesianism, of Malebranchism or of Leibnitzianism. An interest in true science reigns everywhere, and every kind of knowledge has been brought to a very high degree of perfection. There are no old institutions to oppose her views. She has before her a vast field, a space free of all obstacles, upon which to build according to her desires. I do not flatter her, I speak in all sincerity, when I assure her that, from this point of view, her position is more advantageous than ours.

THE ORDER OF STUDIES

After this observation, I shall proceed to compare a course in universal knowledge with a great avenue, at the entrance of which appear a crowd of people, all crying at the same

DIDEROT

time: "Instruction, instruction! We know nothing, teach us."

The first thing that I say to myself is that not all are either capable of following, or destined to follow this long avenue to the end.

Some will go this far; others that far; some few a little farther; but as they advance, the number will diminish.

What then will be the first lesson that I shall teach them? The answer is not difficult. One that will be suitable to all, no matter what their social condition may be.

What will be the second? One which, though of a utility a little less general, will be suitable to those remaining with me.

And the third? One which, even though still less useful than the preceding, will be suitable to the small number who have followed me until then.

And so on until the end of the course, the utility of the instruction will diminish in the same proportion that the number of my hearers diminishes.

I shall classify the sciences as our naturalist M. de Buffon[3] classified animals, and as he would have classified minerals and vegetables. First, he spoke of the ox—the animal about which it is most important for us to know, then of the horse, the ass, the mule, the dog. According to his method, the wolf, the hyena, the tiger and the panther occupy a remote place in natural science because they are far removed from us in nature, and because we derive little benefit from them or have little reason to fear them.

[3] Georges-Louis Leclerc de Buffon, naturalist and author of *Une Histoire naturelle,* which appeared in parts from 1749 to 1789 (1707–1788).

What will be the result? It will be that the sooner he who does not have the strength or the courage to follow his university career to the end abandons it, and the less knowledge he leaves behind, the greater was his need of that which he carries away.

I insist upon this principle. It will be the corner-stone of the edifice. If this stone is badly laid, the edifice will fall; if well laid, the edifice will remain forever unshakable.

Essential Knowledge and Conventional Knowledge

There are two kinds of knowledge: one that I shall call essential or primary knowledge, the other I shall call secondary or conventional. Primary knowledge is necessary to all. If it is not acquired in youth, it must be acquired at a more advanced age. If it is not acquired at all, the penalty will be constant mistakes, or else the need of calling on others for help at every instant.

Secondary knowledge is needed only for the particular state in life which we have chosen.

There is an advantage in the fact that primary knowledge need only be elementary, and that secondary knowledge must be advanced.

Advanced primary knowledge constitutes professional knowledge.

All professions do not require the same amount of the primary or elementary knowledge which makes up the complete course of studies in a university. The laborer needs less than the factory worker, the factory worker needs less than the shopkeeper, the shopkeeper less than the soldier, the soldier less than the magistrate or the ecclesiastic, and these latter less than the statesman.

It is then important that a student should follow more or less of this course of studies, according to the profession for which he is destined. For instance, if a magistrate has acquired, by following the entire course of public education to the end, all the primary knowledge pertaining to his profession, he will less frequently have need to call on experts, and will be better able to judge of their integrity whenever he does need them.

Let us take another example that is less important: the poet. What subject is there in Art or Nature which is not in his province? is it possible to be a great poet without knowing the ancient languages and some of the modern ones? Is it possible to be a great poet without a good background of history, of physics and of geography? Is it possible to be a great poet without a knowledge of the duties of a man and of a citizen, of all that pertains to the laws which govern societies in their relations to each other, to religions, to the different kinds of government, to the manners and customs of nations, to the society of which one is a member, to the passions, to the vices, to the virtues, to character and to ethics? What vast learning in Homer and Virgil! What had they not studied before they began to write? If our poets Corneille and Racine had been less learned, they would not have been what they were. What is it in particular that distinguishes Voltaire from all our young writers? Learning. Voltaire knows much, and our young poets are ignorant. The works of Voltaire are full of things; their works are empty. They wish to sing, they have the voice; but, for lack of knowledge, they sing only melodious trifles.

To be a poet then requires a long period of study. The variety of the primary knowledge which is necessary for him implies that he has advanced very far in the public-school course. He must be in the class nearest the end, and, as the number of students diminishes as the course advances, this class is the smallest. So much the better. I say the same of orators, of scholars and of the other professions which do not suffer mediocrity, and for which instruction is of no avail without genius. Furthermore, even at their best, they are not very necessary to society.

When the knowledge of the ancient languages is given the first place in the curriculum of a public education, it indicates precisely the intention of peopling a nation with rhetoricians, priests, monks, philosophers, lawyers and physicians.

More philosophers than physicians, more physicians than lawyers, more lawyers than orators, almost no poets at all.

The Object of a Public School

The object of a public school is not to make a man profoundly learned in any particular subject, but to initiate him into a great many kinds of knowledge, the lack of which would be detrimental in all states in life, and more or less shameful in some. Ignorance of the laws would be pernicious in a magistrate. It would be shameful if he were a bad judge of true eloquence.

The individual enters school ignorant, he comes out of it a scholar. He makes himself a master by devoting all of his natural capacity and all of his application to some special subject.

What should be acquired in a public school? Good elementary knowledge.

Objection and Reply

What! the course of studies of a university is only the progressive teaching of elementary knowledge?

—Assuredly.

—But this is the means of peopling society with superficial men!

—Not at all. It is to fit them all to become in time learned men; at least such of them as were not born wrong, and endowed with that impertinent presumption which breaks into the conversation of learned men, which thrusts itself at random into all sorts of subjects, saying: "You are speaking of geometry, I am a geometrician. You are speaking of chemistry, I am a chemist. You are speaking of metaphysics, there is no one who is a greater metaphysician than I." Incurable vice! Have no fear that he who possesses the fundamental principles of knowledge will render himself ridiculous. He will not speak inopportunely, without understanding himself and without being understood, if elementary knowledge is well ordered in his mind. No one is vain of a little knowledge, or over-confident in his judgments, or dogmatic, or skeptical at venture, when he has an inkling of all that remains to be known in order to be able to affirm, to deny, to approve or to contradict. He may know some arithmetic without boasting of being an arithmetician, some geometry without arrogating to himself the title of geometrician, some chemistry without interrupting Rouelle or Darcet.[4]

[4] Guillaume-François Rouelle (1703–1770) and Jean Darcet (1725–1801), both famous chemists of their time.

PLAN OF A UNIVERSITY

A Division Common to Every Art and Science

In every science, as in every art, there are three very distinct parts: the general knowledge or account of its progress, which is its history; the speculative principles together with the long chain of consequences that have been deduced from them, which is its theory; the application of the science to practical use, which is its practice.

A more or less extensive knowledge of the history belongs to all. The science, or the sum of the knowledge which constitutes it and the practice are reserved to the members of the trade or profession.

Differences between the Order of Studies in a Treatise and in a School

The arrangement of the order of studies in a school is not at all one that would be suitable in a scientific work.

The writer allows himself to be led by the natural sequence of all facts, which connects them in his mind and brings them under his pen. This method would not be suitable for public teaching.

Or else, he will associate all human knowledge with the principal faculties of the understanding, as we have done in the *Encyclopédie,* by arranging all facts under memory, all the sciences under reason, all the imitative arts under imagination and all the mechanical arts under needs or pleasures. But this view, which is vast and great, and excellent in a general statement of our activities, would be unreasonable if applied to the lessons in a school, where it would reduce everything to four teachers and to four classes: a teacher of

221

history and a teacher of reason, a class in imitation and another in needs. In one case, only historians or philosophers would be trained, in another, only orators, poets or workmen.

There are still two very general points of view from which universal knowledge can be considered: man and Nature, man alone and man in society. But from one of these divisions, I see come forth helter-skelter physicists, naturalists, physicians, astronomers and geometricians; from the other, historians, moralists in verse and in prose, lawyers and politicians; all the science of the robe, of the sword and of the Church. But how many preliminary studies are essential and common to all of these professions!

What should we conclude from this? That, as I have insinuated above, things that are right in theory may be wrong in practice, and that the order of teaching prescribed by the age, by the more or less general needs of the students, the only one that is feasible in a public education, is also the only one that accords with the general and particular interest of all concerned.

Objection and Reply

This plan presents only one difficulty, which is that the relation of a science with the one that precedes it, and also its natural connection with the one which follows it, and of which it would facilitate the study, indicate for it one place in the curriculum, whereas its more or less general usefulness assigns to it another.

But fortunately this contradiction presents itself in only one case, and, furthermore, the science for which the natural order indicates one place and its usefulness another is not a long study. Also the elements of this science are necessary for several important occupations. This is the only case in which we are permitted to deviate from our general principle of assigning to each branch of knowledge its place in the order of studies according to its degree of general usefulness.

After these theoretical observations, upon which I have perhaps dwelt at too great length, I shall pass to their application.

THE PLAN OF THIS LITTLE TREATISE

I shall set forth the order according to which, in my opinion, the sciences should be taught in a public school. I shall first present as vast a plan as possible, and then reduce this plan to the ordinary limits required by usage. I shall give a diagram of both of these plans. I shall then discuss the reduced plan, class by class, applying to each subject that is to be taught the principle of utility, and I shall finish with some observations on schools in general, their administration, teachers, students, textbooks, exercises and buildings.

SUPPOSITIONS

I suppose that he who presents himself at the door of a university knows how to read, write and spell his language fluently, and I suppose that he also knows how to form the digits and symbols of arithmetic. He must have learned these things at home or in the primary school.

DIDEROT

General Plan of Instruction in a University

FIRST COURSE OF STUDIES	SECOND COURSE OF STUDIES	THIRD COURSE OF STUDIES	FOURTH COURSE OF STUDIES
1st Class Arithmetic. Algebra. Combinations or the first principles of calculating probabilities. Geometry.	Parallel to the first and of the same duration.	Parallel to the first two and of the same duration.	Parallel to the first three and of the same duration.
	1st Class The first principles of metaphysics; the distinction between the two substances; the existence of God; the corollaries of this truth.	**1st Class** Drawing. (This class is common to all students.)	**1st Class** Music. Dancing.
2nd Class The laws of motion and fall of bodies. Centrifugal and other forces. Mechanics. Hydraulics.			**2nd Class** Fencing. Riding. Swimming.
3rd Class The sphere and the globes. The terrestrial system. Astronomy and related subjects, such as gnomonics, etc.	**2nd Class** History. Geography. Chronology and the first principles of economics, or of the most advantageous use of time and talents. Household management and the preservation of property.		
4th Class Natural history. Experimental physics.			
5th Class Chemistry. Anatomy.			
6th Class Logic. Criticism. General analytic grammar.			

PLAN OF A UNIVERSITY

GENERAL PLAN OF INSTRUCTION IN A UNIVERSITY
(*Continued*)

FIRST COURSE
OF STUDIES

7th Class
Grammar and
principles of
the Russian lan-
guage.
The Slavonic lan-
guage.

8th Class
Greek and Latin.
Eloquence and
poesy.

SECOND FACULTY	THIRD FACULTY	FOURTH FACULTY
Medicine.	Law.	Theology.
School of Political sci-ence or of public af-fairs.	School of engineering or of military science.	Naval school.
School of agriculture and commerce.	School of perspective. School of drawing. School of painting. School of sculpture and architecture.	

I suppose that his mind is not sufficiently developed, and that the door of the university will not yet be opened to him, if he is not capable of understanding the first principles of arithmetic; which, of all the sciences, is the most useful and the easiest.

I suppose that it is not according to his age, but according to the progress of his understanding that a child should or should not be admitted to a public school of the sciences.

Children are not all able to walk at the same age.

Of this general plan, I suppress the fourth course of exercises, because it is not customary in universities to teach music, dancing, fencing, riding or swimming. If these accomplishments, which distinguish the gentleman, the man of the world from the pedant, are of so little importance in our eyes that they have never been included in the curriculum of any public institution, it is doubtless one of the consequences of the inveterate defect of our monkish education. For nearly nine centuries, we have seen our students only in a cassock or a gown.

I suppress the school of political science or foreign affairs, although such preliminary knowledge is indeed necessary, because we have the right to suppose that the secretaries and counselors of embassies who are sent to foreign courts to achieve their education already possess this knowledge.

I suppress the school of engineering or military science, because Her Imperial Majesty already has a school for cadets, where I presume those youths who are destined to follow the career of arms receive such instruction and practice as are necessary for this profession, while waiting to perfect themselves on the field of battle.

I suppress the naval school, because Her Majesty has her naval cadets as well as her military cadets.

I yield very ridiculously to custom, and I must be strangely subjugated by routine to suppress the school of agriculture and commerce; the two subjects which are the most important to society: the art which produces bread, wine and food of all kinds, which furnishes the raw material for every industry, for consumption, for barter between citizen and citizen and for barter between nation and nation.

PLAN OF A UNIVERSITY

All the schools which I have suppressed are more or less necessary. Whether they are united with those of the university or not, some day, they will nevertheless be established in all the cities of the empire, but isolated, and without being subject to any rational method of teaching—for which they will not be any better.

Faculties

I have just given the plan for a university such as I should wish it to be; then, curtailing this plan to render it practicable, I divide this university into four faculties: first, the Faculty of Arts; second, the Faculty of Medicine; third, the Faculty of Law; fourth, the Faculty of Theology. As the last three faculties are devoted to particular sciences and professions, it is the first, the Faculty of Arts, that comprises all the studies applicable to the generality of those who study.

This faculty is divided into three parallel courses, which are to be followed simultaneously.

The first course, divided into eight classes, comprises the mathematical sciences, the natural sciences, the logical sciences and rhetoric.

The second course, divided into two classes, comprises the first principles of metaphysics, ethics, natural and revealed religion, history, geography and the first principles of economics.

The third course is composed of only one class, in which are taught drawing and the principles of architecture.

DIDEROT

REDUCED PLAN OF INSTRUCTION IN A UNIVERSITY

FACULTY OF ARTS

FIRST COURSE OF STUDIES	SECOND COURSE OF STUDIES	THIRD COURSE OF STUDIES
1st Class Arithmetic. Algebra. Caculation of probabilities. Geometry.	Parallel to the first and of the same duration.	Parallel to two preceding and of the same duration.
	1st Class First principles of metaphysics; the distinction between the two substances; the existence of God, etc.	**1st Class** Perspective. Drawing and first principles of architecture or rather the art of building.
2nd Class Laws of motion and fall of bodies. Centrifugal forces. Mechanics and hydraulics.		
3rd Class The sphere and the globes. Astronomy and related subjects such as gnomonics, etc.	**2nd Class** History and mythology. Geography. Chronology. First principles of economics or of the use of time and talents. Household management and the preservation and increase of property.	
4th Class Natural history. Experimental physics.		
5th Class Chemistry. Anatomy.		
6th Class Logic, criticism. General analytic grammar.		
7th Class Principles of the Russian and Slavonic languages.		
8th Class Greek and Latin. Eloquence and poesy.		
SECOND FACULTY Medicine.	THIRD FACULTY Law.	FOURTH FACULTY Theology.

PLAN OF A UNIVERSITY

I begin the course with arithmetic, algebra and geometry, because in all conditions in life, from the highest to the last of the mechanical arts, the knowledge of them is needed. Everything is counted, everything is measured. The use of our reason often reduces itself to the rule of three. Nothing is more general than number and space.

To know some geometry is a very different thing from being a geometrician. It is given to few men to be geometricians; it is given to all to be able to learn some arithmetic and some geometry. Only ordinary intelligence is needed; and a child of thirteen who is not capable of these studies is good for nothing; he should be sent away from school.

I believe that it is easier to learn arithmetic and elementary geometry than it is to learn to read. The letters of the alphabet have made children shed more tears as characters of writing than as algebraic signs.

Children learn games that require more memory, more combinations and more ingenuity than geometry does.

From the first moment of consciousness to the time of entering school, the daily habits of life have prepared them all for arithmetic and geometry. They have never ceased to add, to subtract and to measure.

Algebra, of which the name no longer causes fright, is only a sort of arithmetic which is more general than that of numbers. It is just as clear and even easier. It is only the same operations but simpler.

Examples of children who were initiated at the age of fifteen or sixteen into the elements of higher geometry and of the calculus of infinitesimals are not rare.

Pascal had discovered a certain number of the propositions of Euclid at the age at which most children call a circle a ring and a point a dot. Why should not other children understand what Pascal invented?

It is hardly possible for a child to be too young to enter the primary school. It is not the same with the schools of the university, where he will remain a longer or shorter time, according to his natural capacity and the progress he makes.

It is never too soon to begin to adjust the human mind by furnishing it with examples of the most obvious and most rigorously exact reasoning. It is with these examples that the child will compare later all others which will be given him, and of which, no matter what the subject may be, he will need to appreciate the strength or the weakness.

It is above all in mathematics that all facts are identical. All the science of calculation is only the repetition of the axiom that one and one make two, and all geometry is only the repetition of the other axiom that the whole is greater than any of its parts.

Geometry is the best and simplest of all logics, and it is the most suitable for fortifying the judgment and the reason.

If a people is ignorant and superstitious, let the children be taught some geometry, and you will see, in time, the effect of this science.

PLAN OF A UNIVERSITY

The first among the ancients who, by means of some rules of trigonometry, showed that the moon was greater than all the Peloponnesus made the priests of paganism grind their teeth with rage.

If, as some believe, the study of mathematics dries up the heart and the mind, it can be true only in the case of habitual study; and yet, is it true?

I have added to arithmetic, algebra and geometry the science of permutations and combinations or the calculation of probabilities; because everything enters into combinations, and, with the exception of mathematics, everything is only probability; because this part of education is of immense use in the daily affairs of life; because it includes both the most important and the most trivial things; because it enters into our ambitions, our projects of fortune and glory and our amusements; and because its elements are no more difficult than those of arithmetic.

The theory of probabilities is of importance even in matters of legislation. It may be asked, for instance, after how long an absence a citizen may be legally presumed to be dead.

It rules all that pertains to insurance, to tontines, to lotteries, to annuities payable on one or more lives, to the major part of financial and commercial transactions.

It indicates the surest or the least uncertain result, and it consoles when the event does not correspond with a well-founded expectation.

Our whole life is only a game of chance; let us try to have the chances in our favor.

DIDEROT

SECOND CLASS

LAWS OF MOTION, FALL OF HEAVY BODIES FREE OR ON INCLINED
PLANES, CENTRIFUGAL FORCES, FORCES OF ATTRACTION, ME-
CHANICS, HYDRAULICS

The laws of the motion and the fall of bodies, perpen-
dicular or oblique, are preliminary knowledge of mechanics,
which is a science of prime utility. There is not a single art
that does not have need of it. We do not take a step in society, on the streets, in town or in the country without meet-
ing machines.

The science of the equilibrium and the motion of fluids
has many applications.

Nothing great or small can be undertaken without a
knowledge of hydraulics; for it is by means of this knowledge that canals, pumps, aqueducts, mills, etc., are controlled.

The art of making use of air, water, fire and earth or
gravity is the art of sparing the time and the strength of
man who has made them his servants.

Here the relation between the sciences themselves and
also their general utility concur in determining the place,
next after arithmetic, algebra and geometry, which I have
assigned to mechanics and hydraulics.

THIRD CLASS

SPHERE AND GLOBES, TERRESTRIAL SYSTEMS, CALCULATION OF
ECLIPSES, MOTION OF THE HEAVENLY BODIES OR ASTRONOMY,
GNOMONICS

The mariner cannot dispense with the preceding subjects,
and still less with these. They are essential to professional

geographers. Every traveller should know something about them.

It would be shameful for an educated man to know nothing about the globe under his feet nor the vault over his head.

If the Creator has manifested nowhere more clearly the greatness of his power than in the ordering of the heavens, man has manifested nowhere more clearly the extent of his intelligence than in the progress of astronomy.

Nothing is simpler nor more ingenious than the art of constructing dials, of tracing a meridian, of erecting a gnomon, of constructing globes and spheres—planispheres which indicate at every moment the state of the heavens, the principal work of the Creator, imitated and reduced by the creature in a space of a few feet.

I admit, however, that, in this case, I may indeed have lost sight of the reason of the more or less general usefulness of the science, and have been guided by the connection of the sciences with each other.

The studies of this class are purely geometric. The students will already have learned all that is necessary as preparation for them. The time that they will take will not be long; it is only a matter of a few months.

Furthermore, there are two ways out of the difficulty. One of these would be to have a part of the students pass directly from the second class to the fourth;[5] the other, to take the studies out of the first course and place them in the second, which is given at the same time, with which they can go abreast, and where they will connect very well with

[5] Probably those students who will certainly have no need of the subjects in question.

geography and chronology. However, I am inclined to leave them where I have placed them.

FOURTH CLASS

NATURAL HISTORY, EXPERIMENTAL PHYSICS

There is nothing more useful nor more interesting than natural history, and no science is more suitable for children. It is a continuous exercise of the eyes, of smelling, of taste and of memory.

Among the more humble occupations, there is not one for which a knowledge of natural history is not more or less useful. Everything that is seen, everything that is touched, everything that is used, everything that is sold and everything that is bought are all derived from animals, from minerals or from vegetables.

It is the catalogue of the riches which Nature has destined for our needs and for our fancy. Animals serve us or harm us, and it is useful to know them, both on account of the benefits that we derive from them and the injuries that we have to fear from them. Minerals are employed in all our workshops; they defend us under the form of arms, they lessen our labors as instruments, and they are convenient as utensils. Vegetables feed us or refresh us.

It is by studying natural history that the students will learn to make use of their senses; an art without which they would be ignorant of many things and, what is even worse, would know badly many others. It is the art of making good use of the only means we have of knowing anything; an art which is, in itself, excellent elementary knowledge, and is prerequisite to every kind of learning.

Experimental physics is an imitation on a small scale of the great phenomena of Nature, and an examination of its principal agents: air, water, earth, fire, light, solids, liquids and motion. There can be no mechanics without some geometry, and no experimental physics without some little knowledge of mechanics.

Experimental physics enters into almost all the arts and crafts. It is a useful, agreeable and easy study. No machines can be made without calculating solidity and fragility, heaviness and lightness, softness and hardness, rigidity and flexibility, humidity and dryness, friction and elasticity. The students would perceive the phenomena, but they would be ignorant of the reasons for them without the preliminary knowledge afforded by the first two classes.

FIFTH CLASS

CHEMISTRY, ANATOMY

Natural history is the introduction to the study of chemistry, just as experimental physics, mechanics and hydraulics are to the study of the human body, the most beautiful of all machines as well as the one that it is most essential for us to know, since it forms a good part of us.

The chemist Becker [6] said that physicists were only stupid animals that licked the surface of bodies. This disdain is not

---

[6] J.-J. Becker, or Becher, born in Speyer (1625–1682).

altogether unjustified. Nothing in Nature is simple; chemistry analyses, composes and decomposes. It is the rival of the Great Artisan; the athanor of the laboratory is a faithful image of the universal athanor. In the laboratory are imitated lightning, thunder, the crystallization of precious stones and ordinary stones, the formation of metals, and all the phenomena which take place around us, beneath our feet and above our heads.

What mechanical art is there into which the science of the chemist does not enter?

Can the agriculturist, the metallurgist, the pharmacist, the physician, the goldsmith, the coiner, etc., do without it?

If there were only three sciences to be learned, and the choice of them were made according to their needs, they would prefer mechanics, natural history, and chemistry.

The mechanical arts are rendered stationary by the ignorance of the workmen, and they degenerate if the advantage of them is not well understood.

The professor of anatomy and physiology should be required to end his course with a few lessons on the means of strengthening the body and of preserving its health. He should not forget the long list of ailments which the intemperate man prepares for himself.

And since the following idea comes to me, it is better that I should state it than omit it.

I should desire that the professor of any subject whatsoever should terminate his course with a brief history of the science, from its origin to the point where he leaves his students. If it were carried further, they would not understand it.

PLAN OF A UNIVERSITY

LOGIC AND CRITICISM, GENERAL ANALYTIC GRAMMAR

Logic is the art of correct thinking, or of making a legitimate use of the senses and of reason, of making sure that the knowledge which has been acquired is true, of guiding the mind well in its search for truth, and of discerning the errors of ignorance or the sophisms of self-interest and prejudice. It is an art without which all knowledge is perhaps more harmful than useful to man; for knowledge without logic makes him ridiculous, stupid or wicked.

It is certainly with logic that education should begin, that is to say, we should begin by perfecting the instrument which is to be used, if such abstract teaching were within the grasp of children; but by the time they reach this class, they will have been prepared for it by adequate exercise of their powers of reason.

Criticism is the art of appreciating the different authorities—often enough contradictory—on which our knowledge rests.

There are:

The authority of the senses and the authority of reason.

The authority of experience and the authority of observation.

The danger of analogy.

The examination of witnesses: the eye-witness, the contemporary historian, the modern historian of ancient events, writers of all kinds, philosophers, orators, poets, nations and tradition.

The examination of facts, both ordinary and extraordinary.

The consideration of probability, of existence, of evidence, of likelihood, of certitude, of persuasion, of conviction and of doubt.

The examination of opinions and systems. In short, the consideration of the philosophical premises.

The elements of logic and of criticism lead to the study of history and of literature. General analytic grammar is the introduction to the study of any particular language.

Whatever apparent diversity there may be among the various languages, if we examine their common object of being the counterpart of all that takes place in the human understanding, we shall soon perceive that they are all one and the same instrument subject to general rules, almost entirely of pure convention, and of which a language of gestures would find the equivalents.

The treatment of these general rules is called general analytic grammar. He who has mastered it possesses the key of the others, and is ready to study intelligently and to learn rapidly any particular language whatsoever.

I have placed this study after logic, which concerns words, their acceptations, their order in a proposition and the order of a proposition in reasoning, because general analytic grammar is only a very subtle application of logic, or the art of thinking, to grammar, or the art of speaking.

If it were considered proper to defer the study of general analytic grammar until after the study of particular grammars and languages, or at least until the students have mastered one foreign language, ancient or modern, with which they can compare the syntax of their own, I should not be opposed to it. The method of deducing general principles from particular facts is perhaps preferable here to that of proceeding from general principles to particular cases.

But when I consider that it is not a question of an entirely new subject, that we all possess a mother tongue, that the long use of speech has disposed us from our very infancy to the study of these principles, to their application to the language which is familiar to us, and of which we have learned the rudiments from our parents when they surrounded our cradle or carried us in their arms; when I see the close connection between this science and logic, I prefer to leave it where I have put it.

SEVENTH CLASS

THE PRINCIPLES OF THE RUSSIAN AND SLAVONIC LANGUAGES

I have made the study of the native language follow that of general analytic grammar, for it is necessary to write and speak correctly one's own language. I shall say nothing about these two languages which are both unknown to me.

I shall remark only that, among all nations, the language has owed its progress to the greatest geniuses. It is the result of the efforts which they made to express their thoughts with force and clearness. It is Rabelais, Marot, Malherbe, Pascal and Racine who brought the French language to the point where it is.

If precision and clearness are the two principal qualities of a language, all should take as a model the French language; if it is energy, it is another matter.

There are almost no mediocre works in French; they are all well, very well or very badly written. Often the beauty or the novelty of the ideas hides the defects of style.

No one is better qualified to finish this paragraph than Her Imperial Majesty. She can enroll herself, when it pleases her, among the patrons of the Russian language.

Literary glory is the foundation of all others. Great actions are forgotten or degenerate into extravagant fables, unless there be a faithful historian who relates them, a great orator who extols them, an inspired poet who sings of them, or the plastic arts which present them to our eyes. No one is then more interested in the birth, the progress and the continuance of the fine arts than good sovereigns.

It is books and monuments that mark the intervals of the centuries. They would overlap and form only a profound darkness, through which later ages would perceive nothing but exaggerated phantoms, if there were no writings of scholars to distinguish the years by narrating the events that took place in them. The past exists only through these writers. Their silence thrusts the universe back into nothingness. Without them, we should know nothing of our ancestors, and their virtues would remain unhonored and without fruit for posterity. The moment when the first chroniclers appear is like the time of the creation.

However, there is a great difference between the one who acts and the one who writes, between the hero and the poet who sings of him. If the former had not existed, the latter would have nothing to say. Certainly it is more difficult to write a fine page than to do a fine deed; but the latter is much more important.

The fine arts do not make good manners; they are only the lustre of them.

There must be orators, poets, philosophers and great artists; but, as they are the children of genius rather than of education, there should be and can be only a few. What is most important is that they should be excellent moralists; otherwise, they would be dangerous corrupters. They would extol brilliant vices and leave modest virtues in oblivion. As adulators of the great, they would debase by their misplaced praise all idea of virtue. The more captivating they would be, the more they would be read, and the more harm they would do.

This is one of the reasons why I have relegated the study of literature to so remote a place in the curriculum. I am going to give many others. I protest against an order of teaching that is consecrated by the usage of all centuries and of all nations, and I hope that I shall be permitted to be a little less superficial on this subject.

Objections

Here are the reasons given by those who persist in placing the study of Latin and Greek at the head of all public or private education.

1. It is necessary, according to them, to teach the science of words at an age when there is much memory and little judgment.

2. If the study of languages requires much memory, it develops it still more by exercising it.

3. Children are hardly capable of any other study.

DIDEROT

Reply

To this I reply as follows: Children's memories can be just as easily and more usefully exercised and developed by the study of subjects other than Greek or Latin words, and as much memory is required to learn correctly chronology, geography and history as to learn vocabulary and syntax. Examples of men who have never known either Greek or Latin, and whose memories are no less reliable nor lesss extensive on this account are not rare. It is false to assume that use can be made only of children's memories; they have more capacity for reasoning than is necessary for the elements of arithmetic, of geometry and of history. It has been proved by experience that they retain everything without distinction; and even if they did not have the capacity for reasoning that is required by the sciences which I have just mentioned, it is not to the study of languages that preference should be given, unless it were proposed to teach them as the mother tongue is taught, that is, by use, by daily exercise—a very advantageous method without doubt, but impracticable in public teaching, in a mixed school of boarders and day-students. Languages are taught by means of elementary and other books, that is to say, by analytic principles, and I know of no science that is more intricate; for it is the continuous application of a very acute logic, a very subtle metaphysics, which I believe is not only beyond the capacity of children, but even beyond the intelligence of the generality of mature men. The proof of this is given in the *Encyclopédie,* in the article entitled *Construction,* by the famous Dumarsais,[7] and in all the articles on grammar. If

[7] César Chesneau, *sieur* Dumarsais, grammarian (1676–1756).

the languages are instrumental knowledge, it is not for students, but for teachers; and it is like putting into the hands of a blacksmith's apprentice a hammer of which he can neither grasp the handle nor overcome the weight. If the languages are keys, these keys are very difficult to seize and very hard to turn, and are of use on very few occasions only. By consulting experience and by interrogating the best students in our classes, it will be found that languages are very badly studied in childhood, and the study of them is exceedingly wearisome and tedious. It occupies five or six years, at the end of which not even technical words are understood. Exact definitions of the terms genitive, ablative, personal and impersonal verbs are perhaps yet to be found; and the precise theory of the tenses of verbs is in no way less difficult than the propositions of the philosophy of Newton. This can easily be verified by consulting the *Encyclopédie,* in which this subject has been excellently treated in the article entitled *Tense.* Thus, young students know neither the Greek and Latin which they have been taught for so long a time, nor the sciences which they could have been taught in this same time, and the more intelligent among them are obliged to study them after they leave school, or else remain ignorant of them to the end of their days. The suffering which these same students have undergone in explaining Virgil, the tears with which they have soaked the humorous satires of Horace have so disgusted them with these authors that they can no longer look at them without shuddering. From all this, I can conclude, it seems to me, that the learned languages, which are so difficult for all and useful to so few, should be postponed until a time when the mind is mature, and placed in the order of studies after a great many other subjects that are not only more generally useful, but also easier; and this with so much the more reason because, at the age of eighteen, more rapid and surer progress is made and more is learned, and better learned, in a year and a half than a child can learn in six or seven years. But let us grant that on leaving school the children know the ancient languages which have been taught them. What becomes of these children? They distribute themselves among the different callings; some become merchants, others soldiers, still others magistrates or barristers. That is to say that nineteen twentieths of them pass their lives without reading a Latin author, and forget what they have so painfully learned.

But this is not all: if the principles of grammar are in no wise within the grasp of children, these same children are hardly more capable of understanding the contents of the books used as texts.

I know that recourse is had to interlinear glosses and other little means of alleviating the imbecility of the students, but I am still ignorant of the results of these methods that are so widely preached by their inventors; and the preservation of morals by the aid of mutilated editions seems to me insufficient, unless, at every line, the teacher makes the students feel the viciousness of a character, the danger of a maxim, the atrocity or dishonesty of an action—a trouble which he will never give himself. If the study of the ancient languages were reserved for a time when the intelligence is more developed and the students more advanced in the knowledge of history, it seems to me that they would meet with fewer difficulties, and that they would have more taste for it, since the facts and personages mentioned by Thucydides, Xenophon, Livy, Tacitus and Virgil would already be known to them.

As any science whatsoever can be taught in the native language, I fully appreciate the inconvenience, but I have still to see the advantage of adding to the difficulty of the subjects themselves the further difficulty of a foreign language, and one in which it is often difficult, sometimes impossible, to express oneself without making use of barbarous constructions and expressions. If the teacher speaks pure and correct Latin, he will not spoil the taste of the students, but they will grow weary of hearing him; if he speaks bad Latin—as is usual and even necessary in the case of a dead language which lacks an infinite number of terms corresponding to our manners, laws, customs, functions, works, inventions, arts, sciences, ideas, etc.—he will be understood, but not without danger to the good taste of the students.

And then, I ask, to whom are these ancient languages of any real use? I should almost dare to answer that it is to nobody, unless it be to poets, orators, classic scholars and other professional men of letters; that is to say, to the least necessary states in life.

Can it be claimed that it is impossible to be a great lawyer without the least knowledge of Greek and with a very small equipment of Latin, when this is the case with all our legal lights? I can say as much of our theologians and our physicians. Our medical men pride themselves on knowing well and writing well Latin, but they are ignorant of Greek, and thus are no more familiar with the language of Galen and Hippocrates than our ecclesiastics are with Hebrew, the language of Holy Scripture.

So much the worse for them, some will say.

But why so much the worse? Do they know any less well anatomy, physiology, natural history, chemistry and the other branches of science that are essential for their profession? Have not the ancient authors' works been translated and re-translated a hundred times? Even if I agreed concerning the advantage of these languages for certain professions, the question would remain no less undecided; for here it is not a matter of their utility, but of the time when it is most suitable to learn them. Is it when the student is a child and a school-boy, or when he is no longer under the rod and wishes to be a master? Should they be placed in the rank of essential or of supererogatory knowledge? Whether they be essential or supererogatory, should they be studied at the age of imbecility, the age when their difficulty surpasses the share of understanding which Nature accords us? Even if they were mastered early, would the authors who wrote in them be understood without the mass of knowledge which precedes them in the order of teaching which we have arranged? Should then a subject be studied at the age of five or six which cannot be well learned at that time, and which will be of no use until the age of twenty-five or thirty, perhaps even later? What I now say concerning the time when the knowledge of Greek and Latin is useful to a physician and the age at which it is most useful to study them, I can say even of the writer, but with this difference, it is impossible to be a man of letters without a knowledge of Greek and, with still greater reason, without a knowledge of Latin. He must be intimately acquainted with Homer and Virgil, with Demosthenes and Cicero, if he wishes to excel. And yet, I am certain that Voltaire, who is not a mediocre writer, knows very little Greek, and that he does not occupy the twentieth nor even the hundredth place among our Latinists.

THE MANNER OF STUDYING ANCIENT AND MODERN LANGUAGES

If I do not agree with usage concerning when to teach the ancient languages, no more do I agree with the philosophers such as Dumarsais [8] and others, who applied the spirit of logic to grammar, concerning how to study them.

If you ask Dumarsais how to learn Greek and Latin, he will tell you to translate the writings of good authors.

—And what else?

—Translate. Continue to translate.

—I agree that it is necessary to translate, but should there be no written exercises or compositions?

—Beware of them.

—And why?

—Because you will double your trouble, and, to loss of time, you will add loss of good taste, by accustoming yourself to vicious and barbarous constructions.

—And what harm would these vices and barbarisms do in the future?

—I do not wish any exercise or compositions, absolutely none. Our ancient writers of grammars and dictionaries did not write exercises, and perhaps nobody to-day knows Latin as they did.

[8] See note p. 242.

TRANSLATION AND WRITTEN EXERCISES

However, in what is the mind engaged when translating? In seeking in the familiar language the expressions that correspond to those in the foreign language which is being translated and studied.

And in what is the mind engaged when writing exercises? In seeking, in the foreign language which is being learned, expressions that correspond to those in the familiar language.

Now, it is evident that in this latter operation it is not the familiar language that is learned, but the one which is not known and is being studied.

This is just as true as in the former operation, which is exactly the opposite of the latter, and in which precisely the contrary is done.

But if these two kinds of translation concur in the progress of the student, and the later cooperates more extensively and more evidently than the former, why separate them?

It is true that in writing an exercise we search the dictionary of our own language, but it is to find the corresponding expression in the foreign language; and it is this expression that is read, this expression that is written. It is according to the syntax of the foreign language that the sentence is constructed; it is its rules that we observe, and its style to which we try to conform. All these operations tend to fix in the memory both the grammar and the vocabulary.

I shall propose then for written exercises and for translation the following method:

1. Translate mentally or make written translations of the writings of good authors.

2. Write exercises according to the method which follows, and which I shall explain in detail.

Take a page from the work of some good author that has been translated into your native language or into some other language that you may know.

Translate this page into the language of the author, and then compare your translation with the original.[9]

In this manner not only words and syntax are learned, but the spirit of the language also is fixed in the memory by being read and written.

ADVANTAGES OF THE STUDY OF THE GREEK AND LATIN LANGUAGES

The Greeks were the teachers of the Romans. The Greeks and the Romans both were our teachers. I have said and I repeat that it is hardly possible to claim the title of man of letters without a knowledge of the languages of these two peoples. As the Greek language had much influence on the Latin, and as its grammar is a little more difficult, it is commonly thought that the study of Greek should come first; but as the student is no longer a child, and his judgment is

[9] This method is slightly different from the one recommended by Roger Ascham—tutor to the Princess, later Queen, Elizabeth —(1515–1568) in his famous work, *The Schoolmaster*. Diderot suggests taking a page that has been translated already by someone else, whereas Ascham would have the student himself first translate the page from the language of the writer into his own, and then after a short time translate it back into the original. It is, however, nearly that of La Chalotais. See p. 101.

mature and his mind is equipped with a sufficiently good provision of elementary knowledge, it is time for him to meditate and reflect. I believe then that the study of the two languages should go side by side. He who knows Greek is rarely ignorant of Latin, whereas it is only too common to know Latin and be ignorant of Greek. He who has learned Latin scarcely ever forgets it, but he who has known Greek, which he learned by translating only, soon forgets it unless he continues to cultivate it without ceasing. In these two languages are to be found such great models of all kinds that it is difficult to acquire excellent taste without knowing them. Go to Rome for painters. Go to Rome and to Athens for men of letters. Anyone who has a little discernment will soon perceive which of the modern writers are familiar with the works of the ancients, and which of them have never had any contact with them. The best translations are only copies without color, without force and without life. To judge the classic writers from these copies of their works is like judging the paintings of Raphael or of Titian from a description.

The Greek and the Latin languages have this in particular: such is their flexibility and, consequently, the variety of style of those who wrote in them, that he who knows perfectly his Homer may understand almost nothing of Sophocles and still less of Pindar, and he who reads readily Ovid and Virgil may be stopped at every line of Pliny the naturalist or of Tacitus the historian.

I shall give a little sketch of the Greek and Latin authors and of their style as well as of the subjects which they treated. This will complete the proof of my contention that such precocious knowledge is little suited to early youth.

(This *sketch* is omitted here. It is, in reality, only a list of Greek and Latin authors and a catalogue of their works, of which the subject matter and nature are given, with a few very superficial comments. It may have been of interest to Her Imperial Majesty; but it is hardly sufficiently so to us to justify its inclusion in this book.)

Almost all these writers are perhaps innocuous in the hands of a mature man; but I question if it is in good faith that we are assured that these authors, difficult in style, profound in content, and often dangerous in ethics, ought to be the first study of early youth; or that we should tolerate under innocent and pure eyes the teachings of Plautus, of which I have not spoken, and those of Terence, which I recall at this moment; Terence, whose elegance and veracity are above all praise, but whose imagery is, for that reason, only more seductive; or again the atheistic teachings of Lucretius. I should much prefer that the students should run the risk of corrupting their taste by reading the stilted, dry and bombastic Seneca the tragedian, to whom I owe this little thrust for the weariness that he has caused me, and whose pardon I beg for the sake of some beautiful pages of our Racine which he inspired.

Do not such studies require more mature intellects and some preliminary knowledge?

Is it of no importance to eliminate their difficulty by means of some general notions concerning the ethics, the customs and the deeds, in a word, by means of the history of the times?

What signification have the letters of Cicero to Atticus, to Brutus, to Cæsar, to Cato, when the tortuous windings of Roman politics are developed under the eyes of a child?

If these famous personages were already known, would not their names be met with more interest when they occur in the works which speak of them? Would not these works be more easily interpreted, would not their charm be better felt, and would not the grammatical thorns be somewhat blunted?

ORDER OF LATIN AND GREEK STUDIES

This order is almost the same as that of our classes, with but one difference, which is that, in ours, the students begin these studies immediately upon entering school, and come out at the end of five or six years very weary, very bored, very chastened and very ignorant, to say nothing of the distaste for these sublime authors which they have acquired and which they rarely lose.

The students have acquired knowledge; it is a question of using it. They have ideas; it is a question of expressing them. They have studied the great models; it is a question of imitating them. They understand the language of historians, of poets and of orators; it is a question of making known to them the principles of composition, of giving scope to their genius, if they have any, and of making of them orators and poets.

ELOQUENCE AND POESY

The fine arts are only imitations of the beauty of Nature. But what is the beauty of Nature? It is that which suits the circumstances.

In one place, a thing is beautiful; in another, it is ugly. A tree which is beautiful on the avenue to a castle is not beautiful at the entrance to a cottage, and conversely. Among the trees to be placed along the avenue of the castle and at the gate of the cottage, there is still a choice.

What I say of the tree is applicable to all objects in Nature and to all creations of Art; from the immense and blazing star which illuminates the universe to the ribbon on the head-dress of a girl or to the least fold of her dress.

Taste is nothing or it includes everything. If the most trivial imitation could be optional, then the most important one could likewise be so.

Art imitates the actions and discourse of man and the phenomena of Nature.

History conforms strictly to the truth.

Eloquence embellishes it and colors it.

Poetry, which is more concerned with the appearance of truth than with truth itself, enlarges upon it and exaggerates it.

The precepts of oratory and of poesy should, therefore, be preceded by:

1. A discussion of the true, of the seemingly true and of fiction, of the absolutely true and of the true by convention.

2. A discussion of the imitation of Nature.

3. An explanation of what natural beauty is and of its choice according to convention.

Above all, these principles should be supported by many examples.

4. A discussion of the good and the beautiful—which is never anything other than the resplendence of the good, of

the sublime—which is only the resplendence of the good or the evil, accompanied by an emotion which arises either from grandeur, danger or interest.

Afterwards harmony will be considered.

Harmony in general and harmony in relation to the organ of perception.

Imitative harmony or harmony relating to the passions of man or to the phenomena of Nature—a harmony which is sometimes inconsistent with the harmony of the ear and shocks it thoroughly.

Harmony which satisfies the organ of perception can be learned; that which comes from feeling cannot be learned. Genius discovers it and submits to it, without being aware of it; and he who seeks it, either by imitation or by ingenuity, gives himself much trouble only to be affected and clumsy.

I have discussed the subject of literature a little more extensively than the others, because it is my own subject and I know it better. Though I am sufficiently fair-minded to give it only the place it deserves among the different branches of knowledge, I have nevertheless yielded to the very natural temptation of speaking of it at a little greater length perhaps than its importance warranted.

Second Course of Studies

This course will begin at the same time as the first course, and will be common to all students, who will follow it until they leave the Faculty of Arts, of which it forms a part.

PLAN OF A UNIVERSITY

The object of the first course is to prepare scholars; the object of this one is to produce upright men; two tasks that must not be separated.

The students will receive in the first class instruction of which the utility will become less and less general, whereas the instruction which they will receive in the second will be of a nature that remains constant.

Whether inept or capable, every student should follow this course for a certain length of time. As a man, he must know what he owes to mankind; as a citizen, he must learn what he owes to society; as a priest, a merchant, a soldier, a geometrician or a tradesman, celibate or married, husband, son, brother or friend, he has duties which he cannot know too well.

For the preceding course the students will be assembled during a part of the morning; for this one, during a part of the evening.

They will not finish either one of them until they leave the Faculty of Arts to enter some one of the higher faculties: medicine, law or theology.

The classes will be less numerous, and the instruction less varied. The first course is divided into eight classes, this one is divided into two only; but the instruction given in these two classes, although remaining the same as to fundamentals, will expand more and more, and will become progressively more detailed and more copious. It would not be possible to go too deeply into these subjects, and the students cannot be too attentive to the precepts.

255

The first course is elementary; this one is not. From the classes of the one, the youth will come forth a student; from the classes of the other, it is to be hoped that he will come forth a master.

Instruction in the sciences has done enough when it has indicated to natural talent the subject that will be its study and its ocupation for the remainder of life. Instruction in ethics, duties and virtue, the laws, honesty and the usual legal procedures is of an altogether different nature.

There is a middle course between absolute ignorance and perfect knowledge; there is none between good and evil; between goodness and wickedness. He who, in his actions, wavers between the two is wicked.

Without knowing history, it is difficult to understand the ancient writers; without knowing general ethics, it is impossible to determine the rules of good taste: and from these two points of view, the instruction given in the second course further affects the instruction given in the first course.

FIRST CLASS

(1) FIRST PRINCIPLES OF METAPHYSICS OR THE DISTINCTION BETWEEN THE TWO SUBSTANCES, EXISTENCE OF GOD, IMMORTALITY OF THE SOUL AND FUTURE PUNISHMENTS. (2) GENERAL ETHICS. (3) NATURAL RELIGION. (4) REVEALED RELIGION

Her Imperial Majesty is not of the opinion of Bayle,[10] who claims that a society of atheists can be just as orderly as a society of deists, and better than a society of the super-

---

[10] Pierre Bayle, philosopher, author of a *Dictionnaire historique* and precursor of the skeptical philosophers (1647–1706).

stitious. She does not think, like Plutarch, that superstition is more dangerous in its effects and more offensive to God than unbelief. She does not define, with Hobbes,[11] religion as a superstition authorized by law, and superstition as a religion which the law proscribes. She thinks that the fear of future punishments exerts a great influence on the actions of men, and that the wickedness which the sight of the gallows does not hold in check can be restrained by the fear of remote punishment. In spite of the infinite harm that religious opinions have done to humanity, in spite of the disadvantage of a system which places the confidence of the people in the hands of the priest—who is always a danger-ous rival of the sovereign—which gives a superior to the head of the Nation, and which establishes laws more vener-able and more sacred than those of the sovereign, she is persuaded that the sum of the little daily benefits which religious belief produces in all countries compensates for the sum of the evils occasioned among the citizens of the same country by the sects, and among the nations by in-tolerance—a species of maniacal fury for which there is no remedy.

It is then fitting that the education of her subjects should conform to her way of thinking, and that the students should be taught the distinction between the two substances, the immortality of the soul and the certitude of a future life, as the preliminaries of ethics or the science which derives all duties and just laws from the idea of true happiness and from the actual relations of man with his fellow-men; for no one can, without committing an atrocity, command me

[11] Thomas Hobbes, English philosopher, author of *The Levia-than* (1588–1679).

to do what is contrary to my true happiness, and it would be useless to do so.

Religion is only the sanction of God's will, revealed and applied to natural ethics.

This course could end with a rigorous demonstration of facts—for, on the whole, there is no better way of obtaining happiness in this world than by being a just man—or by a parallel of the disadvantages of vice, or even by contrasting its advantages with those of virtue.

So few men know how to make use of their talents either to preserve their property or to increase it, poverty is such a powerful enemy of probity, and reverses of fortune are so frequent and have such a disastrous effect on the education of children, that I should add here the elements of the economic sciences or the art of directing household matters—an art which the Greeks and the Romans held in such high esteem.

It would be difficult to speak of wealth without speaking, at least summarily, of agriculture which is the source of all wealth.

Let Her Imperial Majesty not be disturbed by the word *economic;* for there is no question here of that class of good people which has arisen amongst us, and will do us much good or much harm.

SECOND CLASS

HISTORY, MYTHOLOGY, GEOGRAPHY, CHRONOLOGY

I believe that the study of history should begin with the history of one's own nation, and this, as well as all other history, should begin with the more recent times, and then go back to the centuries of fable or mythology. This is the opinion of Grotius.[12] "In general," says he, "do not begin with antiquated facts which are of no importance to us, but with more certain things which concern us more directly, and advance from them, by degrees, toward the beginning of time." This seems to be more in conformity with real teaching, and it is likewise the application of our general principle to the study of facts. Is there any reason why an exception should be made for this study?

Without mythology it is impossible to understand anything of the ancient authors, of monuments, of painting or of sculpture, even of the modern painters and sculptors; for they have exhausted themselves to place before our eyes the vices of the gods of paganism, instead of representing to us great men.

Some will perhaps think that the study of history should precede the study of ethics. I am not of their opinion. It seems to me that it is useful and proper to know the rules of right and wrong before knowing the actions, the personages and the historian even to which they are to be applied.

When it has been said of geography and chronology that they are the two eyes of history, all has been said.

I should wish that the dryness of the study of the globe should be mitigated by some details concerning religions, laws, manners, strange customs, natural products and works of art.

There are ancient geography and modern geography; but two separate studies should not be made of them. It would

[12] Huig van Groot, Latinized Hugo Grotius, Dutch diplomat and scholar and author of several works in Latin on historical, legal and religious subjects (1583–1645).

cost so little effort to add to the name of a city or of a river the name which it bore in ancient times.

Third Course of Studies

Parallel to the first two, and common to all the students throughout the entire duration of their education.

A CLASS OF PERSPECTIVE AND DRAWING

Drawing is of such general utility, it leads so naturally to painting and sculpture, and it is so necessary in order to judge intelligently the productions of these two arts, that I am not surprised that the government has made it a part of public education. However, there should be no drawing without perspective.

There comes to me an idea which perhaps Her Imperial Majesty will not disdain. The greater number of those who enter the public schools write so badly, and those whose handwriting is passable when they enter have so completely lost it by the time they leave, and there are so few men, even among the most educated, who know how to read well—a talent that is always so agreeable and often so necessary—that I am of the opinion that it would be well to associate with the professor of drawing a teacher of reading and writing.

A faulty pronunciation and a bad handwriting are two very analogous defects. The one is to stammer for the ears, and the other to stammer for the eyes.

Drawing is done from a copy, from a cast and from Nature or from a model.

A model seems to me to be necessary only for those students who will become painters or sculptors by profession.

But who does not live in a house? Who is not likely to build and be robbed by a mason or an architect? There is not then a citizen to whom the elements, I do not say of architecture, but of building would not be of some use.

As for the elements of architecture, no man of wealth can be ignorant of them without running the risk of some day consuming immense sums in piling up only shapeless masses of stone.

The more durable public buildings are, the longer they will attest the good or bad taste of a nation, and the more advisable it is that those who preside over this part of the administration should have good and accurate taste.

Three thousand years from now, it will still be seen that we were Goths.

The best means of teaching military or civil architecture would be, in my opinion, to have a great plan which would represent the ground upon which a house, a mansion, a palace or a church would be built. The cellar would be dug, the foundation laid, the building would be erected, story by story, up to the roof. Then the details of interior arrangements and decorations would be considered. In this manner, the students would learn thoroughly and without trouble, merely by using their eyes.

When these three courses of study are completed, the small number of students who have followed them to the end will find themselves on the threshold of the three higher faculties: The Faculty of Medicine, the Faculty of Law and the Faculty of Theology. They will likewise find themselves equipped with the knowledge which I call primary, or suitable to all states of life: to the well-educated man, to the faithful subject and to the good citizen. All of this is preliminary knowledge, and some of it is common to the studies of the three faculties which the students will wish to enter.

Each of these faculties requires a special order of studies with which I shall now concern myself.

Second Faculty of a University:
Faculty of Medicine

If we wish the students to receive in a school of medicine all the instruction they need to practice the science of healing in a manner that will be beneficial to their fellow-citizens, we must remember that public health is perhaps the most important of all subjects. If people are poor, the sovereign takes care of the wretched only; if they are invalids, he takes care of acute cases only.

The different branches of knowledge relating to medicine are very extensive. Half a physician is worse than half a scholar. The latter sometimes wearies, the former kills. Should or should not the members of this profession be numerous? This question has been decided by Dr. Gatti,[13] who divided the hospital of which he was the medical director into two sections: one consisting of patients whom he left to Nature, the other consisting of those on whom he lavished all the resources of medical science. As he had ex-

[13] Professor of medicine in Pisa, afterwards consulting physician to Louis XV, and one of the earliest partisans of inoculation.

pected, many more died among those who received medical care than among those who were left to Nature.

A very interesting problem to solve would be that of determining the relation between the number of physicians and surgeons in a town and the number of other inhabitants. I believe that the solution would vary according to the countries, the manners, the customs, the diet and the climate. Animals are subject to few ailments. The diseases of country people are less numerous and simpler than ours; the further removed we are from the rural life of the earlier ages of the world the shorter the average span of life is. I do not think that it is with physicians as with citizens engaged in other occupations, of whom the need determines the number. It is not possible to take up or leave the science of healing at will. I look upon a bad physician as a small epidemic that lasts as long as he lives. Two bad physicians double this general illness; a body of bad physicians would be a great evil for any nation. With a physician it is not as it is with a manufacturer; a manufacturer of mediocre goods is useful to a great number of people who can afford to pay neither for excellent quality nor for superior workmanship. On the contrary, the lowest of the lowest class of society needs an excellent physician; for he can be cheated only once, and he pays for his mistake with his life. There is, without doubt, some difference between the need of preserving the life of a cabinet minister and the life of a haberdasher in a small way, of an unmarried man and of a father of a family, of a good general and of a bad poet; but neither the sovereign who looks upon us as his children, nor the sentiment of humanity which draws us near to our fellowmen will take this into consideration. Justly or unjustly, it can happen any day that the good physician is called to the unmarried man, and the bad one to the head of a numerous family. It is but the more necessary that physicians should excel in their profession, because the variety and number of the occasions that call them to us do not permit them to exercise their functions to our advantage and to their satisfaction. They are obliged to divide their time and their care among a great number of patients, of whom a single one might sometimes need their assiduous observation and constant presence. A bad physician always comes too soon and stays too long; a good physician can come too late and not stay long enough. An illness is ordinarily so complicated a problem, the effect of so many causes, a phenomenon that varies so much with different patients, that I cannot conceive how a physician who visits fifty or sixty persons a day can treat properly a single one of them. However profound his knowledge of the theory and the practice of the science may be, is it enough to feel the pulse, examine the tongue, ascertain the state of the skin and the stomach, observe the urine, ask a few hurried questions of the patient or of his nurse and then write a prescription? Do physicians not believe in their own science, or do they consider our money more important than our lives?

One disadvantage of the great medical faculties in the capitals, and above all for the great personages in society, is the subjection of the physician to a certain practice or routine of the faculty, under the penalty of risking his reputation and his fortune. If he breaks away from it and success does not attend him, he is ruined; if he succeeds, what does he gain? Nothing, unless it be the epithet of daring. His genius is free only at our bedsides; because his successful or unsuccessful efforts are without consequences for him. We can disappear from among the living, and no one will perceive it.

I have sometimes thought that the charlatans who live in the poorer quarters of the great cities were not so pernicious as is generally supposed. It is empiricism that gave birth to the science of medicine, and it can expect no true progress except from empiricism.

An incurable illness in the midst of a family is like a dead tree in the centre of a garden, and of which the roots are a danger to all the plants around it. The care which tenderness or pity cannot refuse an infirm old man or a sickly child disturbs the order of the duties and fills with bitterness the days of those whom it concerns. A bold empiric, to whom the patient applies when he is abandoned by the members of the profession, kills him or renders to him his health and the enjoyment of their existence to those who take care of him.

Is this the reasoning of a man? No, it is the reasoning of a minister of state. A minister of state disdains the old who are good for nothing, and values children only for what he can expect from them in the future. There is only one life that he really values: that of a mature man; because it alone is useful. His mind is like a bee-hive; according to the example of bees, he exterminates all who cease to produce.

The practice of medicine is a fine subject for a discourse, but here it is a question of the teaching of it; to which I return.

It will be necessary:

1. To appoint a sufficient number of professors, and to pay them in such a manner that they will be able to dedicate themselves entirely to teaching.

2. To establish in the vicinity of the schools a hospital, where the students can be initiated into the practice of their profession.

3. To oblige the teachers to follow a fixed and determined order in the course of studies.

Professors

(There will be seven professorial chairs.)

FIRST CHAIR

ANATOMY AND OBSTETRICS

Midwives will not only be forbidden to practice their profession, but they will not even be permitted to take the examinations of the representatives of the faculty unless they have already attended for several years the courses of anatomy and the practical instruction pertaining to obstetrics.

I shall remark here that there is no country in Europe in which conditions are more favorable to the study of anatomy than Russia, where the intense cold renders it possible to preserve a cadaver long enough for an anatomist to be able to continue to dissect the same one, without interruption, for from fifteen to twenty days.

PLAN OF A UNIVERSITY

SECOND AND THIRD CHAIRS

The Institutes of Medicine [14]

FOURTH CHAIR ..

Surgery

FIFTH CHAIR

Materia Medica and Pharmacy

SIXTH AND SEVENTH CHAIRS

History of Diseases and their Treatment

THE PROFESSOR OF ANATOMY

The professor of anatomy will demonstrate, on the cadaver, the different branches of this science, throughout the entire winter season, and he will certainly have time enough for it. He will discuss the various parts of the human body, their structure, their connections, their functions, their movements and the mechanism by which these latter are executed.

THE TWO PROFESSORS OF THE INSTITUTE OF MEDICINE

Each one of these professors will give, in the space of two years, a complete course in the institutes of medicine. That

[14] In American and English medical schools there was a course in *The Institutes of Medicine* until about 1870, when it was replaced by a basic course in physiology and special courses —not originally given—in preventive medicine, pathology, etc.

is to say, the first year, he will teach physiology and hygiene, and the second year, pathology, preventive medicine and general therapeutics.

The two professors will so arrange their classes between them that each year one of them will give his course in physiology, and the other his course in pathology.

THE PROFESSOR OF MATERIA MEDICA

This professor will include in his course the natural history of every drug. He will describe its particular characteristics in its most perfect condition, in its medium condition and in its defective condition. It would even be desirable that he should have at his disposition a medicine chest containing specimens of each drug in these various conditions.

He will explain each drug and the characteristic qualities discovered in it by chemical analysis.

He will indicate the different processes and manipulations which it undergoes before being used for medicinal purposes, the perceptible effects which it ordinarily produces, the particular cases in which it produces the most salutary effects and, finally, the different pharmaceutical preparations into which it enters.

Officinal preparations are those which are prepared in the pharmacies. The pharmacist leaves the preparation of some of them to the negligence of his assistants, and, as they are badly prepared, they no longer produce the desired effect and fall into disuse. Either he himself or a first assistant attends to the preparation of others, such as those into which minerals or metals enter, and these, consequently, retain their efficacy. This is one of the reasons for the preference that is given to them in practice.

At the end of each year, the same professor will give a course in pharmacy, during which he or an assistant will demonstrate all the different processes which medicines undergo before being used.

THE PROFESSOR OF SURGERY

The professor of surgery will treat of all purely surgical ailments, such as wounds, tumors, ulcers, dislocations and fractures; of which he will describe the nature and the treatment. Every year, he will give a course on operations and instruments, and he will perform himself and have performed by an assistant some operations on a cadaver. From this, he will proceed to the methods of applying bandages of different kinds, either for holding in place parts of the body or for the application of medicinal dressings.

If physical qualities, of which the effects never cease, ought, in time, to give to one country a superiority over others, I dare to predict that some day Russia will provide the other countries of Europe with great anatomists, celebrated surgeons and perhaps even with profoundly learned chemists.

THE PROFESSORS OF THE PRACTICE OF MEDICINE

In order to initiate the students into the practice of medicine, there will be established in a hospital near the school two wards, each containing twenty-five beds; one ward for acute illnesses, and the other for chronic cases.

To this effect, the professors will divide their course in practical medicine into two courses of one year each. The first year they will treat of acute illnesses; the second of chronic maladies.

Then they will explain the nature and the treatment of diseases peculiar to women and children.

They will divide their work in such a manner that each year one of the two professors will treat of acute illnesses, and the other of chronic maladies.

Each one of these two professors, accompanied by his students, will visit the ward of which he has charge. There he will make the students observe the symptoms of each of the diseases which he has to treat, he will indicate to them the means of discovering the causes of these diseases, he will acquaint them with the course which Nature ordinarily follows in such cases, the treatment that seems to be required, and he will give the reasons for the curative methods which he believes he should employ.

If the patient dies, he will be obliged to have the body opened in the presence of the students. No reason or pretext shall ever prevent this.

It would be desirable that he should have the courage to admit it if he has made a mistake; but this frankness, which Boerhaave, Sydenham [15] and Hippocrates had, is almost beyond the strength of man, and we must hardly expect it.

As it is extremely unlikely that cases of all the different kinds of diseases should present themselves in the course

[15] Boerhaave and Sydenham, the former a Dutch physician and chemist (1668–1738); the latter an English physician (1624–1689).

of one or two years, in addition to these demonstrations, each of the two professors will treat in his lectures of all the ailments to which humanity is subject.

But all this instruction must be preceded by two courses which are prerequisite to the study and practice of medicine.

While attending the courses of the Faculty of Arts, the students have acquired some elementary knowledge of natural history and chemistry. This knowledge, though sufficient for a well-educated man, would not be enough for a physician, whose profession requires a profound knowledge of natural substances and their compounds which are his two arsenals. A physician needs to know much less about them than a naturalist by profession, but infinitely more than a man of the world.

Natural history and chemistry will then require two more chairs.

SUBJECTS PREREQUISITE TO THE STUDY OF MEDICINE

NATURAL HISTORY, CHEMISTRY

The professor of natural history and the professor of chemistry will give their courses in conjunction; the one in the morning, the other in the afternoon.

The former will discuss the three kingdoms (animal, mineral and vegetable), but limiting himself to what pertains to the science of healing.

The latter will treat his subject as extensively as he sees fit; avoiding only those subjects that serve merely to excite curiosity.

THE COURSE OF MEDICAL STUDIES

The course of medical studies will be of the duration of seven years.

During the first two years, the students will attend the courses of the professors of natural history, chemistry and anatomy. During this time, they will apply themselves to no other studies.

The third year, while continuing to attend the same courses, they will add to them the course of the professsor of physiology.

The fourth year, they will remain under the professor of anatomy, and will begin the study of pathology.

The sixth year, to these various courses, they will add the instruction of the professor of the practice of medicine who treats of acute diseases. They will attend his lectures in the school, and will accompany him to the hospital.

The seventh year, they will study under the professor who treats of chronic diseases. At the same time, they will be at liberty to return to the lectures of the professors of surgery and of materia medica.

The course will always close with a discourse, pronounced in turn by one of the professors, on the importance of the science of healing, its progress and history, the characteristics and duties of a true physician, the certainty and the uncertainty of the indications of death, and forensic medicine in its relation to the laws; such as the evidences of death by violence or by suicide, of retarded birth, etc., etc.

THIRD FACULTY OF A UNIVERSITY:
FACULTY OF LAW

This faculty will be composed of eight professors:

1. A professor of Common Law.
2. A professor of the History of Legislation.[16]
3. A professor of the Principles of International Law.
4. A professor of the Institutes of Justinian.[17]
5 and 6. Two professors of Domestic Civil Law.
7. A professor of Canon Law and National Ecclesiastical Law.
8. A professor of Civil Criminal Procedure.

The duration of this course of studies will be four years, and, each year, the students will attend the courses of two professors.

First Year of Studies

The students will attend the courses of the professor of Common Law and of the professor of the History of Legislation.

The professor of Common Law will not limit himself to the elements of this subject, but will carry his instruction much further than that which the students have received in the course in ethics which preceded their entrance to this school.

The professor of the History of Legislation will concern himself with the historical aspect of the legislation of the most celebrated nations of antiquity, above all, of the

[16] Development of Statutory Law.
[17] A textbook on the *Justinian Code*.

Greeks and the Romans. On this subject, he will be guided in his work and in his lectures by those who have ably treated of it.

Second Year of Studies

The students will be under the instruction of the professor of International Law and of the professor of the Institutes of Justinian.

The latter will take care to treat but briefly of all that concerns so particularly the Romans that it has no application to modern times; but he cannot treat too extensively of all that concerns obligations. Roman law is the source of the true principles which control every kind of contract pertaining to the rights of individuals. Reason and equity have dictated them, and there is no well-governed nation that ought not to adopt them.

Third Year of Studies

The students will attend the lectures of one of the professors of ancient and modern Civil Law, and of the professor of Ecclesiastical Law, if there be need of it.

The two professors of Civil Law will arrange the subject-matter of their lectures in such a manner as to form a course extending over two years. While one of them is giving the first year of his course, the other will be giving the second year of his. Thus there will always be a course in Civil Law open to students.

Fourth Year of Studies

The students will resume the study of Civil Law. To this

course will be added the study of Civil and Criminal Procedure.

The latter will occupy two semesters: the first will be devoted to Civil Procedure, and the second to Criminal Procedure.

I shall anticipate here concerning the administration of the schools, of which I propose to speak separately later.

At the end of the first, second, or third year of the course, the students will not be admitted to the following year, unless they have given proof of their fitness by public examinations. The professors will not pronounce judgment; their functions will be limited to asking questions. They will take an oath that there is no connivance between them and their students; the examination will open with this ceremony. Her Imperial Majesty will be present at these exercises, or she will appoint as deputies the members of the Senate who are the most fitted to represent her.

When the same men are charged with teaching and are empowered to attest the ability of their students to assume charges and to fill offices in the magistracy; when they have the right to confer degrees in the sciences and letters, to grant diplomas and other certificates, they neglect their teaching, and the students, their patrons or their parents lessen their severity or corrupt them through solicitations, self-interest or fear.

These public exercises will maintain a spirit of emulation among the professors and their students; they will prove the ability of the latter to learn, and of the former to teach.

Independently of these examinatons to determine the fitness of a student to pass from one class to another, it would be expedient that any student who has completed his law course, and who desires to be admitted to the Bar should undergo additional examinations in the presence of the members of the body with which he desires to be associated.

Citizens of all classes should be permitted to be present at these examinations, and it behooves her Imperial Majesty to take care through her representatives that incompetence and vice do not triumph over knowledge and good conduct.

I believe that I mentioned in some of the papers which Her Imperial Majesty did not disdain to place in one of the drawers of her desk, when I had the honor of being received in her cabinet, that the professorships on our Faculty of Law which were awarded by public competition were the most worthily filled.

Each professor will continue to teach the same subject; for instance, the professor of Civil Law will not pass to the chair of Canon Law. This is the only means of perfecting each teacher in his subject.

The salaries of all the professors will be paid by Her Imperial Majesty; no fees will be received from any of the students. Any deviation from this rule would cause numerous abuses. Perhaps it would be possible to encourage the teachers by honorary prerogatives, perquisites and other compensations that would be awarded to merit, without taking into consideration seniority.

Every professor who has held a professorship for fifteen consecutive years without reproach should be assured of an honorable retirement, with the title of professor emeritus. This is customary with us, and it sustains our professors throughout the course of their tedious and difficult task.

Above all, an old professor who is retiring should be forbidden, under serious penalties, to exact a payment from his successor, as often happens with us. The reason for this rule is evident.

One of the honorary privileges of a professor emeritus of law would be, for instance, the right to sit upon the different tribunals of the magistracy. This would be a flattering distinction for the professor, and an advantage for the magistracy, which, by this policy, would continue to recruit without ceasing men who have given proof of probity and of knowledge of the science of law.

Who would be better qualified to serve in the Department of Foreign Affairs than an emeritus of Common Law or of International Law?

What would be more advantageous than to admit to the Council of Ecclesiastical Affairs an able professor of Canon Law?

Who would be more capable of advising a sovereign than a former professor of the History of Legislation?

I submit all these suggestions to the judgment of Her Imperial Majesty, whose benevolence and justice will be the best advocates that merit can have.

I shall only remind her that it is the same, on this point, with public education as it is with private education; a parent who despises the teacher of his son debases him, and the child is badly educated; a sovereign who does not honor the teachers of his subjects debases them, reduces them to the state of pedants, and the Nation is badly educated.

But one thing which must not be overlooked is that branches of public education which will appear superfluous at the present moment may become necessary in time. As the great work of civilization advances, the various interests and the relations between the subjects will multiply. It is this future that Her Imperial Majesty should anticipate by her wisdom, if she fears to leave the continuation of her projects to the ignorance or the caprices of folly. If an unparalleled firmness and courage are necessary to rectify what has been badly established, it will require all her genius to prevent what has once been well established from being destroyed or spoiled.

When a sovereign has Her Majesty's greatness of mind and amazing penetration, he extends his wisdom beyond his own existence, and continues to reign for a long time after he himself is no more.

If there is a sovereign in Europe who is able to form great projects and to draw upon his funds for the solution of all the difficulties that prevent or delay their execution, it is Her Imperial Majesty. However,—as she has done me the honor of telling me—she is swept away by the current of daily affairs. What remedy is there for this situation? Supplement Her Majesty's genius? No, but make up for the time that she lacks by means of the observations and advice of all the able people in the different countries of Europe. I know no one in my own country who would not be honored by her correspondence.

Her ambassadors would also be of great use to her in the execution of her projects. Who better than they could appropriate to Russia the enlightenment and the wisdom of the countries in which they live, and which it is their duty to study?

PLAN OF A UNIVERSITY

This last observation could be added to a page of notes on making some use of her ambassadors, which I left with Her Imperial Majesty.

Fourth Faculty of a University:
Faculty of Theology

A priest, good or bad, is always an equivocal subject, a being suspended between heaven and earth, like that little figure which a physicist makes mount or descend at will, according to the degree of expansion of the bubble of air which it contains. At one moment leagued with the people against the sovereign, at another with the sovereign against the people, he hardly relies upon praying the gods except when he is little concerned about the matter. The people approve little but what is good; the priest, on the contrary, approves little but what is bad. The augustness of his functions inspires him with such pride that here the vicar of St. Roch is greater in his own eyes than the King. The King makes only nobles, dukes, ministers and generals; what is that to one who creates gods? The sovereign bends the knee before the altar, and bows the head beneath the hand of the priest like the humblest of slaves. All are equal in the churches where the priest presides. In our religion and in the religion of Her Imperial Majesty, the head of the State goes to confess and to blush for the faults of which he is guilty, and the priest absolves or binds. In important and unimportant matters, in public and private affairs, in everything, he controls minds, openly or clandestinely, according to his audacity or his pusillanimity. His calling inclines him to harshness, to mysteriousness and to secrecy. If he were asked what a king is, and he dared to reply frankly, he would answer: *He is either my enemy or my lictor*. The holier he is, the more he is to be feared; a dishonored priest can do nothing. His avidity, his ambition, his intrigues and his bad conduct are more harmful to religion than all the efforts of unbelief. It is the contradiction of his principles by his conduct that emboldened men to examine and contemn the former. If he had been a peace-maker between fathers and children, between parents, a consoler of the afflicted, a defender of the oppressed and an advocate of the poor, however absurd the dogmas of so useful a class of citizens might have been, who amongst us would have dared to attack them? A priest is intolerant and cruel; the axe with which Agag [18] was hewn into pieces has never fallen from his hands. His justice or that of God, like that of the Inspired Books, depends upon circumstances. There are no virtues that he cannot blast, and no crimes that he cannot sanctify; he has the authority to do both.

I do not hate the priest. If he is good, I respect him; if he is bad, I despise him or I pity him. And if I depict him here in such frightful colors, it is because it is necessary to disregard exceptions and to know him as he is by profession, in order to make him what he should be; I mean to say a saint or a hypocrite. Hypocrisy is a virtue in a priest; for the most pernicious scandals are those which are given by priests.

[18] Agag, King of Amalec, who was captured by Saul, and hewn into pieces by the hands of the High-priest Samuel. I Kings, Ch. 15 (Douay), or I Sam., Ch. 15 (King James).

In Spain, where merit leads to the episcopate, and the patronage of the bishop to the subordinate functions, the higher clergy is learned and respected, and the lower clergy ignorant and base. In France, where, on the contrary, the higher places in the Church are obtained by birth and patronage, it is the lower clergy that is learned and respected.

The preparation of a priest may be considered from three general points of view: conduct, knowledge and functions; and the functions under two other aspects: public functions and private functions; by the latter I mean what pertains to his domestic life.

To separate the seminary [19] from the schools would be to separate the theory from the practice. It would be to give preference to learning rather than to conduct. However, it is evident that a priest, if not ignorant, at least very moderately learned, can be a good priest; and, just as easily, a very scholarly priest can be a very bad priest.

Nothing is less important and so dangerous as to have a numerous clergy. I should not wish it to be either rich or poor.

The relief of the poor is the common duty of all citizens. The administration of alms corrupted the leaders of the primitive Church.

The most serious part of the preparation of a priest is that which concerns the character and the conduct which become him.

Each calling has its special mannerisms. The demeanor of a priest should be serious, his appearance reserved, his

[19] By *seminary* must be understood the place in which the theological students live. The schools, where they attend classes.

figure imposing, his habits austere. One who is too familiar outside the temple is not sufficiently respected within it.

I mean by public functions all that pertains to the administration of the Sacraments, to the celebration of the Holy Mysteries, to the ceremonies of the Church, to preaching and to chanting.

By his private exercises, I mean prayer, meditation and reading.

These occupations should proceed in conjunction with the professional training, and follow it without interruption.

If a candidate for the priesthood has completed the entire course in arts, he will know both Latin and Greek.

A knowledge of the Latin language is indispensable for him; a knowledge of the Greek language is less so than for a physician.[20]

As for Hebrew, which is the language of Holy Scripture, it is professional knowledge. Therefore, two chairs of Hebrew must be established; one for teaching the language, the other for literal explanation of the original text.

The teaching of theology can be comprised in the following divisions: study of the Holy Scriptures, dogmatic theology, moral theology,[21] and Church history.

Holy Scripture

Two professors will treat, either in Latin or in the vernacular, of the authenticity and of the inspiration of the Sacred Books and of the canon of the Scriptures.

[20] It is to be feared that Diderot did not know as much as he should have known about the needs of the clergy of the Greek Orthodox Church; of which the Russian Church is a branch.

[21] No further reference is made to moral theology.

As our doctrines and worship differ only in a few unessential details from those of the Schismatic Greek Church, our good authors can be used in the schools.

Explanations of the most difficult passages of Scripture could be dictated to the students. But, because dictation is a pure loss of time, because I exclude it from all the schools, and because the extent of the subject-matter often renders it impracticable, it must be supplemented by printed works.

The second professor of Hebrew will take the students after they have had some months of instruction in Hebrew grammar with the first professor. They will know enough of the language to understand his literal explanation of the Bible.

I believe, however, that only the small number of students who give evidence of special ability should be admitted to the courses of these two professors. In the case of priests, mediocrity of talent is less to be feared than defects of character. All faults should be excused, except those of demeanor and conduct. The best of priests is a holy priest, a good priest is a decent priest.

The teaching of dogmatic theology should be simplified as much as possible. It is the cause of all heresies and disputes and of the most baleful troubles of society.

Nothing should be permitted that tends to the reconciliation of the Greek Church with the Roman Communion. Learning might gain by it perhaps, but it would be a danger for the State. It would be imprudent to allow a part of the subjects, so powerful as the clergy, to recognize, in whatever manner it might be, a foreign head. It would be a source of perpetual division between the Church and the Senate. There should be no appeal other than to the Sovereign, no council outside the Empire, no head of the Council other than the head of the State.

Dogmatic Theology

It is enough to know what Holy Scripture, the Councils of the Church and the Fathers have pronounced concerning each particular dogma. Research for the satisfaction of curiosity and systems that produce only errors and parties should be forbidden.

Scholastic theology, which is of use only in countries where there might be disputes with heretics, can be of no use in Russia, where whosoever wishes to do so is free to be a heretic and damned.

There should be two chairs of dogmatic theology: the first destined for the defense of religion against atheists, deists, Jews and Mohammedans.

The second professor of dogmatic theology will devote himself to explaining clearly and succinctly the dogmas of religion and their proofs.

The only points upon which it would be important to insist a little more perhaps are the divinity of Christ and His real presence in the Eucharist. The first is the basis of the Christian beliefs and worship; the second the principal cause of the great schism. It would be shameful if a priest should remain silent in the presence of Socinians, whom he will meet at every step, and of Lutherans and Calvinists, with whom he is surrounded.

In a country where the religion requires confession—which is well enough when the confession is made by a sincere penitent, and heard by an upright man—and where people go to the first priest they find to ask absolution—which is always bad—there must be two professors who will give instruction concerning advice to penitents, judgment of actions and the nature of reparations and expiations.

Things concerning the political order do not pertain to theology.

The first of these teachers will establish and develop the principles of the natural law in relation to conscience. He will treat of the nature of the laws, of their origins, of the obligations which they produce, of the causes which suspend them or cause them to cease, of oaths, of contracts, etc.

The second will enter into the details of the duties that are common to all men, and his teaching could be, strictly speaking, only an analytic commentary of the Decalogue and the commandments of the Church; just as that of his colleague could be, strictly speaking, only an analytic commentary on the Creed.[22]

He will treat later of the precepts of the Church and of ecclesiastical punishments; taking care to avoid all the ridiculous and dangerous subtilities of the casuists of the last century.

Church History

Finally, the professor of Church history will undertake to explain the origin and the successive progress of the ecclesiastical hierarchy, and, I shall not say the origin and successive progress, but at least the development of the dogmas: a task that is difficult enough.

---

[22] Just what connection there could be between laws, their nature, origins, effect, etc., and the Creed is not clear.

This professor will then pass to the elucidation of the most important facts concerning the Church, paying special attention to those of the first centuries, and calling the attention of his hearers to the perpetuity of the faith, the unbroken chain of tradition and of the ministry, the ancient form of ecclesiastical government, its vicissitudes, its present form, the rise of heresies, the origin of abuses, the relaxation of discipline, etc.

It is thus that a good and learned ecclesiastical would be trained in Italy, in France, in England, in Spain, and in Portugal. Is there any need of changing much in this education, either in regard to the scientific or the moral part, for another country, for Russia? I do not know.

It appertains to Archbishop Platon to revise all this part of public education. It will be his task to reconcile the form and the objective with the customs, the laws, the manners and the needs of the Russian Empire, and it will devolve upon Her Imperial Majesty to correct all that professional zeal—which secretly dominates the most learned and the best-intentioned men—might suggest of a dangerous or irregular nature to the Archbishop.

In addition, I beg Her Imperial Majesty to consider that there must be either no priests or good priests, that is to say, learned, edifying and peaceable priests; and that, if it is difficult to do without priests wheresoever there is a religion, it is easy to have peaceable ones if they are paid by the State, and threatened, at the least fault, with being dismissed from their positions, deprived of their functions and stipends, and cast into poverty.

The bulk of a nation will always remain ignorant, timorous and, consequently, superstitious. Atheism can be the doctrine of a small school, but never of a great number of citizens, still less of a nation a little civilized. The belief in the existence of God—the old trunk—will remain always. Who knows what monstrous things this trunk, if abandoned to its free vegetation, could produce? I should not, therefore, maintain priests as depositories of truth, but as obstacles to possible errors that might be still more monstrous; not as teachers of sensible people, but as guardians of lunatics; and I should let their churches remain as asylums or Bedlams for a certain class of imbeciles who might become violent if they were entirely neglected.

I could not then approve of a policy which would consider the clergy with the same indifference as it does other corporations, and would permit anybody to become a good or bad priest, as in some countries that are well enough governed, so that every citizen may, without hindrance, take advantage of his talents, anybody is permitted to become a good or bad shoemaker.

This Faculty of Theology cannot then be totally suppressed.

I should have finished my task, if I had limited myself to the order and extent of the studies of a university; for here is the plan and the justification of the plan, but its execution requires superiors, inferiors, teachers, students, textbooks, instruments, buildings and regulations. All of which subjects I shall discuss summarily.

The Profession of Scholarship

A nation that is not learned may perhaps be numerous and powerful, but it will be barbarous, and I shall never allow myself to be persuaded that barbarity can be the happiest state for a nation, nor that a people advances towards misfortune to the same extent that it becomes enlightened or civilized or that the rights of property become more sacred to it.

The ownership of property and personal freedom or civil liberty presuppose good laws, and, in time, bring about the cultivation of the earth, increase in population, industries of every kind, arts, sciences and the great century of a nation.

Among the arts and sciences, some are the children of necessity or need; such as medicine, law, the first elements of mathematics and of physics; others are born of ease and perhaps of laziness; such are poesy, eloquence, and all the branches of speculative philosophy.

A father, who has enriched himself by commerce, has many children; among these children, there is one who wishes to do nothing. On account of his weak and delicate arms, he has an aversion to the shuttle, the saw and the hammer. He rises late, he remains seated with bowed head, he reflects, he meditates, he becomes a poet, an orator, a priest or a philosopher.

A nation must be very numerous or very rich to be able to have, without disagreeable consequences, many of these individuals who think while others work.

This lazy class must be very numerous, and learning must have already made great progress amongst a nation in order to give rise to academies.

What is an academy? It is a body of scholars that constitutes itself just as society in general constituted itself; the latter in order to struggle with greater advantage against

Nature; the former by the same instinct or on account of the same need: the acknowledged superiority of united efforts against ignorance.

In the beginning, neither the one nor the other of these associations had either code or laws. An association of scholars subsists under a species of anarchy until a sovereign, who foresees its usefulness, takes it under his patronage, endows it and makes himself its law-giver.

To call foreigners to form an academy of scholars is to neglect to cultivate one's own land, and buy grain from one's neighbor. If we cultivate our own fields, we shall have grain.

An academy or body of scholars should only be the product of enlightenment which has reached a certain degree of perfection and is very widely spread. Otherwise, if it is supported by the State, it costs it a great deal, subsists only by means of recruits [23] and produces no results. It publishes fine collections of work which no one buys or reads; because no one understands them. Some few volumes of these collections are distributed abroad, which does not compensate for the expenses; and the rest of the Nation remains at the same point of ignorance or learning.

It is not the same with public instruction. Affecting all classes of an empire, and spreading enlightenment everywhere, its final effect is the creation of academies which are lasting, as they are incessantly renewed from national sources.

To found an academy before having provided for public education is in fact to begin a building at the top.

[23] Recruits from abroad is probably meant; for no society of any kind could subsist other than by means of recruits, unless it were hereditary.

All things considered, the profession of a scholar is agreeable. Men will always be naturally inclined to it wherever knowledge is to some extent rewarded and greatly honored.

Establishments for public education should foster the progress of the population in general. A multitude of such institutions would be a species of calamity. Let there be few colleges but good ones.

Hardly had the University been established amongst us, when the number of its colleges began to increase immeasurably. Great lords followed the example of the sovereign and founded some of those which we are to-day destroying.

I do not think that the time has yet come for Russia to encourage this sort of emulation among the great. If they should acquire it, perhaps it would be necessary to put a stop to it.

There are two kinds of public schools.

The primary schools are open to all the children of the people, as soon as they are able to walk and talk. In these they should find teachers, books and bread; teachers who will teach them reading, writing and the principles of religion and of arithmetic; books which perhaps they would not be able to procure for themselves; bread which authorizes the authorities to force the poorer parents to send their children to school.[24]

On leaving these primary schools, the children will either return to their homes to learn some trade, or they will

[24] It is interesting to note that Diderot evidently felt that education was not such a fundamental need that parents could, with justice, be required to send their children to school and provide them food at the same time.

present themselves at the colleges of the University of which I have presented the plan, and of which I shall briefly outline the administrative policy.

GENERAL ADMINISTRATION OF A UNIVERSITY AND SPECIAL ADMINISTRATION OF A COLLEGE

A university should have a head or general inspector of conduct and studies.

This function should be entrusted to a distinguished, experienced and wise statesman. It is to his tribunal that will be submitted all contestable matters, which will be decided, as a last resort, by Her Imperial Majesty or by her Council.

The first step of wisdom in our time is to relate everything to the cultivation of the earth; the second step which remains to be taken is to realize the importance of public education or the cultivation of the human intelligence.

Let there be no innovations, either in the order of the studies or in the regulations, without the express sanction of the sovereign.

These regulations should be examined and confirmed every five years; not in order to change the order of instruction, which should be permanent if it is good, but to perfect the application of it.

In each college, if there are several, there should be a principal whose function would be to supervise the teachers and control all the household administration.

There should be under the principal a prefect or supervisor of students, a bursar and a chaplain.

The prefect will supervise the students only when they are not in class; he will be a sort of police officer.

I shall not dwell on the duties of these superiors, as they will be given in detail in the regulations, and there is nothing which distinguishes them from the duties which Her Imperial Majesty has prescribed for the masters who direct her other establishments under different names.

Each class of students will have its special and separate enclosure, both during the time of study under the professors and out of the hours of classes.

Out of classes, the students will be under the control of another kind of masters, whom we shall call house-masters or tutors.

Each class will have its tutor or house-master, just as it will have its professor.

The functions of the house-master will partake of those of the professor and of those of the prefect. He will be in charge of the maintenance of order like the prefect, when bad weather confines the students indoors and the recreation is not taken in the open air.

He will preside over the studies out of class, and he will make the students repeat their lessons. It is he who will be responsible to the professors for the diligence and the progress of the students, and to the prefect for their conduct. It is he who will grant permissions by day or by night.

To understand well the functions of a house-master, it will be necessary to have a clear idea of the daily program of the student.

In the classes, the students will be under the control of the professor. Out of the classes, during general recreation and out of doors, they will be in the care of the prefect.

At study out of the classes, they will be under the house-master. During special indoor recreations, they will also be under the house-master.

When the students are out of class, either at silent study or are repeating orally the lessons which they have had in class, the house-master exercises indoors precisely the same functions as a professor.

Until the age of fifteen, the students will assemble for study out of class in a large common room. Each class will have its own hall. After the age of fifteen, each student will have his own little private study.

The house-master should be almost as learned as the professor, for one of his duties will be to replace the latter when he is absent; just as it will be the duty of the prefect to replace, in similar cases, the professor and the house-master.

The house-master or tutor will expect to become a professor when a chair becomes vacant, and, if there is nothing serious with which to reproach him, his expectation should not be frustrated. He should hold the reversion of a professorship; but only of the class of which he has been the tutor.

I have followed thus far the order and discipline of our colleges, because I have learned from my own experience their usefulness for the promotion of good conduct and the progress of learning.

The Daily Program of a College

An ancient philosopher said: "I rule all Greece, because I rule Aspasia, who rules Pericles, who rules all Greece."

There is in every community house a subaltern, who rules an Aspasia, who rules despotically everybody; and this Aspasia is the bell. The bell rules the superiors, the teachers, the prefects, the tutors, the students and the servants.

The bell rings, and *ad hoc* the servants repeat, each morning, its supreme command at all the doors, at which they knock until they receive an answer.

The hours of rising and of retiring should be fixed for winter and for summer. In our colleges, the students rise at half past five. A little more sleep may be allowed the students of the lower classes.

The students will be awakened at half past five, and by six o'clock prayers will have been said in each dormitory.

At six o'clock, they will dress themselves, and then study individually until a quarter before seven.

At a quarter before seven, lessons will be heard by the house-master until a quarter before eight.

At a quarter before eight, the students will breakfast, and then take recreation indoors, each class in its own hall, until half past eight.

At half past eight, they will go to the classes of the first course of studies, each in his own class and under his professor, where they will remain until half past ten.

At half past ten, they will return indoors, where they will take recreation for a moment, and will then apply themselves to their individual studies until a quarter before twelve.

At a quarter before twelve, they will dine. Dinner will last until a quarter before one.

At a quarter before one, there will be general recreation for all the students together in the open air, if the weather is fine, or indoor recreation for each class in its own hall, if the weather is bad. This recreation will last until half past one.

At half past one, the students will return indoors, if they are outside, or silence will be commanded in the hall, and they will study individually until half past two.

At half past two, they will betake themselves to the classes of the second course, and will remain until half past four.

At half past four, they will pass to the third course of studies; that is to the class in drawing. They will remain in this class until a quarter past five.

At a quarter past five, there will be a light lunch, followed by general or individual recreation until six o'clock.

At six o'clock the students will return for individual study until a quarter before seven.

At a quarter before seven, they will repeat with the masters the lessons of the first course of studies until eight o'clock.

At eight o'clock supper will be served, and will last until a quarter before nine.

By nine o'clock, prayers will have been said, at a quarter past nine, all will be in bed, and the day's study will be finished.

VACATIONS FROM CLASSES AND INTERRUPTION OF WORK FOR MASTERS AND FOR STUDENTS

The classes will be closed and work will be suspended, both for teachers and for students, on Wednesdays and Saturdays; but only in the afternoons and until six o'clock.

At six o'clock, the students will return for individual study until a quarter before seven.

At a quarter before seven, they will repeat their lessons with the house-masters until a quarter before eight.

These two half-days will be spent in playing all sorts of games. Rest is necessary for the teachers, and exercise for the students.

Among the students, the children from the country are more robust than the children from the towns; among the children from the towns, those of the common people and of artisans are more vigorous than those of the rich middle class; the weakest and the least healthy are the children of the nobles. Everything has its compensations.[25]

The sedentary life of a studious man and meditation—which is the occupation the most contrary to Nature—are both sources of particular illnesses; the stagnation of the humors causes them to deteriorate, and the body becomes corrupt while the spirit is being purified. This is sad.

Objection and Reply

Some will say that this is a very laborious day.

That may be; but what does it matter? Is it so very necessary, after all, that there should be a great number of scholars? Is the day of a factory worker, of a merchant, of a magistrate or of a farmer any less laborious? Can learning be acquired while reclining on a pillow?

Furthermore, the work is interrupted by relaxations, and

[25] It would be interesting to know upon what Diderot based these conclusions. If indeed he based them upon anything other than a sort of cheering philosophy. If they were true, they would be a terrible arraignment of modern industrial civilization.

the studies are varied. It is assiduous application to a single thing that bores, wearies and disgusts both men and children.

Quintilian, who was a writer of great understanding, assures us that a child will be less tired after four different lessons a day than after a single one that would last as long as the four together.

The Students

There will be no fixed age for entering the schools. The education of our ancestors hardly began before the age of fifteen. Before concerning themselves with the cultivation of the mind, they gave thought to the strength of the body.

The only thing that will be required of a child who presents himself will be that he should know those things which should have been learned at home or in the primary schools.

He will be examined in order to ascertain whether he knows how to read, whether his handwriting is good, whether he can spell passably, whether he knows the arithmetical figures and is acquainted with the principles of his religion.

There will be three kinds of students: boarders, day scholars and holders of scholarships.

The boarders will live in the college. The cost of their board, lodging and tuition will be borne by their parents.

The day scholars will receive only instruction in the school. They will live in the homes of their parents.

The holders of scholarships will live in the college, and they will differ from the other boarders only in that their board, lodging, tuition and other expenses will be paid through the beneficence of some rich men who have endowed the scholarships which they hold.

Great lords cannot be too much encouraged to make so worthy a use of their superfluous wealth. Her Imperial Majesty will certainly not fail to set them an example.

But such scholarships absolutely must not be in the gift of their founders. Their offers should be declined if they are unwilling to renounce a privilege which would fill a school with the favored unfit.

Scholarships should be awarded by public competition or granted to merit that has been proved by a rigorous examination. Time and pains should not be wasted in cultivating the limited intelligence of a child whom Nature has fitted only to work with his hands, and who would at the same time be kept away from some useful employment.

It would be advisable that all students who live in the college, both boarders and holders of scholarships, should be distinguished from the day scholars by a special costume; for fear lest, in the tumult of leaving the classrooms, the former, by mingling with the latter, might elude the vigilance of the door-keeper and escape.

The prefect should be present when the students enter and leave the classrooms.

An important point, upon which I shall insist, is that deputies from the Senate shall visit each class four times a year. They must require all the professors and housemasters to swear to tell the truth; these latter will then inform them of any delinquent students who should be excluded from the school and sent back to their parents.

I mean by a delinquent student one who is neither willing nor talented. It is better to run the risk of misleading genius than to divert from subordinate occupations a multitude of children, and thus deliver them to all the vices which come from ignorance and laziness.

This regulation will diminish in succession the number of students in each class from the first to the last—the class of the ancient languages, in which poets and orators are produced. So much the better!

All the classes should be considered as one large one consisting of different divisions. The length of time that a student should remain in each of these divisions should depend only on his progress. There are some students who are precocious and who learn quickly. There are others who are backward and whose progress is slow. There are the attentive and the inattentive. Consequently, some should be kept in the same division, and others promoted to the next higher.

No student should be permitted to advance one step in the course unless he knows all that has preceded it as well as he is capable of learning it.

At the end of the year, each class will be composed of new and of old students. None should be permitted to remain in the same class three years.

It is frequently the custom here to add to the third class the study of the languages and the class in rhetoric.

It is better to know a little well, or even to be ignorant, than to know badly. False knowledge engenders obstinacy and overconfidence; whereas absolute ignorance inspires docility and cautiousness.

Let the students be thoroughly convinced that the duration of their studies depends entirely upon their assiduity. The rigorous application of this regulation will temper the ambition of parents who are desirous of withdrawing their children from the subordinate occupations which they themselves follow, and of having them educated for the priesthood, medicine or law.

Nothing is more fatal to society than this disdain of parents for their own calling and these senseless migrations from one state in life to another.

There should be nothing optional in regard to the subject-matter of the lessons or to their duration.

There should be nothing optional in regard to punishments or to rewards.

There should be no corporal punishments. To reward the good is to begin the punishment of the bad.

A little penal code for offenses against discipline or good conduct and failure in studies would obviate misplaced partiality and severity, as well as spare the masters the hatred of the guilty who are punished by the law. This code would also make known to the students their duties and the punishments which they will incur if they fail in them.

Offenses against discipline should be more severely punished than misconduct, and the latter more severely than failure in study.

I am inclined to suggest that the faults of the students should be reported by the masters to the chaplain.

The function of the chaplain, on feast-days and Sundays, after the celebration of the Divine Office, would be to encourage the students in wisdom and virtue.

In his capacity of exhorter and censor, he would praise publicly, and by name, the students who had distinguished themselves during the preceding week; and he would also name the ignorant, the lazy and the vicious, whom he would upbraid unsparingly. It would be desirable that the chaplain should be a man of some zeal and eloquence.

He would finish his exhortation and censure by reading the articles of the code against which the students had offended. He would likewise impose punishments and distribute the prizes for knowledge and virtue.

His text for the day would be the utility of the rules which had been violated and the justice of the punishments incurred. If there were some act of virtue to be rewarded, he would also laud this virtue.

On other days, he would speak of the duties of superiors, of masters, of students and even of servants.

On Saturday mornings, there will be a general review and examination on the work of the entire preceding week, the results of which will determine the places of honor or of dishonor that will be assigned to the students.

Marks of distinction for diligence must be instituted, prizes must be awarded, and it is a little more important, it seems to me, to give a reward for a good action than for a lesson well learned. It would seem that virtue counted for nothing in the laws of the schools as well as in those of peoples.

Above all, hopes for the future must be inspired by appointing to public offices, when they leave school, those students who have distinguished themselves. One of the defects of our education is that it leads to nothing, to no special position in society.

Four times a year, there will be an examination in the presence of the senators or the magistrates. This examination will precede the administration of the oath to the masters and the expulsion of the unfit.

Twice a year, there will be public exercises in each class. Printed programs will indicate the nature of these exercises, and will invite all citizens to be present. What is even more important still is that all the students in the class, whether ignorant or learned, be required, without distinction, to answer the questions of those present. This is an excellent means of honoring the diligent students and punishing the lazy, as well as of sustaining the emulation of the teachers.

These public exercises will be in the work of the three parallel courses of public education.

There is another advantage in a varied instruction. All students have not an equal aptitude for every study. One, who is endowed with a prodigious memory, will make rapid progress in history and in geography. Another, who is more given to reflection, will understand with ease questions concerning number and space, and will learn almost without effort arithmetic and geometry. If only one subject is taught during the whole time, the student to whom Nature has given little or no aptitude for this study will be constantly humiliated and discouraged; but if the instruction comprises several subjects at the same time, after his moments of shame, will come his moment of triumph and glory, and his parents will return from the public exercises with some consolation.

In our schools, in which, for five or six consecutive years, only the ancient languages are taught, three or four distinguished students stifle all emulation in the others.

PLAN OF A UNIVERSITY

In the course of the day's study, each one of the students will show his natural aptitude; consequently there will be none who will always be superior, and they will all have a motive for mutual esteem.

THE TEACHERS

A sure means of judging a school is to see whether the students who are being educated in it give promise of being some day good teachers themselves. If it tends to this result, it is good; otherwise, it is bad.

What are the qualities to be desired in a good teacher? A profound knowledge of the subject which he is to teach, and a spirit of honesty and understanding.

If the position of a teacher is important on account of the salary attached to it and the distinguished place it occupies among the various professions, if this salary is the teacher's only resource, and, consequently, by dishonoring his profession, he would at the same time ruin himself, he will have or will pretend to have the necessary virtues. Let us then obtain from selfish motives what we should prefer to obtain from good qualities.

There should be no priests among the teachers other than in the schools of the Faculty of Theology. Priests are rivals by profession of the secular power, and they are rigorists in their ethical views, which are also narrow and gloomy.

The difficulties of the married state do not prevent a workman from following his trade, a lawyer from attending court nor a magistrate or senator from looking after public affairs. They will be no greater obstacles for a housemaster or for a professor.

Professors or house-masters may then be either married or unmarried. If they have children, so much the better; as fathers, they will be more gentle and more compassionate in their dealings with the students.

The unmarried masters will or will not live in the college according to their preference.

The married men will have their lodgings outside. There should be no women in a college; for the mingling of the two sexes soon has a bad moral effect and causes dissensions. But because a master who is burdened with a numerous family ought not to have fewer advantages than an unmarried one, the rental of his lodging should be paid for him. This rule should likewise apply to all who are employed in the college.

I ask nothing more of a teacher than the same good conduct that is expected of every citizen, the knowledge necessary to teach in his school, and a little patience which he will not fail to have if he will remember that he too was at one time ignorant.

The students will pass from one class to another, but each teacher will remain in his own.

There should be no inspector of education who would have absolute power other than the State. It pertains to the State to appoint, to retain or to change the rector and the principals, to remove the professors, to dismiss the tutors or house-masters and to exclude from the schools incapable or vicious children.

If the University were composed of several colleges, I should not hesitate to require the students or their parents to pay a small quarterly tuition. The exemption of public instruction from cost has debased our professors. In effect, of what importance is it to them if they have few or many students, if they perform their functions well or ill? They have less trouble and receive the same salary.[26]

Another advantage of this little expense is that it would diminish the number of students, which will never be other than too great, no matter what may be the future state of the Nation. The facility of entering the public schools, the ambition of parents, their avarice—which makes them prefer to any other apprenticeship the one that costs nothing—withdraw a multitude of children from the calling of their fathers. Great commercial establishments disappear, important manufactures decline or deteriorate, trade corporations are impoverished. And why? To make a Doctor!

A fault of a master should never be considered a matter of little importance. There should be no pardon for a vicious master. Fathers, misplaced indulgence for the instructors of your children will fall on them and on you. Sovereigns, misplaced indulgence for bad instructors will fall on the hope of your Nation and on you.

I shall say only a word concerning the method of teaching, which is that if students understood better the toil of the teachers, they would endure their own more easily. Instead of affecting a superiority of knowledge, it would be better for a teacher to appear to study and work with his students. In this manner, while learning, they would become familiar with the art of teaching.

For instance, if a teacher who is solving a problem in arithmetic or geometry for a student would make a false supposition, then retrace his steps and start over again until

[26] Here Diderot is not consistent; *cf.* p. 276.

he has finally discovered the solution, I think that he would instruct the student better than he would if he reached the same conclusion by a rapid, sure and unhesitating procedure.

There is a very great difference between an error due to ignorance or to carelessness and an intentional one. The latter serves to keep the student on his guard; if he perceives it, his little vanity is satisfied; it accustoms him to mistrust; it trains him imperceptibly for the research of truth; and it inspires him with the spirit of investigation. The former, on the contrary, wastes time and inspires only contempt. An intentional error will sometimes palliate an involuntary error and dispense the teacher from blushing.

This method of teaching, though in appearance perplexing, dubious and vacillating, is entirely Socratic.

It is not enough that the masters should receive adequate salaries, it would also be advisable to provide for the time of old age and infirmities. The assurance of a pension upon retirement after a certain number of years of faithful service would render them attentive to their duties, attach them to their positions, and prevent them from becoming disgusted with their occupations.

I do not dare say anything about permitting or forbidding masters to receive gifts or other gratuities from the parents of students. The permission to do so would authorize abuses, whereas, to prohibit them would not prevent them; and a prohibitory law that cannot be enforced is a bad law.

And how are teachers to be procured? For the time being, they are called from all countries; no matter whether they be good, mediocre or bad, provided their conduct be good, and they are well paid.

PLAN OF A UNIVERSITY

Students are sent to Leyden, to Leipzig, to London and to Paris, where they are placed under the care of a respectable man, who lodges them all in the same house, and watches over their conduct and progress in the sciences.

By means of prizes, the study of the Russian language is encouraged in all enlightened countries.

A certain salary is offered to a man who is qualified to teach geometry, and who knows enough Russian to do so in this language, if he will go to Moscow or to Petersburg. Similar offers are made to those who know Russian, and are capable of teaching medicine, law or the fine arts. We may be sure that if these invitations are constantly repeated and the promises faithfully kept, they will have their effect.

Let us plan our edifice for the present time, and, for the future, lay the foundations, erect some pieces of wall, and leave to our successors the remainder of the operation.

TEXTBOOKS

Almost all the textbooks are still yet to be made. For lack of these aids to study, students everywhere study much and with difficulty; they learn little and they learn badly. There must be books for all ages and for all branches of knowledge. However, there are excellent treatises of all kinds, and a good textbook is only a well-made abridgement of one of these great treatises.

Why are these abridgements so rare? It is because they can be the work of a methodical and profoundly learned man only. No semi-scholar, nor even every scholar, has the gift of being able to arrange facts, to define terms, to distinguish what is elementary and essential, and of being clear and precise.

Those who could have rendered this service have been more interested in their personal glory than in the public needs, and have preferred to advance knowledge by one step rather than to trace the steps which it has already made.

A good textbook implies that the art or the science is already approaching perfection. Now is the time for this work. A sovereign who wishes to do so can accomplish anything, and I dare to affirm that within three or four years all kinds of textbooks would be written, if Her Imperial Majesty so desired.

This is a task that should be distributed among the scholars of Europe. Let Her Imperial Majesty commission M. d'Alembert [27] to prepare all the textbooks in the science of mathematics, and M. d'Alembert will prepare them, and prepare them well.

BUILDINGS

Each faculty should have its own separate group of buildings like that of the Faculty of Arts, which will serve as a model for the others.

There will be:

The lodging of the principal.

The lodging of the bursar.

The lodging of the prefect.

The lodging of the chaplain.

[27] Jean Le Rond d'Alembert, philosopher and mathematician, one of the original contributors to the *Encyclopédie,* of whom Diderot was another (1717–1783).

PLAN OF A UNIVERSITY

A chapel.

Separate lodgings for the professors.

Separate rooms for the house-masters or tutors.

Common study halls for the lower classes.

Common dormitories for these same lower classes.

Private and separate rooms for the older and more advanced students.

Classrooms; as many separate classrooms as there are different professors or sections in the entire course.

Halls for indoor recreations.

A vast outdoor space, shady and covered with sand, for general recreations.

A library for all kinds of studies, with a lodging for the librarian.

A collection of mathematical and astronomical instruments and of appliances for experimental physics.

An amphitheatre for anatomical demonstrations.

A collection of prepared anatomical specimens.

A chemical laboratory.

A medicine cabinet arranged as we have prescribed.

A hospital adjacent to the schools of medicine.

A seminary adjacent to the schools of theology.

This is all I know concerning the best means of establishing a university.

It appertains to Her Imperial Majesty to add to this plan whatever is necessary that I may have omitted, and to eliminate whatever she may consider useless. I entreat her, however, to take into consideration the fact that many things may appear to her superfluous for the present which will become necessary in time, even before the end of her reign, if it lasts as long as she promised me it would. I shall be satisfied with my work if she recognizes in it a proof of my entire devotion to her orders and of my lasting gratitude for her benefactions. I am indebted to no one for the good or bad ideas which constitute this plan for public schools; it is the defects of my own education which have suggested them all. It would have been easy for me to have been more brief, but it would have been still easier to have written at greater length.

IV

MARIE-JEAN-ANTOINE-NICHOLAS CARITAT
DE CONDORCET

*REPORT ON THE GENERAL ORGANIZATION
OF PUBLIC INSTRUCTION*

Translated from the text edited by Gabriel Compayré,
Hachette, Paris, 1883.

CONDORCET (1743–1794)

and his

REPORT ON PUBLIC INSTRUCTION

MARIE-JEAN-ANTOINE-NICHOLAS CARITAT, Marquis de Condorcet, mathematician, philosopher and one of the leaders of the Revolution, was born on September 17, 1743, at Ribemont in Picardie.

He was educated at the Jesuit College in Rheims and at the *Collège de Navarre* in Paris. At an early age, even before finishing his studies in college, he gave evidence of his great ability as a mathematican, and when he was only twenty-six years old he was elected to the Academy of Sciences, to which he contributed a number of papers on mathematical as well as various other subjects.

An ardent protagonist of the philosophical ideas of the eighteenth century, he was associated with d'Alembert in the preparation of the *Encyclopédie,* and was also in close relations with Voltaire and Turgot.

In 1777, he was elected perpetual secretary of the Academy of Sciences, and became a member of the French Academy in 1782. He was also an associate of many foreign academies.

He was the author of a great number of mathematical treatises, which it would be impossible to enumerate, and of which many, says his chief biographer, Arago, were never included in his collected works, as they were buried in the archives of various learned societies. Perhaps the most important of them all was an *Essai sur l'application de l'analyse aux probabilités des décisions prises à la pluralité des voix,* which was first published in 1785, and of which an enlarged edition was published in 1804, under the title *Éléments du calcul des probabilités et son application aux jeux de hazard, à la loterie et aux jugements des hommes, etc.* The application of the theory of probabilities to popular votes and the factors which must be taken into consideration in determining their results is most ingenious.

From a purely literary point of view, Condorcet's best works are perhaps his life of Turgot, which was published anonymously in London in 1786, and his life of Voltaire, which was published in Geneva in 1787.

Condorcet began early to take interest in social questions, and during the ministry of Turgot he combated in favor of reforms. He was also greatly interested in the revolt of the English colonies in North America and in the establishment of the new republic. He wrote several essays on this subject, among which may be mentioned his *Lettres d'un citoyen des États-Unis sur les affaires présentes,* his *Lettres d'un bourgeois de Newhaven à un citoyen de la Virginie* and his *Réflexions sur l'esclavage des nègres.*

Naturally, he was an enthusiastic partisan of the Revolution. He was elected to represent the city of Paris in the Legislative Assembly, and became its secretary. It was he who composed the greater part of the addresses which it directed respectively to the European Powers in 1791, and to the French people in 1792. He was appointed a member of the committee on public instruction, and drew up the plan which we here present.

At first there was much opposition to the general plan, because Condorcet was accused of desiring, by the creation of the National Society of Sciences and Arts, to deliver education into the hands of a corporation which would constitute a state within the State. Pierre Daunou, however, defended him successfully by claiming that for Condorcet it was first of all a matter of withdrawing public education from the influence of the King, and for this reason he had constituted the teaching body an autonomous body. "Condorcet, the enemy of kings, wished to add, in the balance of public authority, one more counter-balance to the royal power," said Daunou. [1]

The plan was first submitted to the National Assembly on April 20 and 21, 1792, and on May 25, Condorcet completed his report by presenting an estimate of the costs of the project. However, by this time the attention of the Assembly was occupied with other affairs, and the entire matter of national education was adjourned. It was resumed later by the Convention, which ordered that Condorcet's report should be reprinted, and this report formed the basis of the deliberations of the committee on education which was appointed by the Convention.[2]

As might be expected of "the enemy of kings," Condorcet was one of the first to declare himself in favor of the republic, and he prepared the memorandum which led to the suspension of the royal power and the convocation of the National Assembly. When the King, Louis XVI, was being tried for his life, Condorcet voted against the death sen-

[1] *Grande Encyclopédie,* Vol. XII, p. 359, Lamirault, Paris. Article *Condorcet.*
[2] G. COMPAYRÉ, History of Pedagogy, p. 379.

tence, advocating instead "the severest punishment that there be after the death penalty" [3] . . . which was a perpetual sentence to the galleys! The King of France a galley slave! Great indignation was excited among royalists everywhere, and, on account of this vote, the Empress Catherine of Russia and the King Frederick-William II of Prussia ordered Condorcet's name removed from the lists of the members of the Academies of St. Petersburg and Berlin.[4]

It was not to be long before Condorcet himself was to be a fugitive from the tribunal which he had helped to create, and was likewise to be condemned to death by it.

In February, 1793, Condorcet had offered to the Convention a draft of a constitution, which it had rejected in favor of one prepared by Hérault de Séchelles. Later, Condorcet attacked this constitution as not offering guarantees sufficient for liberty, and, in consequence, the Convention decreed his arrest on July 8, 1793. As he well knew what he had to expect from his judges, Condorcet made his escape. He was condemned to death in contumacy on October 3, 1793. For some time he remained concealed in the house of a Madame Vernet—a relative of the painter Claude Vernet—who gave him refuge, and is reported to have said that the Convention could declare him outside the law, but not outside humanity.

It was during the time that he was hiding in the house of Madame Vernet in Paris that he wrote his best-known

[3] *Grand Dictionnaire Universel,* Vol. IV, p. 879, Librairie Larousse, Paris. Article *Condorcet.*

[4] *Biographie Universelle,* Vol. IX, p. 22, Thoisnier Deplaces, Paris, 1852. Article *Condorcet.*

work: *Esquisse d'un tableau historique des progrès de l'esprit humain,* upon which his reputation as a philosopher is principally based. The fundamental idea of this work is that mankind is destined to progress continuously until it finally attains perfection. The excesses of the Revolution— of which, by now, he had had some experience as victim— he attributed to bad institutions, of which humanity would ultimately rid itself. According to his conception, the history of mankind should be divided into nine epochs, beginning with the primitive life of hunting and fishing and passing through the pastoral to the agricultural age. The third period ends with the invention of the alphabet and the beginning of authentic history. Next come the epochs of Greece and of Rome, and then the Middle Ages, which he divides into two periods: one closing with the Crusades, and the other with the invention of printing. The eighth epoch extends to the philosophical revolution brought about by Descartes, and the ninth, to the Revolution and includes the discoveries of Locke, Newton and Rousseau. In the tenth epoch—which is that of the future—he predicts that man will abolish all inequalities, and foresees the perfection of individual human nature. He considered popular education the basis of all progress. One of the main features of this work is an intense animosity against all religion— Christianity in particular—and against monarchy.

After he had been about eight months in the home of Madame Vernet, Condorcet received a letter telling him that there was to be a search made of the house in quest of fugitives from the South, and that he would find a safe retreat with the ex-academician Suard at Fontenay-aux-Roses. Therefore, he resolved to leave Paris, which he did disguised as a workman. For some reason that has not been fully explained, either he failed to go to Fontenay-aux-Roses, or did not remain there—some accounts state that Suard was unwilling to shelter him—and was obliged to pass two nights in the quarries of Clamart. When, finally, he was forced to go to an inn to seek food, his fatigued appearance aroused the suspicions of some individuals present who reported him to the Vigilance Committee of Clamart, and he was arrested. Condorcet gave the name Pierre Simon, and was imprisoned under this name at Bourg-la-Reine. The next day, the gaoler found him dead in his cell. The medical inspector gave a verdict of death from apoplexy; but it was nevertheless supposed that Condorcet had committed suicide by means of a poison which the celebrated physician Cabanis had prepared for him, and which he carried for a long time concealed in a ring.

His fate remained unknown for several months, as his friends believed that he had escaped to Switzerland. However, when the story of the prisoner who had died at Bourg-la-Reine came to the ears of those interested in Condorcet, the identity of the prisoner with him was established by means of a watch and a copy of Horace's *Epistles* which had been found on the dead man.

At the request of his widow, the death certificate of the pretended Pierre Simon was rectified to that of Condorcet by a decree dated 12 Ventôse of the year III.

Condorcet was dominated by two ideas: the infinite perfectability of the human race and a passion for liberty. He proposed milder means than most reformers in dealing with those who were so blind to their own interests as to differ from him. He merely proposed to let Nature take

its course, and, in time, the recalcitrant—if any remained—
would die out. In the meanwhile, he had a scheme by
which the coming generation would be caught while still
young, and trained to think correctly. That he really believed in his own theories is evident; for he seems to have
thought that it would suffice merely to afford people of
all ages and all conditions the opportunity of frequenting
the schools and lectures that a paternal—and propagandist
—government would provide for them. If Condorcet was
ingenuous enough to fail to see the necessity of a law making attendance obligatory if it is desired that children
should frequent schools for the indoctrination of ideas
contrary to those accepted by their parents, it is only a
proof that he really believed implicitly in the excellence of
his doctrines, and that it would be enough to make them
known for them to prevail. Certainly, he lacked the knowledge which the present generation has of the experience of
nearly a century of nationalistic and party propaganda by
means of government-controlled schools. Had he realized
the necessity, he might, in his zeal for liberty, have reme-
died this defect in his plan and advocated compulsory attendance; as the Directory did a little later.[5]

In proposing to constitute the teaching body, an autonomous and self-perpetuating one, Condorcet was making
sure that, even if the Revolution should fail, revolutionary
ideas would long continue to be taught in the schools; for
such a body, once constituted of men favorable to the
Revolution—and at that time none others would have been

[5] A.-F. THÉRY, *Histoire de l'éducation en France depuis le
cinquième siècle jusqu'à nos jours,* Vol. II, p. 191, Dezobry, E.
Magdeleine et Cie., Paris, 1858.

chosen, would take care in the future to admit none but "right thinkers."

It is difficult to know what to think of Condorcet's plan for the training of physicians:

While enough of the elementary theory of the science of medicine for the practice of this profession is being taught in the institutes (the institute would correspond to the *lycée* of the present day, which is somewhere between the high school and the college in the States), the physicians from the hospitals can teach the practical part, and give instruction in surgery. In this manner and by multiplying the schools in which elementary but correct knowledge will be imparted, it will be possible to assure the poorest citizen the aid of well-informed men trained by a good method, instructed in the art of observing and free from the prejudices of ignorance as well as from those of systems.

When we compare such an inadequate provision for medical training with the exhaustive course proposed by Diderot,[6] we are almost forced to conclude that Condorcet must have held that a complete knowledge of republican principles would contribute largely even to the making of a physician.

We need not marvel at his animosity towards the classics. Educational reformers, of whatever epoch they be, somehow usually begin or end by attacking these studies; and yet they survive.

The greatness and strength of French secondary education has always lain in the sincere devotion to the classical tradi-

[6] See p. 262 *et seq.*

tion. In spite of numerous attacks levelled against this tradition from the Revolutionary period to the present day, faith in the educative value of the classics in general and for France in particular remained unshaken.[7]

From the beginning to the end of his plan, Condorcet never once lost sight of his chief objective: what to-day we call civic education. Everything else was subordinate to this aim, and it was to be achieved not only by means of instruction in the schools, but also by species of lay sermons delivered by the schoolmasters, by the celebration of national holidays, by the commemoration of great events where they took place, and of the anniversaries of great men at their birthplaces. It is legitimate to presume that great care was to be taken in selecting only such events and men to be thus glorified as would best serve to further republican ideals.

To analyse the whole plan in detail would require an entire book. Indeed, chapters have already been occupied with it; and the conclusions usually depend—as in most similar cases—upon the idea which the writer had in the beginning. Albert Duruy, in referring to it together with other educational schemes of the Legislative Assembly, writes: "Here we are no longer in the realm of the real and the possible; we are sailing in the absolutely fantastic, we are soaring in space to heights which ideology alone could attain." [8] On the other hand, Gabriel Compayré

[7] I. L. KANDEL, *The Reform of Secondary Education in France,* p. 5, Teachers College, Columbia University, New York, 1924.

[8] A. DURUY, *L'instruction publique et la Révolution,* p. 80, Hachette, Paris, 1882.

writes: "We think that an attentive perusal of Condorcet's report will convince the most indifferent, and will rally their sympathy, their admiration even, to the work of the French Revolution." [9] We shall attempt no such analysis in the present work. We give the report in full: let each one form his own opinion.

[9] G. COMPAYRÉ, *Condorcet, Rapport et projet de décret sur l'organisation générale de l'instruction publique,* Hachette, Paris, 1883. See introduction.

REPORT ON THE GENERAL ORGANIZATION
OF PUBLIC INSTRUCTION

Presented to the National Assembly on behalf of the Committee on Public Instruction, April 20, and 21, 1792

GENTLEMEN:

To offer to all individuals of the human race the means of providing for their needs, of assuring their welfare, of knowing and exercising their rights, of understanding and fulfilling their obligations.

To assure each one the facility of perfecting his skill, of rendering himself capable of the social functions to which he has the right to be called, of developing to the fullest extent those talents with which Nature has endowed him; and thereby to establish among all citizens an actual equality, thus rendering real the political equality recognized by the law.

This should be the first aim of any national education; and, from such a point of view, this education is for the government an obligation of justice.

To direct the teaching in such a manner that the perfecting of the industries shall increase the pleasures of the generality of the citizens and the welfare of those who devote themselves to them, that a greater number of men shall be capable of exercising the functions necessary to society, and that the ever-increasing progress of enlightenment shall provide an inexhaustible source of help in our needs, of remedies for our ills, of means of individual happiness and of general prosperity.

In short, to cultivate in each generation the physical, intellectual and moral faculties, and thereby contribute to the general and gradual improvement of the human race—which should be the final aim of every social institution.

This, likewise, should be the object of education, and it is for the government a duty imposed on it by the common interest of society, by that of all mankind.

But, while considering from these two points of view the immense task which has been entrusted to us, we have felt from the very first that there is one part of the general system of education which it is possible to isolate without hurt to the whole, and that it is even necessary to do this, in order to hasten the creation of the new system: that is the distribution and general organization of establishments for public instruction.

In fact, whatever differences of opinion there may be concerning the exact content of each grade of instruction, concerning the methods of teaching, concerning the greater or less degree of authority accorded to parents or granted to teachers, concerning the assembling of students in boarding schools established by the government, concerning the means by which may be joined to education properly called the development of the physical and moral faculties; nevertheless, the general organization can be the same. Moreover, the necessity of designating the locations for such establishments and of having elementary books prepared long before these institutions can function, obliges us to urge the enactment of a law concerning that part of the work which has been entrusted to us.

We have felt that in this plan for a general organization, our first care should be to make education, on the one hand, as general, on the other, as complete as circumstances will permit. All should receive equally such education as can be given to all, but, at the same time, no group of citizens should be denied a higher grade of instruction than can be given to the mass. In the first case, because it is useful to those who receive it; in the second, because it benefits even those who do not receive it.

As the first requisite of all education is that only the truth be taught, all institutions established by the government should be as free as possible from all political control, and, since this independence cannot be absolute, it results from the same principle that they must depend only on the Assembly of the Representatives of the People. Because, of all political bodies, this is the least subject to corruption, the least likely to be influenced by personal considerations, the most easily guided by the opinions of enlightened men, and, above all, as it is the one from which necessarily all changes emanate, it is the least inimical to the progress of enlightenment, the least opposed to the improvements which this progress should bring to pass.

Finally, it has seemed to us that education should not cease when the individual leaves school. It should be of concern to all ages; for there is no age at which it is not possible and profitable to learn, and this later instruction is even more necessary because the education received in childhood was confined to the narrowest limits. In fact, one of the principal causes of the ignorance in which the poorer classes of society are to-day plunged is that it is easier for them to obtain a primary education than to preserve the advantages derived from it.

We do not wish that henceforth a single man in the realm may be able to say: "The law assures me an entire equality of rights, but I am denied the means of knowing them. I should be subject only to the law, whereas my ignorance makes me subject to everything around me. In my childhood, it is true, I was taught all I needed to know, but, as I was obliged to work to earn my living, I soon lost the little learning that I had, and now nothing is left to me but the sorrow of knowing that my ignorance is not due to a decree of Nature but to the injustice of society."

We believe that the government should say to the poorer citizens: "The poverty of your parents prevented you from obtaining any but the most indispensable knowledge, but you are assured the means of preserving and understanding it. If Nature has given you talents, you can develop them, and they will not be lost, either to you or to your country."

Thus, education should be universal. That is to say, it should be within the reach of all classes of citizens. It should be equally shared, in so far as is compatible with the necessary limitations imposed by the cost, by the distribution of the population, and by the greater or less amount of time that children can devote to it. It should, in the various grades, comprise the entire sum of human knowledge, and should assure to all, of whatever age, the possibility of preserving knowledge already obtained or of acquiring new.

Finally, no branch of the government should have the authority, or even the means, of preventing the teaching of new truths or the development of theories contrary to its special policies or its momentary interests.

These have been the principles which have guided us in our work.

We have distinguished five grades of instruction under the names: (1) primary schools; (2) secondary schools; (3) institutes; (4) lyceums; (5) the National Society of Sciences and Arts.[1]

In the primary schools will be taught all that each individual will need to know for his personal guidance and for the enjoyment of the fullness of his rights. This instruction will also suffice even for those who will profit by the lessons intended to render men capable of fulfilling those simpler duties for which it is desirable that all good citizens be qualified; such as juryman, municipal official, etc.

Every village of at least four hundred inhabitants will have a school and a teacher.

As it would be unjust that in a department where the dwellings are dispersed or in small groups the inhabitants should be deprived of equal advantages, a primary school will be located in every district wherein will be found villages distant more than two thousand yards from another containing four hundred inhabitants. In these schools will be taught reading and writing—which, of necessity, will require some knowledge of grammar. To this will be added the rules of arithmetic; simple methods for measuring a plot

---

[1] These terms, as used by Condorcet, have not the same signification that they have to-day. By *secondary schools* he means what is called in France to-day the higher primary schools. *Institutes* would correspond to the *Lycées* of the present time, and *Lyceums* refers to the faculties of the universities. The *National Society* was meant to replace the *Académie*.

of ground, for estimating the height of buildings; an elementary description of the products of the country, of agricultural and industrial procedures; the fundamental moral concepts and the rules of conduct which are derived from them: in short, those principles of social order that can be made comprehensible to children.

This instruction will be divided into four courses, each of which can be completed in one year by a child of normal capacity. Such a period of four years, which permits a convenient division for schools where it will not be possible to have more than one teacher, also coincides nearly enough with the interval, for children of the poorer classes, between the time when they begin to be capable of learning and that when they can be employed in some useful work or can be regularly apprenticed.

Every Sunday, the village schoolmaster will deliver a lecture for citizens of all ages. We have considered these lectures a means of giving the young people the necessary knowledge which it has not been possible to include in their primary education. In these lectures, the principles and rules of ethics will be further expounded, as well as those of the laws of the Nation which every citizen must know, or else he would not know his rights and would, therefore, be unable to exercise them.

Thus, in these schools, the fundamental truths of the social sciences will precede their application. Neither the French Constitution nor the Declaration of the Rights of Man will be presented to any class of citizens as tables handed down from heaven that must be worshipped and believed. Enthusiasm will not be founded on prejudice or on habits acquired in childhood; and it will be possible to say: "This Declaration of the Rights of Man, which teaches you, at the same time, what you owe to society and what you have the right to demand of it; this Constitution, which you should maintain at the risk of your life, are only the development of those simple principles dictated by reason, of which you have learned, in your first years, to recognize the eternal truth." As long as there are men who will not obey reason alone, who will receive their opinions from others, in vain will all chains have been broken. Even though these borrowed opinions be true, the human race would remain no less divided in two classes: those who think and those who believe; that is to say, masters and slaves.

By thus continuing to learn throughout life, it will be possible to prevent knowledge acquired in school from being quickly forgotten, a helpful mental activity will be maintained, and the people will be taught such new laws, such agricultural practices, and such economic methods as they will need know. It will even be possible to teach them how to learn for themselves: how to look for a word in the dictionary; how to use the index of a book; how to follow, on a chart, on a plan, or on a design, narrations or descriptions, notes or extracts. These means of learning, which in a more extensive education are acquired by habit alone, must be taught directly, in an education limited to a shorter time and to a small number of lessons.

So far, we have spoken, both for children and for adults, only of direct instruction; as this is the only kind of teaching whose procedure, arrangement and extent must be determined before undertaking the organization of the institutions for public education. Other educational means will be considered in another part of our work.[2]

Thus, for instance, the national holidays, by recalling the glorious epochs of liberty, by perpetuating the memory of men whose virtues have honored their country, by celebrating acts of sacrifice and courage of which it has been the scene, will teach all men, in the cities and in the country alike, to cherish the duties which have been made known to them. Besides, in the schools, care will be taken to teach the children to be good and just. They will be made to put in practice, in their relations with each other, the principles which have been taught them. In this manner, while they are being made to acquire the habits of regulating their conduct according to these principles, they will learn to understand them better and to feel more profoundly their usefulness and justice. Books will be especially prepared both for adults and for children: books which they will find easy to read and will be disposed to procure for themselves because of their utility or their interest. Place before the simplest men interesting and easily acquired information, above all, useful information, and they will profit by it. It is the discouraging difficulty of most studies; it is the uselessness of those to which a preconceived opinion had given the preference that indisposed men to learning.

Gymnastics will not be forgotten, and care will be taken to direct the exercises in such a manner that all the powers will be equally developed, and the ill effects of habits produced by certain kinds of work will be corrected.

[2] It would seem that an additional report was intended.

If this plan is criticized for comprising too extensive an education, we can reply that with well-prepared elementary textbooks destined for the use of children, and by taking care to supply the teachers with special books from which they can learn to demonstrate a principle, to accommodate themselves to the intelligence of their pupils and to make the work easier, there need be no fear that the extent of this education will be beyond the ordinary capacity of children. Moreover, there are means of simplifying methods, and of bringing facts within reach of the most untrained minds. It is after due consideration of these means and of the results of experience, that we have prepared this plan for an elementary education that should be offered to everyone, and that all are capable of acquiring.

We might also be criticized for having, on the contrary, restricted too much an education intended for the generality of citizens. The necessity of having, in most cases, only one teacher for each school—due to the large number of schools required in order that they may be within reach of all the children—as well as the fact that the children of the poorer families can devote only a few years to study, has obliged us to confine this elementary education to narrow limits. It will be easy to extend them when an improvement in the condition of the people, a more equal distribution of wealth—both the necessary consequences of good laws— render it possible: when, at last, the decrease of the national debt and of superfluous expenditures permits a larger portion of the public revenues to be applied to really useful purposes.

The secondary schools are intended for children whose families can do without their work for a longer time, and can devote to their education a greater number of years and even a certain sum of money.

There will be a secondary school in each district, and also in each town of four thousand inhabitants. An arrangement, similar to that of which we have spoken in reference to the primary schools, will prevent any inequality in the distribution of these establishments. The course of study will be the same in all, but each school will have one, two or three teachers, according to the number of children that will be expected to attend.

Some knowledge of mathematics, of natural history, of applied chemistry, a more extensive development of the principles of ethics and of the social sciences, and elementary instruction in commerce will form the main part of the teaching.

The teachers will deliver weekly lectures which will be open to all citizens. Each school will have a small library and a small museum containing a few meteorological instruments, a few models of machines and looms and some natural history specimens. This will provide a new source of information. Without doubt, at first, these collections will be of almost no value, but they will be enlarged in time; they will be increased by gifts and exchanges, and will create a taste for observation and study; which, in turn, will contribute to their progress.

This grade of instruction may, in some respects, be regarded as general, or rather, as necessary to establish in the general instruction a more absolute equality. The rural populations are, it is true, really excluded from it, unless they are of sufficient means to be able to send their children away to school; but in such cases, those who are destined to trades must, of necessity, finish their apprenticeship in the neighboring towns, where they will receive in the secondary schools at least such instruction as they will need the most. On the other hand, farm-workers have in the year periods of rest, of which a part can be devoted to the acquirement of knowledge; whereas artisans are deprived of this leisure. Thus the advantage of private and voluntary study compensates in one case for the advantage of more extensive instruction in the other; and, in this manner, equality is still maintained, rather than destroyed, by the establishment of secondary schools.

Furthermore, as industrial processes are perfected, the work becomes more and more subdivided, and there is an increasing tendency to give each individual a purely mechanical task limited to a small number of simple movements; a task which is better and more easily done, but through habit alone, and in which the mind almost entirely ceases to function. Hence, the perfecting of the industries will become, for a part of the human race, a cause of stupidity, will produce in every nation a class of men incapable of rising above the grossest interests, and thus introduce both a humiliating inequality and the seed of dangerous troubles, unless a more extensive education offers to individuals of this class a resource against the inevitable effects of the monotony of their daily occupations.

So the advantage which the secondary schools seem to give the towns is, in reality, only another means of rendering the equality more complete.

The weekly lectures proposed for these first two grades must not be considered of little value as a means of instruction. In forty or fifty lessons a year, a great deal of knowledge can be acquired, and, as the most important subjects will be repeated every year, and the others every other year, in the end it will be entirely assimilated so that it will never be forgotten. At the same time, another part of the instruction will be entirely new, since it will treat either of new procedures in agriculture or the mechanical arts, of new discoveries and observations, or of the interpretation of the general laws as they are promulgated, of explanations of the acts of the government, when they are of universal interest. This will tend to excite curiosity, to render these lectures more interesting, and will maintain a public spirit and a taste for work.

It need not be feared that the seriousness of this teaching will repel the people. For a man occupied with physical labor, rest alone is a pleasure, and a certain intenseness of thought is a real relaxation; it is for him what bodily exercise is for the scholar who is devoted to sedentary studies— a means of preventing those of his powers that are not sufficiently exercised by his habitual occupations from becoming numb.

The farmer in the country, the artisan in the city will not disdain knowledge when once he has realized, either from his own experience or from that of others, that it is useful. If at first he is attracted by curiosity, soon he will be held by interest. Frivolity, distaste for serious things, disdain for what is only useful are not the vices of poor men; and that feigned stupidity which is born of subjection and humility will soon disappear when free men find at hand the means of breaking the last and most shameful of their shackles.

The third grade of instruction will comprise the elements of all human knowledge. This instruction, considered as a part of general education, is absolutely complete. It includes all that is necessary to enable a man to fit himself to fulfill those public functions which require the highest degree of enlightenment, or to devote himself successfully to the most abstruse studies. In these schools will be prepared the teachers for secondary schools, and also those for primary schools who were prepared in the secondary schools, will receive further training.[3]

The number of institutes has been fixed at one hundred and ten, and they will be established in all departments.

In them will be taught not only what it is useful to know as a man, as a citizen, no matter what profession one may intend to follow, but also all that can be needed for each of the great divisions of these professions; such as agriculture, mechanical arts, military science: and even such medical knowledge as is necessary for simple practitioners, for midwives and for veterinarians will be added.

In glancing over the list of professors, it will perhaps be noticed that the subjects to be taught have not been assigned according to a philosophic division, and that the physical and mathematical sciences occupy a very great place, while the subjects which dominated in the old system of education appear to be neglected.

We have considered it best to apportion the sciences according to the methods which they employ, and, consequently, according to the grouping of knowledge which exists most usually among men of learning, or which it is easiest for them to complete.[4]

---

[3] Condorcet makes no provision for Normal Schools.

[4] The division adopted by Condorcet contains four categories of subjects: (1) the mathematical and physical sciences; (2)

A philosophic classification would probably be only embarrassing and almost impracticable in application. In effect, should the divers faculties of the mind be taken as a basis? But the study of each science exercises them all, and helps to develop and perfect them. How is it possible to ascribe a certain part of human knowledge to memory, to imagination, to reason, if, for instance, when a child is required to demonstrate at the board a geometrical proposition, he cannot succeed without making use, at the same time, of his memory, his imagination and his reason? Without doubt, the knowledge of facts would be placed in the category attributed to memory; then natural history should be classed with the history of nations, the study of the arts with the study of languages; they would be separated from chemistry, political science, physics and metaphysics—all sciences with which the knowledge of facts is closely connected; both by the nature of things and by the method itself of treating them. Should then the nature of subjects be taken as a basis? But the same subject, according to the manner of considering it, belongs to absolutely different branches of science. Sciences, thus classified, require qualities of mind that are rarely united in the same person; and it would be very difficult to find, perhaps to train men capable of adapting themselves to such divisions of teaching. Certain sciences would not be relevant to certain professions, branches of them would not be interesting to the same mind, and these divisions would be wearisome for teacher and pupil alike.

the moral and political sciences; (3) applied sciences; (4) literature and fine arts. This division is based upon the methods employed in each category.

Whatever other philosophic basis be chosen, there would still be obstacles of this kind. Moreover it was necessary to assign a certain limit to each part, and maintain among them a sort of equilibrium. With a philosophic classification this could be done only by bringing together in teaching what had been separated in classification.

We have then imitated in our distribution of subjects the order which the human intelligence has followed in the development of knowledge, without attempting to compel it to follow another conforming to that which we should assign for teaching. Genius wishes to be free, all servitude brands it, and we often see it bearing still, when it is in all its vigor, the mark of the irons which were placed on it when its first germ was developing in the exercises of childhood. Thus, since a distribution of studies is absolutely necessary, we were obliged to prefer that which has spontaneously developed in the last half-century, during which all branches of human knowledge have made rapid progress.

It is for several reasons that a certain preference has been given to mathematical and physical sciences. In the first place, for men who do not devote themselves to prolonged meditation, who do not make a special study of any branch of knowledge, the study—even though elementary—of these sciences is the surest means of developing their intellectual faculties, of learning to reason correctly and to analyse well their ideas. It is without doubt possible, by close application to literature, to grammar, to history, to political science, to philosophy in general, to acquire accuracy, method, and a sound and profound knowledge of logic, and, nevertheless, be ignorant of the natural sciences. Great examples have

337

proved this; but elementary knowledge of these same subjects has not this advantage: it makes use of reason but it does not develop it. This is because, in the natural sciences, the ideas are simpler, more circumscribed, the language is more perfect, the same words are used more consistently to express the same ideas. The elements constitute a real part of the science, confined to narrow limits but complete in itself. Again they provide a means of training the mind, which is within the grasp of a greater number of intelligences, especially in youth. There is not a child—unless he is absolutely stupid—who cannot acquire to some extent the habit of application by means of elementary lessons in natural history or agriculture. These sciences are a remedy for prejudgments and narrowness of mind, which, if not surer, is, at least, more universal than philosophy itself. They are useful in all professions, and it is easy to see how much more so they would be if they were more uniformly diffused. Those who follow the progress of the sciences see the time approaching when the practical utility of their application will reach an extent which no one would have dared hope, when the progress of physics ought to bring about a happy revolution in industries; and the surest means of hastening this revolution is to spread a knowledge of the sciences among all classes of society, and to facilitate the study of them.

Finally, we have yielded to the general attitude of mind which, in Europe, seems to incline more and more to these sciences. We have felt that, on account of the progress of the human race, these studies which offer its activity an eternal and inexhaustible aliment were becoming the more necessary, as the improvement in the social order must leave less scope for ambition or for greed; that, in a country where they wish to unite at last peace and liberty in eternal bonds, it ought to be possible, without tedium, without sinking into idleness, to consent to be only a man and a citizen; and that it was important to turn towards useful objectives the need of action, the thirst for glory for which the state of a well-governed society does not afford a vast enough field of action, in short, to substitute the desire to enlighten men for the desire to govern them.

In the part of the former system of education which corresponds to this third grade of instruction, only a small number of subjects were comprised. We ought to include them all. It seemed formerly that only theologians or preachers were to be prepared. We aspire to produce enlightened men.

The former system was no less vicious in its divisions of classes than in the choice and distribution of subjects.

Throughout six years, a progressive study of Latin formed the basis of instruction. In connection with this study were taught incidentally the general principles of grammar, some knowledge of geography and of history, and some notions of the art of speaking and writing.

Four professors are now designated to teach these subjects; but the subjects are separated, and each teacher teaches only one branch of knowledge. This arrangement, as it is more favorable to the progress of the students, will more than compensate for the reduction in the number of teachers.

Some may find that the Latin language is too much neglected. But from what point of view should a language be considered in a general education? Is it not enough if students are brought to the point where they can read the really useful books written in the language and are able to make further progress without teachers? Can a profound knowledge of a foreign language and of the beauties of style offered by the works of men of genius who have used it be regarded as general knowledge which every educated man, every citizen who is destined to fill the more important positions in society must have?

By right of what special privilege should Latin alone be more extensively taught, when the length of time available for instruction and the very aim of education oblige us to limit it in all branches to elementary knowledge, and to let the inclination of the students guide them freely in the choice of the subjects which they wish to cultivate afterwards? Is it to be considered the universal language of scholars, in spite of the fact that it is losing every day this advantage? But an elementary knowledge of Latin suffices to read their books; but there does not exist a single really important work on science, on philosophy, on politics which has not been translated; but all the facts which these books contain can be found, better explained, together with new facts, in books written in the vernacular. Reading originals is rightfully useful only to those whose object is not the study of the science itself, but of its history.

Finally—since all must be said—as all sorts of preconceptions should now disappear, a prolonged and assiduous study of the languages of the ancient peoples, a study which would require the reading of the books which they have left us, would perhaps be more harmful than useful.

We seek, in education, to make known facts, and these books are full of errors. We seek to train the mind, and these books can lead it astray. We are so far removed from the ancients, we are so far ahead of them on the road to truth that we must have well-fortified minds if these precious relics are to enrich them without corrupting them.

Even as models of the art of writing, of eloquence, of poetry, the works of the ancients can be of use only to minds already fortified by previous studies. Of what use, in fact, are models which cannot be imitated without constant changes, rendered necessary by the differences of customs, of language, of religion, of ideas? I shall cite only one example. Demosthenes spoke from the tribune to all the Athenians assembled before him. The law which his eloquence obtained was voted by the Nation itself, and copies of it circulated afterwards slowly among the orators and their pupils. Now, a speech is made not before the Nation, but before its representatives; and this speech, made known by the press, has as many dispassionate and severe judges as there are citizens in France who are interested in public affairs. If a captivating, passionate, deluding eloquence can sometimes lead astray popular assemblies, those who are deceived by it have only themselves to consider; the consequences of their fault will affect them alone. But the representatives of the people who, deluded by an orator, would permit themselves to be guided by anything but the dictates of their reason would betray their trust, as they are obliged to consider the interests of others, and would soon lose the public confidence, on which alone every representative constitution is based. Thus, this same eloquence which was necessary to ancient constitutions would be to ours a germ of corruption and destruction. It was, at that time, permissible, useful perhaps, to arouse the emotions of the people. We owe it to them to seek only to enlighten them. Consider first all the influence that this change in the form of the constitutions, all that the art of printing can have on the rules of the art of public speaking, and decide afterwards whether, in the early years of youth, the ancient orators should be given as models.

You owe the French Nation an education on the level with the spirit of the eighteenth century, with that philosophy which, while enlightening the present generation, presages, prepares and already anticipates the superior intelligence to which the necessary progress of the human race is leading the future generations.

These are our principles; and it is according to a philosophy that is untrameled, independent of all authority, free from all old habits, that we have chosen and classified the subjects of public instruction. According to this same philosophy, we have considered the moral and political sciences an essential part of the common instruction.

In fact, how is it possible to hope to raise the ethical standards of a people, unless the standards of the men who are able to enlighten it, who are destined to guide it are based on a rigorous and exact analysis of the moral sentiments, of the ideas which result from them, and of the principles of justice which are the consequence?

"Good laws," said Plato, "are those which the citizens love more than life." Indeed, how could laws be good, if to enforce them, it were necessary to employ any means contrary to the will of the people, and thus uphold justice by tyranny? But, in order that citizens may love the laws without ceasing to be truly free, in order that they may preserve that independence of spirit without which devotion to liberty is only a passion and not a virtue, they must know the principles of natural justice—these essential rights of man—of which the laws are only the development and the application. It is necessary to know how to distinguish in the laws the consequences of these rights from the means which have been more or less happily devised to enforce them; to love the former, because they were dictated by justice, the latter, because they were inspired by wisdom. It is necessary to know how to distinguish that devotion of the reason which is due to laws that it approves from that submission, that formal support which the citizen still owes the laws, even though he recognizes that they are imperfect or dangerous. It is necessary to know how to judge the laws and still love them.

Never will a people enjoy a stable and assured liberty if instruction in the political sciences is not general, if it is not independent of all social institutions, if the enthusiasm aroused in the souls of the citizens is not guided by reason, if they are capable of being inspired by anything but truth, if, while attaching men by habit, by imagination, by sentiment to the constitution, to the laws and to liberty, you do not prepare for them, by a general education, the means of achieving a more perfect constitution, of making better laws, and of acquiring a more complete liberty. For it is the same with liberty, with equality, with these great political subjects as it is with the other sciences: there exists in the order of things possible a limit which Nature wishes us to be able to approach, but which it is impossible for us to attain.

This third grade of instruction will give those who profit by it a real superiority that is rendered inevitable by the diversity of the functions of society. The necessity of such a superiority is only an additional motive for desiring that it be one of reason and of true enlightenment, and, consequently, for endeavoring to procure learned men and not clever men, finally, for not forgetting that the inconveniences which are caused by this superiority diminish as the number of individuals who share it increases, that the more enlightened they are, the less dangerous it is, and, therefore, a superiority of reason and enlightenment is the only remedy for a superiority of mere ability which, instead of giving help and guidance to ignorance, seeks only means of leading it astray.

The instruction will be given in different courses, some related, others independent, though given by the same professor. These courses will be distributed in such a manner that it will be possible for a student to follow four of them at the same time, or to follow only one, to complete the entire curriculum in five years, if he has great ability, or, if he is less apt, to limit himself to only a part of it in the same period of time. It will even be possible to stop at a given point in each science, to devote to it more or less time. In this way, different combinations can be arranged to suit all variations of talent or personal needs.

Once a month, the professors will deliver public lectures. As these lectures are intended for the more learned who are able to acquire knowledge for themselves, they need not be more frequent. They will treat principally of scientific discoveries and experiments, of new observations and procedures useful to industries. By *new* is meant what is not yet a matter of common knowledge, of generally accepted procedure, but still not beyond the range of elementary instruction. Each college will have its library, its museum, its botanical and agricultural gardens. These institutions will be under the care of a curator, and it is evident that all who possess already some small amount of knowledge will be able to acquire more from these collections and from the elucidations which the curator or the professors will not refuse to give.

Finally, as in this grade of instruction the teaching must not be limited to simple explanations, and the students must be trained by means of demonstrations, discussions, or even compositions—for it will be necessary to ascertain whether they understand, whether they retain what they have learned, and whether their intellectual faculties are acquiring activity and strength—a certain number of seats should be reserved in each classroom for those who, while not being regular students, and, consequently, not subject to the questions or the work demanded of the class, might wish to follow a course of instruction or be present at a few lessons.

This sort of publicity, regulated in such a manner that it will not disturb the order of the teaching, would have three advantages. First, it would afford a means of instruction for those of the citizens who have not been able to receive a complete education, or who have not sufficiently profited by it, and make it possible for them to acquire at any age such knowledge as may be useful to them. Thus the immediate benefit which can result from the progress of the sciences would not be exclusively reserved for scholars and for youth. Second, parents could be present at the lessons of their children. Third, the young people, placed to some extent before the eyes of the public, would be more inspired with emulation, and would early acquire the habit of speaking with assurance, with facility and with propriety; a habit which a few solemn exercises could not fail to make them acquire.

In garrison towns, the professors of military science can be required to deliver weekly lectures for the soldiers. The principal subject of these lectures would be explanations of the military laws and regulations, care being taken to dwell on their spirit and motives; for the soldier's obedience to discipline ought not to differ from the citizen's submission to the law: it should be equally enlightened, and, to the same extent, commanded by reason and love of country rather than by force and fear of punishment.

While enough of the elementary theory of the science of medicine for the practice of this profession is being taught in the institutes, the physicians from the hospitals can teach the practical part, and give instruction in surgery. In this manner, and by multiplying the schools in which elementary but correct knowledge will be imparted, it will be possible to assure to the poorest citizens the aid of well-informed men, trained by a good method, instructed in the art of observing and free from the prejudices of ignorance as well as from those of systems.

In seaports, special professors of hydrography and of pilotage can teach navigation to those students who have already been prepared by the courses in mathematics, astronomy and physics which will form a part of the general instruction. Elsewhere, with the aid of these same courses, a small number of teachers will suffice to train other students in architecture and engineering. In all subjects, this system of common instruction will render simpler and less expensive all kinds of special training which will be needed for the public welfare.

The principles of ethics that will be taught in the institutes will be those which, being founded on natural sentiments and on reason, are common to all men. The Constitution, by recognizing the right of each individual to choose his religion, by establishing a complete equality among all the inhabitants of France, does not permit the introduction into public instruction of any teaching which, by excluding the children of a part of the citizens, would destroy the equality of social advantages, and give to particular dogmas an advantage contrary to the liberty of opinions. It is then absolutely necessary to separate ethics from any special religion, and not to permit in public instruction the teaching of any religious creed.

Each religion should be taught in its own temples and by its own ministers. Parents can then, whatever may be their opinions concerning the necessity of one religion or another, send, without reluctance, their children to the national schools; and the government will not have usurped rights over consciences under pretext of enlightening and guiding them.

Besides, how much better it is to base ethics on the principles of reason alone! Whatever changes the opinions of a man may undergo in the course of his lifetime, principles established upon this basis will remain always equally true, they will be always as invariable as their basis, they will protect him against attempts to lead his conscience astray, they will preserve his independence and his rectitude; and there will no longer be seen the distressing sight of men who imagine that they fulfill their duties by violating the most sacred rights, and that they obey God by betraying their country.

Even those who still believe in founding ethics on some particular religion should approve of this separation; for without doubt it is not the truth of the principles of ethics that they make depend on their dogmas, it is only that they think that men will find in these dogmas more powerful motives for being just. Will not these motives acquire more power over every mind capable of reflecting, if they are used to fortify only what reason and inner feeling have already dictated?

Can it then be said that the idea of such a separation is too far above the present stage of enlightenment of the people? No, surely not; for, since it is here a question of public education, to tolerate error would be to become party to it; not to proclaim truth would be to betray it. Even if it were true that political considerations should still continue for a time to defile the laws of a nation, even if this insidious and weak doctrine should find an excuse in the stupidity which it pleases some to attribute to the people in order to have a pretext for deceiving and oppressing them, at least that education which is to hasten the coming of the time when such considerations will be unnecessary must concern itself with the whole truth and nothing but the truth.

We have given the name *lyceum* to the fourth grade of instruction. In this grade, all the sciences will be taught in their entirety. It is in the lyceums that scholars will prepare themselves—those who will make of the cultivation of their minds, of the perfecting of their own faculties one of the chief occupations of their lives, also those who intend following one of the professions in which great success can be obtained only by assiduous study of one or more of the sciences. The professors also will be prepared here. It is by means of these institutions that each generation will be able to transmit to the following generation what it has received from the preceding, and what it has been able to add.

We propose to establish in France nine lyceums. Learning, by proceeding from several centres at the same time, will be spread with greater equality, and will be distributed among a great number of citizens. This will be a sure means of retaining in the departments a greater number of enlightened men who, if they were obliged to go to Paris to complete their studies, would be tempted to remain there. According to the wording of the Constitution, this consideration is very important.

In effect, the law requires that deputies be chosen from the citizens of each department, and, even if this were not obligatory, the common welfare would nevertheless render it necessary at least in the greater number of cases. The judges and government officials are likewise appointed in the departments where they exercise their functions. How could it be maintained that everything has been done to prepare for the Nation men capable of fulfilling the most important functions, if one city alone afforded them the means of preparing themselves? How could it be possible to assert that the means of developing themselves have been offered to all talents, that none have been neglected, if, in as extensive a realm as France, these means could be found in only one place?

349

Besides, it would not be without detriment to the success, and, above all, to the equality of the general education to open for professors only one school, and that one in Paris. The number of lyceums has been fixed at nine because, by comparing this number with that of the great universities of England, of Italy and of Germany, it seemed to correspond with the needs of the population of France. In fact, without the number of students being so great that it will be detrimental to the teaching, one man in every sixteen hundred will be able to attend a lyceum. This proportion is sufficient for an education required for only a small number of professions, and that will concern itself with only the more advanced instruction.

The instruction which we propose to provide is more complete, the curriculum is more in accord with the present state of the sciences in Europe than in any establishment of learning in foreign countries. We have felt that no sort of inferiority would befit the French Nation; and, since each year brings new progress in the sciences, not to surpass what has already been done would be in itself an inferiority.

Some of the lyceums will be situated where they will attract young people from abroad. The commercial advantage of this is of small importance to a great nation; but the advantage of spreading wider the principles of liberty and equality, the reputation that a people acquires by the concourse of strangers who come to it to seek light, the friends that this people gains among these youths reared in its bosom, the immense advantage of rendering its language universal, the fraternity among nations that can result; all these of a nobler utility should not be over-looked.

Some of the lyceums must then be located within a short distance of the frontiers, and, in their general distribution throughout the realm, care should be taken to avoid too great a disproportion in the distances between them. Those cities which already possess great establishments devoted either to teaching or to science have the right to a prefer-ence based on economic reasons and the interest of educa-tion as well.

Finally, it has seemed to us that the less important cities, where the general attention of the citizens would be drawn to these institutions, where the spirit of science would not be stifled by great business interests, where public opinion would not be strong enough to exert a dangerous influence on teaching and subject it to local views, would offer more advantages than the great commercial cities, from which the higher cost of living would keep away the children of poorer families, and of which parents would fear the more powerful seductions and the more numerous occasions for dissipation and expense. We have felt, however, that these considerations should not apply to Paris. The unanimous judgment of Europe, which for the past century has held this city to be one of the capitals of the learned world, would not permit it. It is with due regard for these divers considerations, and by yielding more or less to each of them that we have determined the locations of the lyceums.

The lyceum of Paris will differ from the others only in the fact that it will provide a more complete instruction in the ancient and modern languages, and perhaps by having some institutions dedicated to the fine arts—subjects which, by their very nature, require only one school for all France. We believed that an institution where all known languages would be taught, where men of all countries could find an interpreter, where it would be possible to analyse and compare all the methods by which men have formed and classified their ideas ought to make some important discoveries, and facilitate the creation of a closer union between peoples; a union which should no longer be regarded as a philosophic chimera.

In the lyceums, young men whose minds have already been trained will learn by studying the ancients. There will be no danger to them in these studies; as they will be capable of estimating the effects of the differences of customs, of government and of language, as well as of the progress of opinions and ideas, and they will be able, at the same time, to feel and to judge the beauty of their models.

The instruction in the lyceums will be open to both students and auditors. More than once in Paris, members of the Academies have been seen frequenting regularly courses at the Royal College of France, and, still more often, present on occasions when the subject of the particular lesson possessed for them some special interest. Besides, the more complete libraries, the more extensive museums, the greater botanical and agricultural gardens will be still another means of instruction; to which may also be added the public lectures and discussions of the professors, because in them it will be possible to treat questions which special circumstances render interesting, and which cannot enter into lessons necessarily subject to a regular routine.

In these four grades of instruction, the tuition will be absolutely free.

A constitutional enactment decrees that the tuition shall be free in the first grade: and the second, which can also be regarded as general, must likewise be free, or there would be created an inequality in favor of the richer classes who are taxed according to their wealth, but who would pay for education only according to the number of children that they would send to the secondary schools. As for the other grades, it is important to afford the children of the poorer classes, who are the most numerous, the possibility of developing their talents. This is not only a means of assuring the country more citizens able to serve it, the sciences more men capable of contributing to their progress, but also of reducing that inequality due to difference of wealth, and of bringing together the classes which this difference tends to separate. The natural order creates in society no other inequalities than those of wealth and education,[5] and by extending education the effects of both of these causes of inequality will be lessened. The advantages of education, if no longer the exclusive privilege of opulence, will be less obvious and, consequently, less dangerous to equality. The advantage alone of being born rich will be counterbalanced by the equal, even the superior knowledge which will naturally be acquired by those who have an additional incentive.

Moreover, as the different lyceums and institutes will not each attract an equal number of students, there would be

[5] Certainly a most extraordinary assertion!

353

too great a difference in the salaries of the teachers if the tuition were not free. The opulent cities, the fertile districts would have all the able teachers and would, therefore, possess still another advantage. Some branches of science— and not always the least useful—will attract fewer students than others; hence it would be necessary to devise some different manner of paying the teachers, or else permit too great an inequality among them, which would be harmful to that equilibrium among the several branches of human knowledge that is so necessary to their real progress.

Let us further observe that a student in an institute or a lyceum where the tuition is free can follow at the same time a great number of courses without increasing the expenses of his parents, that he is able to vary his studies, to test his inclinations and his abilities; whereas, if each new course calls for new expenditure, he is obliged to restrict his activities to narrow limits, to sacrifice often to economy an important part of his education. A disadvantage which exists, moreover, only for the less wealthy families.

Besides, since the teachers must receive fixed salaries while the tuition demanded of the students should necessarily be very small, there would be no great economy; and the voluntary expenditure that would result would be less of a burden to the wealthy families than to those who make sacrifices in order to procure for their children, who have given evidence of talents in their early years, the means of cultivating them and using them to advance their fortunes.

Moreover, the spirit of emulation, which would make professors desire to increase the number of their students—

and at the same time increase their revenues—does not proceed from sentiments so exalted that we may permit ourselves to deplore its loss. Ought it not rather to be feared that the results of this emulation would be rivalries between institutions of learning, that the teachers would seek to shine rather than to teach, that their methods—even their opinions—would be based on the desire to attract a great number of students, that they would yield to the fear of losing them by combating certain prejudices, by attacking certain interests?

After having freed education from all kinds of authority, let us be careful not to subject it to public opinion: it should anticipate it, correct it, form it, and not follow and obey it.

Above the primary schools, education ceases to be absolutely general. But we have felt that the double objective of assuring the country all the talents that could serve it, and of not depriving any individual of the advantage of developing those with which he has been endowed would be attained, if the children who show the most aptitude in a given grade of instruction should be chosen to enter the next higher, and maintained at the expense of the national treasury; they would be called National Scholars. According to the plan proposed by the committee, 3850 children, or thereabouts, would receive a sum sufficient for their maintenance. Of these, 1000 would attend the institutes and 600 the lyceums. About 400 would come out each year to take up useful employments in society or to devote themselves to the sciences. Never in any country has the government opened for the poorer classes a more abundant source of prosperity and learning; never has it used more powerful means to maintain the natural equality of man. Not alone will the study of the sciences be encouraged, but also that modest industry which seeks only to make easier the admittance to a laborious profession will not be neglected. As it is desirable that there be also rewards for diligence, for love of work and for integrity, even when not accompanied by brilliant qualities, the government will provide for other National Scholars their apprenticeship in industries of general utility.

In the primary and elementary schools, the choice of elementary textbooks will be the result of a competition open to all citizens—to all who are desirous of contributing to public education; but the authors of such books for the institutes will be designated. No restrictions will be placed on the professors of the lyceums save that of teaching the science of which the courses confided to them bear the name. The scope of the elementary books for the institutes, the desire to see celebrated men assume the task of preparing them, the improbability that they would be willing to do this unless they were assured that their works would be adopted, the difficulty of judging in these cases, have led us to determine not to submit these books to a competition. We have argued that if a man justly renowned in any branch of science is disposed to prepare an elementary book in this science, and looks upon the task as a proof of his zeal for public education, for the advancement of knowledge, the work will be good. As this has reference to a man renowned in Europe, there need be no fear of making a mistake in the choice. If, on the contrary, a competion were held, what assurance should we have of obtaining a good book? How is it possible to decide among ten books, for instance, each one an elementary course in mathematics or physics in two volumes? Is it absolutely certain that the judges would take the trouble to make a careful examination? Is it absolutely certain that it is even possible for them to judge correctly? Might not some philosophic views, some subtle and ingenious ideas in a book incline them in its favor at the expense of method or clearness?

In the first three grades of instruction, the elements alone will be taught to a greater or less extent: there is for every subject, and for every one of its branches a limit that must not be passed. The government should, therefore, designate the books which are suitable; but, in the lyceums, where all of a subject is to be taught, the professor should choose the methods. There is an inestimable advantage in this: it will prevent education from ever being corrupted; for it is certain that if, by a combination of political circumstances, the elementary textbooks should be infected by dangerous doctrines, the freedom of the teaching in the lyceums would counteract the effects of this corruption; thus, it need never be feared that the language of truth will be silenced.

Finally, the last grade of instruction is the National Society of Sciences and Arts; instituted to supervise and direct the educational establishments, to concern itself with the perfecting of the sciences and arts, to seek, to encourage, to apply and to spread abroad useful discoveries.

It is no longer the special instruction of children, or even of adults, that is under consideration, it is the instruction of the entire generation, the general perfecting of the human intelligence. It is not a matter of providing more extensive knowledge for such and such an individual in particular, it is the entire mass of knowledge that must be enriched by new facts, it is for the human intelligence that new means of hastening its progress, of multiplying its discoveries must be prepared.

We propose to divide this society into four classes which will hold their meetings separately.

A single society, if too large, would be inactive, or if reduced to too few members for each science, would not excite emulation; and the unfortunate choice of members—which it would be impossible to avoid always—would be too dangerous.

Moreover, it would be formed of too many heterogeneous parts; the scholars who would compose it would speak in manners too diverse, and the greater number of the lectures and discussions would be uninteresting to too great a number of the hearers.

On the other hand, we have wished to avoid the multiplicity of divisions: a single group occupied with the same science is too disposed to acquire a personal spirit, to become a sort of corporation.

Finally, it is of importance to the progress of the sciences to bring together rather than to separate those which have common interests. While each science makes progress and enriches itself by discoveries of its own, these points of contact multiply, and the application of one science to another offers a fruitful harvest of useful discoveries; and such should be the effect of this increase of knowledge that soon no science will be isolated, none will be foreign to any other.

It is according to these views that we have arranged the

divisions of the National Society. The first class comprises all the mathematical sciences.[6]

For a century, no learned society has thought of separating them. Passing by imperceptible degrees from those which make use only of reckoning to those founded only on observation to-day, almost all can use the two means of extending human knowledge; and it is desirable that those who know best how to use the one or the other of these means of discovery should help one another, should teach one another, that the chemist, the physicist, should prevent the botanist from confining himself to the simple listing of names, to too bare a description of plants; or should recall to more useful work the geometrician who might be passing his time with questions of numbers, with metaphysical subtilities.

The second class includes the moral and political sciences. It would be superfluous, without doubt, to prove that they ought not to be separated and that they ought not to be associated with the others.

The third class comprises the sciences of applied mathematics and physics.

Here we are more at variance with the commonly accepted ideas. This class contains medicine, mechanical arts, agriculture and navigation.

But, in the first place, we have felt obliged to treat the usual applications of the sciences as we have treated the sciences themselves.

We have found that the divergency was even less great and the points of contact more numerous. A physician in

[6] Condorcet includes physics and chemistry, because they use mathematics.

charge of hospitals, for instance, who would be concerned with the moving of patients in certain illnesses for serious operations or the dressing of wounds, would derive advantage from contact with mechanicians and constructors. A distinction as marked as that between pure mathematics and certain branches of the physical sciences cannot be made in this case, and medicine could not be separated from veterinary surgery or agriculture, nor agriculture from construction or hydraulics without severing useful connections.

It remained then to be seen whether any one of these branches could require for itself alone the creation of a separate society. Medicine, agriculture, and navigation were the ones that appeared to have the greater claims, and it could even be alleged in their favor that such institutions have already existed.

But in the first place, a naval society, for instance, could not subsist unless all the sciences on which navigation is based were included in it. It would then be a society of the sciences specially applied to marine affairs, and there would be duplications of some of the functions of other societies. In the same way, a medical society could maintain itself only by calling on anatomists, botanists and chemists. An agricultural society would need botanists, mineralogists and specialists in political economy and commerce.

Now, what would be the result? A lessening of esteem for these particular societies; because the scholars of whom they would be composed would naturally consider membership in the society which would comprise the generality of the sciences an object more worthy of their ambition.

It would then be necessary either that a man should

belong to two or three societies at the same time—which would have no other advantage than to feed his vanity, and would be detrimental to equality—or else that he should be permitted to pass from one society to another— which would produce continual changes, hurtful to those societies enjoying less consideration which would, in consequence, be habitually abandoned—or finally that he should remain irrevocably attached to one of them—which would have the no less great disadvantage of excluding from societies devoted to a single science men who might be candidates for those in which all the sciences are united.

Moreover, I ask how many men are there, for instance, who, without being great enough geometricians or able enough mechanicians to be admitted to such a learned society, could nevertheless hasten the progress of naval science? How many agriculturists who, without having a reputation as botanists, have really contributed to some great improvement in agriculture? How many physicians and surgeons are famous as such, and not for their discoveries in science? A talent for an applied science distinct from a talent for the pure science is not possessed by a sufficiently great number of men to justify the formation of a special society; and, far from being detrimental to these important branches of science, it would, on the contrary, be an advantage for them to be united in one great society in which each of them would have a few members.

Besides, these societies, if separate, would become to some extent a power over those who follow the corresponding professions; whereas, if united, they would not have power over the generality of citizens divided among these various professions.

The fourth class includes grammar, letters, fine arts and classics.

In public education and in the National Society, the fine arts as well as the mechanical arts should be considered only in relation to the theory of the art. The object is to bridge the space which separates the abstract science from the practical—the philosophy of an art from the simple practice of it. It is in the studio of the painter, as in the workshop of the craftsman or the workman, that the art or craft itself should be learned by means of actual practice. Thus, our schools will not replace work in the studio, but will teach the principles of which the application must be learned elsewhere.

This will be the means of creating for all the arts, for all the crafts even, a more enlightened procedure, of uniting by the bonds of a common motive men whose occupations keep them farthest apart. For never have we lost sight of the idea of destroying all kinds of inequality, of multiplying among men whom Nature and the law attach to the same soil and the same interests, relations which will render their union more harmonious and more intimate.

The distribution of work in the great societies creates between the intellectual faculties of men a distance which is incompatible with that equality without which liberty is for the less enlightened classes only a deceptive illusion; and there are only two means of eliminating this distance: to stop everywhere, if it were possible, the progress of the human intelligence, and condemn all mankind to eternal ignorance—source of all evils—or else, to leave to the intellect all its activity, and establish equality by spreading knowledge. This is the fundamental principle of our work, and we need not fear in the eighteenth century any reproach for having preferred to lift up and set free, rather than to level by casting down and keeping down by force.

This teaching of the arts and crafts, progressing by degrees from the primary schools to the lyceums, will give to all classes of society the knowledge of the principles that should guide the practice of these same arts and crafts. It will make known promptly everywhere new discoveries and new methods, and will make known only those whose value has been proved by experience. It will arouse the industry of the workers and, at the same time, by preventing it from going astray, will forestall the ruin to which their activity and their talents expose them when ignorance of the theory leaves them to their imagination. Nothing perhaps will hasten more the coming of the time when the French Nation will reach the point to which it would have risen long ago, if the defects of its laws and constitution had not arrested its efforts and restrained its industry.

According to the plan which we propose for the National Society, each individual can be a member of only one class, but may, however, pass from one class to another. There is no objection to this, because each class will be too limited to admit scholars who do not essentially belong to it, because no class would admit any member who naturally belongs to another, because, finally, no class will be considered inferior to another. For these reasons, passing from one class to another will be very rare.

We have already stated that each class of the Society will hold its meetings separately. These meetings will be open to the public; but only in order that those who cultivate the sciences may listen to the papers and follow the discussions. There will be no necessity of being understood by the audience, of keeping within the limits of their capacity, of interesting or amusing them, to influence the order of the meetings, the form of the discussions or the choice of the papers read.

The members of one class will have the right to sit with all the others, to take part in discussions, read reports and have their works included in the collections published by each one. Thus, the rule permitting membership in only one class will deprive of no real advantage either the sciences or those who cultivate several of them at the same time. Vanity alone will lose the advantage of adding to a name some few more words.

Each class will be divided into sections. Each section will consist of a fixed number of members, of whom one half will reside in Paris, the other in various departments.

This division into sections is rendered necessary by the fact that the National Society is charged with the supervision of education. It is likewise useful in order to make sure that no branch of science will ever be neglected even for a short time. This is one of the greatest advantages that can result from the establishment of a learned society.

In fact, each science has its periods of favor and disfavor. Minds are naturally inclined to those in which new means offer a vast field for brilliant and useful discoveries; whereas, in others, talent has almost exhausted all known methods, and waits for genius to discover new ones. Thus, these divisions will be useful until the time when the sciences, passing beyond their present limits, will approach and, to a certain extent, penetrate each other so that they will form only a single one.

The fixing of the number of members seemed to us equally useful. Otherwise, a learned society is no longer a cause of emulation; moreover, it ceases to be able to govern itself, it is forced to confide its scientific work to a committee, and equality within it is abolished.

This can be seen in the Royal Society of London. How could seven or eight hundred members have an equal right to read papers and have reports printed, or to judge which of them deserve preference? Is it not evident that a very great majority of them would not be capable of producing good works or even of judging them? It is then necessary either to restrict the number of members or to have, as in London, an aristocratic committee, or else the result will be an absolute nullity.

One half of these scholars will reside regularly in the departments. This is a more equitable distribution, and is necessary for scientific observation—of which there is an immediate need. It will likewise have the advantage of spreading knowledge more uniformly, of bringing it within reach of a greater number of citizens, of creating a more general taste for study and for useful research, of making the rewards of talent and of knowledge better known, of providing everywhere teachers and aids for the ignorant, enemies to charlatanism—who will be quick to expose and to conquer it, of leaving prejudice no refuge where it can take root anew, strengthen and spread.

The members of the National Society will elect the new members. If, at its foundation, the Society is composed almost entirely of enlightened men, we may rest assured that it will continue to be such an assembly. During the past two years, much has been written against the dominating spirit of the Academies, but in vain has been sought a single example of a real discovery that they have rejected, of a man whose reputation has survived him who has been excluded other than in consequence of political or religious intolerance, of a scholar renowned for works known in Europe who has suffered repeated refusals. It is because the selection of members was based on publicly known documents—documents that do not disappear, because errors of judgment can be proved, because scholars and men of letters depend on public opinion, and, above all, because they are answerable to all Europe for their choice. This last observation is borne out by experience, which has proved that the more experts in any branch of science there were in foreign countries, the less open to criticism were the choices made. This is still another one of the reasons which have caused us to limit the number of the members of the National Society. In fact, as long as the list can be almost entirely filled by names known throughout Europe, there need be no fear of unsatisfactory choices. However, additional precautions have been taken. First, a public list of the candidates will be made, so that all who cultivate or are interested in the sciences, by knowing who are the candidates, may be able to judge the choice made, and exercise over the Society the only censorship that is of any real use—that of public opinion armed with the power of truth alone.

The entire class, composed of scholars in several subjects who will be influenced by the reputation of the candidate as well as by their own judgment, will reduce this list to a smaller number of eligible names; then, the section directly concerned will choose. Thus, the responsibility will finally rest upon a small number of men who will be required to judge only the qualifications of the candidate—which they must know—and who will be sufficiently restrained by this responsibility. The members of the National Society who reside in the departments will participate in the election of new members on an entire equality with those who reside in Paris. This will necessitate the adoption of some method by which the selection of the candidates and the election can each be accomplished by a single vote. The example of the Italian Society, which is composed of dispersed members, suffices to prove the possibility of this.

Each class of the National Society will elect, by the same procedure, the professors of the lyceums who are to teach the subjects which pertain to it.

The professors of the lyceums will appoint those of the institutes, but the municipalities will have the right to reduce the list of those who are eligible.

As for the teachers in the secondary and primary schools, the list of those eligible will be made by the professors of the institutes in the district, and the choice will be made, in the former case, by the municipal corporation of the place where the school is situated, in the latter, by the heads of families in the district of the school.

In fact, the teachers, like the professors, should possess knowledge which the administrative bodies are not qualified to judge, and which can be appraised only by men who can justly be supposed to be of a higher degree of instruction. The list of candidates, which attests their capacity, ought, therefore, to be prepared by members of a higher institution. But, though in choosing a professor from among those eligible, the more learned, the more able should be preferred, in the case of teachers for younger children, who will be more influenced by the moral qualities of the teacher, and where it is only a question of imparting very elementary knowledge, the opinion of those to whom Nature has entrusted the coming generation, or at least of their nearest representatives, should be taken as a guide. It is for this reason that the right to reduce the list of candidates eligible to professorships in the institutes is given to the municipalities. Personal and local considerations are of some importance, and this right of exclusion suffices to guarantee that they will not be too flagrantly ignored. Committees composed of members of the National Society and of the faculties of the lyceums and institutes will be charged with the regular inspection of institutions of a lower grade. In important cases, the decision will be made by one of the classes of the National Society or by the assembly of the professors of either the lyceum or the institutes.

By this means the independence of instruction will be assured, and there will be no need of creating, for the purpose of inspection, any special organization in which the spirit of domination might be feared. As the National Society is divided into four classes corresponding to scientific divisions, and, on every important subject, the right of decision belongs to only one class, it can be seen how, without prejudice to the surety of inspection, there need be no fear of seeing the teaching bodies set up a new power in the State.

Unity is not destroyed, because general questions that would concern an entire institution can be decided only by laws which must be demanded of its legislative body.

If we count all the sums used for the literary foundations that are replaced by the new institutions, the endowments of the teaching orders and of the colleges, the salaries that the cities paid the professors, all the different kinds of income that the schools received, and then add what it cost the people to pay the teachers of these schools, we shall find that the expenses of the new organization of public instruction will not greatly exceed, perhaps not even equal, what the old institutions cost the Nation. Thus, a complete and general instruction, superior to that which exists among other nations, will replace, at less cost even, a system of public education whose crude imperfections offered a contrast, so shameful for the government, with the enlightenment, the talents and the genius which have been able to break the bonds of prejudice amongst us, as well as to overcome the obstacles created by the political institutions.

We have presented in this plan the organization of public education as we have believed it ought to be, but we have not considered at all the manner of creating the new institutions. It seemed to us that the National Assembly should determine what it wished to do before we concerned ourselves with the means of fulfilling its wishes.

In the villages where there will be only one primary school, children of both sexes will be admitted to it, and

369

will receive the same instruction from the same teacher. If a village or a town has two primary schools, one of them will be in charge of a mistress, and the children of the two sexes will be separated.

This is the only arrangement concerning the education of women that we have made in our preliminary work. Their education will be the subject of a special report; for, if we take into consideration the facts that in the families of moderate means the home-training of the children is almost entirely left to their mothers, and that out of twenty-five families occupied in agriculture, commerce or some industry, one at least, has a widow as its head, we shall realize the importance, both for the common welfare and for the general progress of knowledge, of this part of the work that has been entrusted to us.

This system of organization may be reproached with not respecting sufficiently the equality among men devoted to study, and granting too much independence to those who belong to the system of public instruction.

But, in the first place, it is not a question of a distinction to be made, rather of a public function which it is necessary to confer on certain men, the number of whom will be determined by law, and whose meetings will be subject to a regular procedure. Reason requires that men who are charged with the instruction either of children or of adults should be chosen by those who can be supposed to have equal or superior knowledge. Does not the supervision of the educational institutions also require this same equality, in the case of lyceums; this superiority, in the case of the institutions of a lower grade? It was then necessary to find some group of men who could satisfy this essential condition. Should the choice of these men be left to the entire body of those who cultivate the sciences—or claim to do so? It might just as well be left to the generality of citizens; for, if the pretension of learning sufficed for the exercise of this right, it would be enough to belong to some society that claims to be a learned body; and it is very evident that this condition would exclude neither profound ignorance nor the most absurd doctrines. Besides, this would be the same as to authorize veritable corporations—properly called wardenships; for any free association, to which any public function whatsoever were confided, would necessarily assume this character.

It is not ignorance alone that would need be feared, it is charlatanry which would soon destroy both public instruction and the arts and sciences as well, or, at least would use for their destruction all that the Nation would have provided for their progress.

Finally, if the government should choose one of these societies, it would substitute for a group composed of very enlightened men one more numerous but less enlightened, in which men of mediocre ability could enter with more ease, and would be less easily restrained by the ascendancy of genius and of superior talents, and in which would reign at length an ostracism all the more appalling in that mediocrity is readily the dupe or the accomplice of charlatanry, and does not extend to it that hatred of all brilliant and durable success which is so natural to it. If all kinds of free associations were recognized, every class of charlatan would have its own. It would not be modest ignorance that would judge talent according to commonly accepted opinions—which would already be a sufficiently

CONDORCET

great evil—but presumptuous ignorance that would judge it according to its pride and interest.

On the contrary, according to the plan that we propose, the free associations can have only a salutary effect. They will serve as censors of the National Society, which will exercise over them at the same time a censorship no less useful. Those associations in which charlatanism will dominate will soon cease to exist, because no hope of captivating public opinion will sustain them. Each society will seek, in its own sphere of activity, not to lag behind the National Society, which also will not wish to be considered inferior to them. They will be, above all, the natural judges of the choices made by the National Society, and thereby they will contribute more to assure its success than if they cooperated with it in a more direct manner.

In short, the society commissioned to supervise national education, to concern itself with the progress of the sciences, of philosophy and of the arts in the name of the government should be composed entirely of scholars, that is to say, of men who have devoted themselves to a science to its fullest extent, who have penetrated its depths or have enriched it by discoveries.

Without such a society, since the knowledge of the principles of all the arts is still foreign to almost all those who cultivate them, since their history is known to only a small number of scholars, how should we then not expect to see the citizens and the Nation welcome, reward and put in practice, as so many useful discoveries, procedures or means long known and rejected for a sound reason or abandoned after unfortunate experience?

The free associations cannot exist unless they admit at

372

the same time both scholars and those who are merely interested in the sciences; and it is by this means especially that they create a taste for these subjects, that they help to make them more widely known, that they maintain and perfect good methods of studying them. It is thus that these societies encourage the arts without protecting charlatans, that they form for the sciences an opinion common to enlightened men, which it would be impossible to disregard, and of which the National Society will be no more than the interpreter.

At the same time, every citizen being free to establish an educational institution, there will result for the national schools the absolute necessity of maintaining themselves on at least as high a level as these private establishments; and liberty, or rather equality will remain as complete as it can be in a public institution.

The National Society such as we have conceived it must not be confused with the learned societies which it replaces. The real equality which is its basis, the complete liberty of opinion which it shares with all citizens, the functions relating to public instruction which are assigned to it, a distribution of work which forces it to concern itself only with useful subjects, an equal number of its members dispersed in the departments: all these differences assure that it will not deserve the reproaches—often exaggerated but sometimes just—of which the Academies were the object. Moreover, under a constitution founded on equality, there will be no need to fear that a society of enlightened men will easily acquire that class spirit; so dangerous but so natural at a time when everything depended on privilege. At that time, every man endeavored to obtain prerogatives, or to increase those which he already had; to-day, everyone knows that citizens alone have rights, and that the title of public official carries with it only duties to perform.

This state of independence of all external authority, in which we have placed public education, need cause no fear; since any abuse would be instantly corrected by the legislative power, which has direct authority over the entire system of education. Does not the existence of independent instruction and of independently established learned societies also oppose to this abuse a force of opinion so much the more important because, under a popular constitution, no institution can exist unless public opinion adds its strength to that of the law? Besides, there is a final authority which, in all things pertaining to the sciences, nothing can resist: the general opinion of enlightened men in all Europe; an opinion which it is impossible to mislead or to corrupt. On it alone depends any brilliant and enduring celebrity; it is its approval that added to local celebrity gives it greater solidity and brilliance. It is, in a word, for scientists, for men of letters, for philosophers, a sort of anticipated posterity whose judgments are as impartial and almost as sure as those of posterity itself, and a supreme power, from whose authority they cannot attempt to escape.

Finally, the independence of instruction is, in a manner, a part of the rights of the human race. Since man has received from Nature a perfectibility whose unknown limits extend—if they even exist—much beyond what we can yet perceive, and the knowledge of new truths is for him the only means of developing this happy faculty—the source of his happiness and of his glory, what power could have the right to say to him: "This is what you need know; this is as far as you may go"? Since truth alone is useful, since every error is an evil, by what right would any power, whatever it be, dare to determine wherein lies truth, wherein lies error?

Besides, any power which would forbid the teaching of an opinion contrary to that which has served as a basis for the established laws, would attack directly the freedom of thought, would frustrate the aim of every social institution: the perfecting of the laws, which is the necessary consequence of the combat of opinions and the progress of knowledge.

On the other hand, what authority could prescribe the teaching of a doctrine contrary to the principles which have guided the legislators?

There is only one means of avoiding, on the one hand, a superstitious respect for the existing laws and, on the other, the possibility of an indirect attack which, being made against these laws in the name of one of the authorities instituted by them, could weaken the respect of the citizens for all law. This means is the absolute independence of opinions in all teaching beyond the elementary schools. There would then exist, side by side, voluntary submission to the laws and the teaching of the means of correcting their defects, or rectifying their errors, without this liberty of opinion being in any way harmful to the public order, without this respect for the law shackling the intelligence or arresting the progress of enlightenment and sanctioning errors. If it were necessary to prove by examples the danger of subjecting education to any extraneous authority, we could cite the cases of those peoples who were our first teachers in all the sciences: the Hindoos and the Egyptians, whose ancient knowledge still astonishes us, and among whom the human intelligence made such progress at a time of which we cannot even determine the epoch, and who fell into the most shameful ignorance as soon as the religious authority seized the right to teach. We could cite China, which preceded us in the arts and sciences, and whose progress the government suddenly arrested thousands of years ago, by making public education one of its functions. We could cite that deterioration into which fell, all at once, intelligence and genius among the Greeks and Romans, after having risen to the highest peak of glory, when education passed from the hands of the philosophers into those of the priests. After these examples, we should fear all that might hinder the advance of the human intelligence; for, whatever point it may have reached, if any power whatsoever interrupts its progress, nothing can prevent its return to the grossest errors: and, at the very instant that it is forbidden to examine or judge any subject, this first restriction placed on its liberty should make us fear that soon nothing would be wanting to its complete enslavement.

Moreover, the French Constitution itself makes this independence a positive duty. It recognizes that the Nation has the inalienable and imprescriptible right to reform all its laws. It wishes then that, in national education, everything should be submitted to a rigorous examination. It decrees that no law should be irrevocable for more than ten years. It wishes then that the principles of all the laws should be discussed, that all political theories be taught and contested, that no system of social organization be presented to enthusiasm or to prejudice as the object of a superstitious veneration, but that all should be presented to the reason as different systems; among which it has the right to choose. Would this inalienable independence of the people be respected, if to any particular opinions could be added all the weight that a general teaching could give? Would not the authority which would assume the right to choose these opinions really be usurping a part of the national sovereignty?

The plan which we present to the Assembly has been prepared in conformity with the results of an examination of the present state of knowledge in France and in Europe, together with what we have been able to learn from the observations of several centuries concerning the progress of the human intelligence in the sciences and in the arts, and, finally, with what can be expected and foreseen of its further progress.

We have sought all that could more certainly help to assure it a steadier advance and more rapid progress.

A time will come, without doubt, when learned societies instituted by governmental authority will become superfluous and, thenceforth, dangerous; a time when even any public establishment of instruction will be useless. This will be when there will no longer be any general error to be feared; when all the motives which appeal to interest or to the passions in behalf of prejudices will have lost their influence; when enlightenment will be equally spread both over all parts of a same territory and among all classes of a same society; when all the sciences and all the applications of the sciences will be equally delivered from the yoke of all superstitions and from the poison of false doctrines; when, at last, each man will find in his own knowledge, in the soundness of his mind, arms sufficient to repulse all the ruses of charlatanry. But this time is still distant, and our object should be to prepare for it, to hasten the epoch of its coming. Thus, while working to create these new institutions, we have necessarily been occupied, at the same time, in hastening the coming of the happy moment when they will become useless.

INDEX

A

Abuses in colleges, 155
Academies, 288, 366
Acquaviva, Claudius, 62
Adult education, 328, 332, 344, 345, 352
Agriculture, 58, 291, 335, 360
Aiguillon, Duke d', 29 ff.
Alembert, Jean Le Rond d', 32, 189, 308
Alfred the Great, 214
Algebra, 229
Allain, Abbé, 18 ff.
Analytic grammar, 237
Anatomy, 235, 266
Annales de l'Éducation, 193
Architecture, 261
Arithmetic, 225, 229
Astronomy, 88, 232

B

Baillet, Adrien, 82
Batteux, Charles, 103
Bayle, Pierre, 256
Becker, J.-J., 235
Boerhaave, Herman, 148, 270
Boileau, Nicholas, 106

Bossuet, Jacques-Bénigne, 138
Bourges, University of, 11
Brothers of the Christian Schools, 35, 60
Buffon, G.-L. Le Clerc de, 147, 216
Buisson, F., 10
Business affairs, 147, 258

C

Cahors, University of, 11
Cambridge Modern History, 10
Canisius, St. Peter, 52
Canon law, 273
Catechism, 51, 180
Catherine II, 189 ff., 316 ff.
Celsus, 153
Chambers' Encyclopedia, 189
Charlemagne, 214
Charles XII, 124
Chemistry, 235, 271
Choisy, Abbé de, 84
Chronology, 116, 258
Church, history, 285
  and primary instruction, 17, 24

379

INDEX

INDEX

INDEX

Faculty of Theology, 210

Peasants, education of, 65

Petites écoles, 18 ff.

Pharmacy, 267

Philosophy, 136

Physical education, 147, 330

Physicians, 263 ff., 320, 335, 346, 359 ff.

Physics, 86, 88, 112, 234, 337, 359

Plato, 94, 151, 342

Plutarch, 133

Poesy, 240, 252

Political sciences, 359

Popular education before Revolution, 16 ff., 39

Porphyry, 153

Port-Royalists, 13

Practice of medicine, 269

Pradon, Nicholas, 141

Primary schools, 16 ff., 290, 327

Primary teachers before Revolution, 19

Probabilities, calculation of, 229

  logic of, 135

Protestantism, 3

Public exercises in schools, 275, 302

Public instruction, 178, 206, 323 ff.

Public school, 205, 214, 219

Q

Quintilian, 297

R

Racine, Jean, 111, 141

Rambaud, A., 1

Randon d'Hannecourt, 188

Ratio Studiorum, 62

Reading, 18, 76 ff., 260, 327

Religious instruction, 15, 18, 51, 147 ff., 180, 256, 347

Retirement of professors, 276

Revelation, 149 ff.

Revolution, French, 2, 24

Rights of Man, Declaration of, 328 ff.

Ris, Clement de, 188

Rollin, Charles, 14, 196, 202

Rousseau, J.-J., 4, 16, 39, 78

Royal Council on Education, 178 ff.

Royal Society of London, 365

Russian Church, 198, 283 ff.

Russian language and literature, 239

Russian University, 227 ff.

  buildings, 308 ff.

  Chaplain, 300

  daily program of college, 293 ff.

  Faculties, 227

  Faculty of Arts, 229 ff.

383

INDEX